DOME RAIDERS

How Scotland Yard Foiled the Greatest Robbery of All Time

DOME RAIDERS

How Scotland Yard Foiled the Greatest Robbery of All Time

Jon Shatford and William Doyle

First published in 2004 by
Virgin Books
Thames Wharf Studios
Rainville Road
London W6 9HA

ISBN 1 85227 194 9

Design and typesetting by Phoenix Photosetting, Chatham, Kent
Printed and bound by Mackays of Chatham, Chatham, Kent

It seemed unfathomable; this jewel, that you could hold between your finger and thumb, seemed unfathomable as the heavens themselves.

We set it in the sun, and then shut the light out of the room, and it shone awfully out of the depths of its own brightness, with a moony gleam, in the dark.

The Moonstone: A Romance (1868)
Wilkie Collins

Contents

Contents

Dedication

To the men and women of Scotland Yard, and to the officers who served in Operation Magician.

This story is based on actual events. Some details have been altered to protect privacy and security. An asterisk indicates that a name has been fictionalised. The fictional names used bear no connection whatsoever to any other person of the same name.

About the Authors

Jon Shatford is a 29-year veteran of London's Metropolitan Police. From 1998 to 2001 he was operational head of the Flying Squad, the elite Scotland Yard strike force that targets London's most dangerous top-tier criminals. In that role, he led the investigation into the Millennium Dome robbery.

Shatford has worked on undercover drug operations, murder and kidnapping investigations, anti-organised-crime initiatives and hostage rescues. He has been commended fifteen times for his bravery and detective ability. Today, as Detective Chief Superintendent, he is Head of Homicide Investigations for North and East London.

William Doyle is author of *Inside the Oval Office* and *An American Insurrection.* In 2002 he won book awards from the American Bar Association and the American Library Association, and was a finalist for the Robert F. Kennedy Book Award. In 1998 he won the Writers Guild of America Award, one of television's highest writing honours. He has also served as director of original programming and executive producer for HBO in New York.

Glossary of London Police and Criminal Terms

ARV	armed response vehicle
Backer	a criminal who will provide funding money
Bent copper	corrupt police officer
Bird	term of imprisonment
Blagger	armed robber
Caked	having plenty of money
Carrying	in possession of firearms
CIB3	Anti-Corruption Command
CID	Criminal Investigations Department
Crops Officer	Officer trained in rural surveillance
Dirty	actively corrupt criminal or officer
Eyeball	to have someone or something under observation
Face	criminal
FIB	Force Intelligence Bureau
Flying Squad	Scotland Yard's anti-robbery unit
Gun ship	fast, unmarked Flying Squad car with armed officers
Guv'nor	Police Officer of, or above, inspector rank
Happy bag	armed robber's bag of weapons
Heavy mob	Flying Squad
Hendon	Metropolitan Police Training School
ID	identification
Intel	Intelligence
MPS, Met	Metropolitan Police Service
MSU	Marine Support Unit
Nicked	arrested
OP	observation post
Operation Magician	Scotland Yard operation to catch Dome gang
Over the pavement	act of a criminal crossing the pavement to rob

Patsy	someone set up by criminal to take the rap
Pavement ambush	pouncing on robbers in the act
Plot	location of robbery or criminal activity
Roll	when a criminal reveals the names of the other gang members in the hope of getting a reduced sentence
Safe House	location thought to be unknown to police
SIO	Senior Investigating Officer
SFO	Specialist Firearms Officer
SO11	Scotland Yard Surveillance Unit
SO19	Scotland Yard Force Firearms Unit
SWAT	Special Weapons and Tactics Team
Thief taker	officer with reputation for arresting thieves
Tooled up	carrying firearms
Slaughter	where stolen proceeds are divided or stored
Snout	police informant
SOCO	Scenes of Crime Officer
Sweeney	Flying Squad, from 'Sweeney Todd'/'heavy mob'
The Yard	New Scotland Yard
Third eye	someone watching the robbers' backs

Metropolitan Police Ranks

Commissioner of Police
Deputy Commissioner

AC	Assistant Commissioner
DAC	Deputy Assistant Commissioner
	Commander
DCS	Detective Chief Superintendent
	Detective Superintendent
DCI	Detective Chief Inspector
DI	Detective Inspector
DS	Detective Sergeant
DC	Detective Constable

Note: For non-CID ranks, remove 'Detective'

List of Plates

List of Plates

Plate 1 – courtesy of The Steinmetz Group and De Beers LV
Plates 2–5 – courtesy of De Beers Images
Plates 6, 7, 8, 9, 10, 14–33, 35, 36 – courtesy of The Metropolitan Police
Plates 11 and 12 – courtesy of Solo Syndication Ltd
Plate 13 – courtesy of Jon Shatford
Plate 34 – courtesy of the *Sun* newspaper, News International

Prologue: Millennium Eve

Greenwich, 31 December 1999, 11.45 p.m.

The Queen was looking for a diamond.

Somewhere in the darkness before her, surrounded by 10,000 of her subjects, was a jewel so large, so beautiful and so rare that professional diamond cutters would swoon when trying to describe it.

She was a tiny figure in a cinnamon coat, standing near the centre of an enormous enclosed structure on the banks of the River Thames. It was made of white, Teflon-coated, glass-fibre fabric and was pierced by a dozen 150-foot-tall yellow pylons. The brand-new Millennium Dome was supposed to be a breathtaking, hyper-futuristic monument to England's role in the new millennium.

It was certainly a startling building, almost magnificent in some ways, but it was fast becoming a political disaster and a national joke, dismissed by critics as 'the docking station for some sort of alien ship', 'a giant mushroom' or 'a very bad hair transplant'.

The Dome cost £750 million of taxpayers' money to build, and it was already well-poised to approach technical insolvency in just a few weeks, due to a drastic shortfall in visitors.

Prince Charles reportedly hated the place, and would soon be quoted in a *Sunday Times* article as privately calling it a 'crass waste of money', 'commercial and banal' and 'a monstrous blancmange'. It reminded him of 'a giant greenhouse', the article quoted him as telling a friend, 'except that would be an insult to fertiliser'.

The Prince avoided the evening's public ceremony at the Dome by ringing in the New Year in private at his country estate with Camilla Parker-Bowles.

Standing next to the Queen that night was the man who built the Dome, Tony Blair. Against the advice of his own cabinet, Blair had championed the project he inherited from his Conservative predecessors, hoping it could strike a transforming vision of his 'New Labour' philosophy.

Two weeks before, he had proclaimed the Dome was 'a triumph of confidence over cynicism, boldness over blandness, excellence over mediocrity'. But in the face of Blair's exuberance, a series of cock-ups and minor disasters was plaguing the Dome's unveiling on England's Millennium Night.

A celebratory Concorde flight over London was rendered invisible by heavy cloud cover. The giant 'London Eye' Ferris wheel malfunctioned and was shut down for safety concerns. The 200-foot-tall 'River of Fire' display that was supposed to explode across the Thames, from Vauxhall Bridge to Tower Bridge, fizzled out unimpressively.

And, worst of all, bad logistical planning condemned some 3,000 furious invited guests and journalists to be stuck for hours in the London Underground waiting for trains to take them to the remote site of the Millennium Dome, near Greenwich in South-east London, which, in a baffling omission, had no provision for car parking[1]. 'It was like launching a new restaurant,' one government official lamented, 'and giving everyone food poisoning the first night.'

For now, though, most of the million people lining the banks of the Thames seemed happy as clocks ticked towards midnight and there was a mass countdown.

The Queen held a glass of champagne and smiled as she watched a group of eight children scamper to pull down the chord of the Dome's roof curtain, and Prince Philip prepared to plant a kiss on her cheek.

At exactly 11.50 p.m., she watched intently as a laser beam was fired at the heart of a 2-inch-high polished stone on a pedestal at the centre of a display in the Dome.

The stone being targeted was the De Beers Millennium Star, a jewel described by the press as 'the largest perfect diamond yet found', and 'arguably the most beautiful diamond in the world'.

It was the crowning achievement of the 118-year-old business empire of the De Beers Consolidated Mining Company, the dominating commercial force in modern diamond history.

In the audience that night was a man who was godfather to the jewel – an improbably young-looking former Israeli Army Intelligence Officer and Tom Cruise lookalike, Nir Livnat. He was the Chief Executive Officer of The Steinmetz Group of Companies, a leading trader of rough diamonds and manufacturer of polished stones, and the largest single client of De Beers.

[1] This design feature was apparently omitted for the purposes of reducing auto congestion and encouraging visitors to use the North Greenwich Underground Station.

Livnat and his team of master diamond cutters had been selected by De Beers to sculpt the rough 777-carat jewel into the exquisite 203.04-carat, pear-shaped masterpiece.

Livnat could remember how he felt five years beforehand, when he first held the rough diamond in his hand. He was, quite simply, flabbergasted. The beauty of the stone was mind-boggling, and so was its size. It was, he thought, the biggest, most perfect diamond he would ever see; the kind of gem that came out of the earth perhaps once every millennium.

As Livnat and his master diamond cutters studied the stone, they realised it was something none of them had ever seen before and rarely even heard of.

It was an absolutely perfect giant diamond.

For days they peered into it in wonder, looking for internal imperfections. There were none. Not a single flaw could be detected with either a fully corrected 10-loupe or binocular microscope. There were no carbon flaws, no dead areas and no 'glatzes' or cracks in the stone.

Its colour registered at the ultimate level of perfection – D Colour, or colourless. It was what diamond experts called 'ice' – so clear and transparent that even under very high magnification you couldn't see its structure lines.

For three years they studied, sculpted and polished the jewel, carrying it to laboratories in Johannesburg, Antwerp and New York. Everything had to be custom-designed to accommodate the stone's size.

They built a sterile, operating-room-style chamber to work on the diamond. They designed new cutting plates and tangs to hold it. They created over 200 mock diamond replicas to practise on.

'When you cut a diamond, it's like cutting your own nerves,' said Mates Witriol, the chief designer in charge of finishing the stone. 'If you apply a fraction of extra pressure or temperature or vibration, it will shatter.' The financial risk on a stone like this was so great there was no insurance to cover mistakes.

In finishing the gem, the diamond cutters achieved a near-impossible goal – they made it perfect both internally and externally. Every one of its 54 external facets was flawless. It had never been done before in a jewel of this size. And the finished diamond was the rarest of creatures in the gem world – 'full flawless'.

The ninety-year-old retired Chairman of De Beers, Harry Oppenheimer, said the jewel was 'perhaps the most beautiful diamond I've ever seen in all my long lifetime of looking at diamonds. You see,' he marvelled, 'it's perfect – perfect in colour, perfect in purity and in its brilliance which means that it's superbly well cut.'

A few months previously, the jewel had been previewed to the press at De Beers' London headquarters, in the hands of movie actress Sophie Marceau, star of the new James Bond film *The World Is Not Enough*. The movie featured an opening speedboat chase that culminated in Pierce Brosnan falling onto the Dome by helicopter.

And now the stone was making its full debut, on New Year's Eve, before the Queen, the Prime Minister and a multitude of revellers in the Dome, at the moment the New Millennium arrived.

There was only a handful of cut diamonds larger than the De Beers Millennium Star, and two of them belonged to the Queen. The world's biggest, the 530-carat Great Star of Africa, or Cullinan, was mounted in the Imperial Sceptre (used at her 1953 coronation), and the 317-carat Second Star of Africa, or Cullinan II, was mounted with 2,868 other diamonds in the Imperial State Crown (worn annually to open Parliament).

Surrounding the Star that New Year's Eve were 11 other rare De Beers diamonds, including the electric blue 27.64-carat Heart of Eternity, the largest vivid blue diamond in the world.

The combined actual value of the collection, called the 'Millennium Jewels', was incalculable, but some experts estimated it at a staggering £250 million. The BBC called it 'the most spectacular collection of diamonds ever put on public display, anywhere in the world'.

At exactly midnight, as a flurry of laser beams bombarded the De Beers Millennium Star, the Queen and her people gazed in amazement as a thousand years of history and empire dissolved, and the Dome was filled with an infinity of dancing, sparkling fragments of light.

1. The Attack

Nine Elms, 11 February 2000, 6.35 a.m.

'Get back. It's a raid.'

A man in a black mask pointed the long-barrelled silver revolver at the face of a customer at a drinks stand. The voice was calm and commanding. A few feet behind the gunman was a giant security van loaded with £10 million in cash.

The van was stopped dead in its tracks, blocked by a stolen BMW, from which another masked man had jumped out and was now pointing his gun at the driver.

In the pre-dawn gloom, the amber glow of streetlights revealed glimpses of an armed gang of ten men, in matching black combat outfits, launching a complex, military-style assault on a heavily defended Securicor vehicle.

One of the largest cash robberies in history was beginning.

Three lorries were manoeuvring into blocking positions across three nearby main street entrances to this grim, industrial corridor of the Nine Elms section of South-west London, home to the sprawling ruins of the Battersea Power Station and the site of a Securicor high-security depot.

The blockade created a 'sterile corridor' that sealed off traffic in and out of the area. A sniper crouched in the cool damp of a nearby roof top, ready to spray bullets towards the police if they penetrated the barricades.

Twenty-five minutes earlier, inside the Securicor depot around the corner, two security officers had leaned into the vault security hatch and begun the methodical process of loading the cash into the van.

The cash was stacked high in nine sealed, heavy steel cages which they wheeled on trolleys to the tail-lift on the back of the van. They scanned the cash amounts into a hand-held computer.

It was a regular Monday to Friday route, delivering piles of money to London's banks. The driver was a thirty-year company veteran.

In theory, it was nearly impossible to blow open the van.

The specially modified HGV featured blast-resistant doors that could only be opened by multiple sets of keys which were held at different locations. Since only one set was held by the officers, there was no way they could access the cash vault when it was in transit, even from inside the van.

And the armoured tail-lift folded up to provide an extra layer of protection for the back doors, blocking anyone trying to force their way in.

If the van's outer shell *was* pierced, a high-tech alarm and tracking system were triggered. Various other alarms, security codes and cloaking measures were built into the vehicle, some so secret even the officers didn't know about them.

They locked the tail-lift into place, secured the van and activated an anti-hijacking system that would immobilise the vehicle if it was attacked.

At 6.30 a.m., they pulled out of the Securicor depot and, as the driver made a left into Kirtling Street, he noticed a small tipper-type lorry parked near the entrance to a cement works. It had a white sheet draped over the back and, for some reason, the driver thought it seemed out of place.

Fifty yards further on, as the van approached the junction with Cringle Street, it was having to move slowly to manoeuvre through the side street packed tight with parked cars. A trickle of people was arriving for their early morning shifts in the locale.

From the shadows, a green BMW cut in front of the Securicor van and slowed to a dead stop. The Securicor driver, thinking the car was stalling, flashed his lights at the BMW, which lurched forward then reversed back and pinned itself against the cab and driver's door. The Securicor driver tried to reverse his rig but the gears were sluggish.

'I can't select the gear,' the driver exclaimed nervously to his partner.

It was now 6:35 a.m., and ten men in the attack team were fanning around to perform specialised tasks. One gunman took charge of crowd control, waving his weapon at a pocket of stunned bystanders who were frozen in place at the tea-and-coffee stand at the junction of Kirtling and Cringle Streets. Other gang members were jumping out of jack-knifed lorries, blocking traffic from the side streets.

In his wing mirror, the Securicor driver could see two masked men jumping out of a white transit van. They were carrying petrol-powered industrial cutters that could cut through concrete, and running towards the back of his van.

Like the rest of the gang, they were dressed in black, wearing black crash helmets, bomber jackets and black trousers tucked into their boots, looking like a SWAT team. But these two were wearing what looked like DIY goggles.

They dived under the van and started slashing away at the cables.

The BMW driver, a stocky, imposing figure who appeared to be the leader, pointed his gun at the Securicor drivers through the windshield.

His helmet and black balaclava hid any facial expressions but the message was clear – freeze.

The security officers threw their hands in the air. A feeling of abject terror seized one of them, a British military veteran who had a flashback to his days in Northern Ireland.

The BMW driver calmly patrolled the area, keeping his gun low, checking his team working under the van, and striding back and forth to check on the officers trapped in the cab.

When the gang leader wasn't looking, the Securicor driver pressed a panic switch that triggered an alarm back at the Securicor depot.

The gang was so cool, quiet and professional that some pedestrians assumed they were workmen. Bystanders were innocently blundering into a crime-in-progress. A few employees arriving at the nearby Securicor depot even assumed it was some kind of training exercise.

A motorcycle driver arrived on the scene, slowing down to check things out. He was waved off by a gang member pointing a pistol at his head.

'Fuck off,' said the gunman. 'Keep moving.'

A fifty-year-old man with short white hair strolled by on the pavement and peered through a gap in the parked cars at two pairs of legs sticking out from under the van. He was greeted with a gun to his temple and a masked man jerking his head for him to move on. 'Keep moving. You haven't seen anything.' The man slowly stumbled away, his hands in the air.

Other pedestrians, now sensing the gravity of things, scampered around a corner and stayed there, popping their heads in and out to see what was going on. Under the Securicor van, one gang member continued slashing through the brake and power cables while his partner struggled to force down the armoured tailgate. The gang struggled to lower the tailgate and expose the metal shell of the back door.

A screeching alarm erupted from the van, but even now some observers didn't grasp the situation. The sound was a familiar one in this neighbourhood, since alarms were often tested or went off accidentally in the nearby Securicor loading bay.

Some 50 ft behind the cash van, a giant, sharp metal spike protruded out of the back of a flatbed lorry stuffed with Christmas trees – the vehicle spotted by the Securicor driver a few minutes earlier with a white sheet over the back.

The spike had been welded into the chassis, reinforced with concrete and was now pointing at the cash van. It was a giant battering ram. And it was going to be reversed at high speed into the Securicor van.

At £10 million this would not only be one of the biggest cash robberies in British history, it would rank in the stratosphere of cash robberies of all time, which rarely exceeded £5 million. The two largest cash robberies in history, both in America, in 1997, had hit the magic £10 million. But that was rare.

The leader of the gang stood in the middle of the road, checking a stopwatch. They had no time to spare. They forced down the tailgate, fully exposing the metal skin of the van's back door.

While all this was happening, a commuter strolled up from an adjacent street and saw that his parked car was completely pinned against the pavement by a lorry filled with Christmas trees. Incredibly annoyed, he surveyed the scene and noticed that the truck door was open.

'Take his keys,' shouted a bystander.

The commuter peered into the truck and saw that the keys were in the ignition. He decided to have a few words with the driver. He grabbed the keys and wandered off to find him. By some fluke, the commuter was completely oblivious to the attack which was taking place a few dozen yards away on Nine Elms Road. He was walking south, away from the attack.

Seconds later, a masked gang member sat in the cab of the ramming truck.

In total horror, he realised there were no keys in the ignition.

As the rest of the gang hurried over, he frantically patted his pockets and checked the cab.

They all looked at each other – where are the keys?

They hadn't the slightest idea.

Every man in the team was just seconds from being a tax-free millionaire, but there was no way to get their hands on the cash.

The gang leader checked his stopwatch again.

They were about to hit the five-minute mark.

In the distance, police sirens were wailing.

They'd lost it.

He gave the signal by waving his hands – ABORT! ABORT!

The gang members calmly placed their power tools on the pavement.

They fanned out to their vehicles, ignited incendiary devices hidden inside and set off towards Battersea Power Station.

Three terrific explosions rocked the area. The BMW exploded into flames . . . then the flatbed truck . . . then the white van.

Columns of thick black smoke were billowing into the Securicor van. The security officers, still in the cab, were afraid they might be burned alive.

Somebody was yelling, 'Call the police'.

The gang members burst through a security gate at a nearby cement works and trotted down towards Battersea Pier.

There, a high-speed inflatable speedboat was waiting for them, its engine revving.

2. The Detective

New Scotland Yard, 11 February 2000, 6.55 a.m.

He got to work early that day.

He had a mountain of files to read through, and he wanted to get an early start.

Jon Shatford bought his usual cup of tea at Bruno's, the busy Italian café in St James's Park Underground station, and walked across Broadway towards an aluminium-coated office complex just off Victoria Street.

He passed the revolving square sign reading 'NEW SCOTLAND YARD', and entered the headquarters of the Metropolitan Police Service of London.

Detective Superintendent Shatford was the operational head of Scotland Yard's Flying Squad, an elite strike team of detectives who pursued the most dangerous, top-tier criminals involved in armed robbery.

The building opened in 1967, although its name dated back to 1839, when the London police headquarters opened near a courtyard in Whitehall, called Great Scotland Yard, which some thought came from the name of its owner in the Middle Ages, a man named Scott. It was also the site of a residence used by visiting kings of Scotland and, over the years, Scotland Yard became the popular name for both the Metropolitan Police headquarters and its criminal investigations department (CID).

Shatford's first stop that morning was the Flying Squad reserve office on the fifth floor, where he flipped through the robbery report, a ring binder holding the typewritten details of overnight armed robberies. Nothing unusual.

He walked down a long corridor, past the kidnap squad desk and into his office. Like most Scotland Yard workspaces it was surprisingly cramped, and the shelves were overloaded with files with labels like 'Firearms Authorities' and 'Cash in Transit Robberies'.

On the wall was a poster: 'Adapt or Die'.

Shatford's office overlooked Victoria Street but, like all New Scotland Yard windows, the glass was tinted to the outside to protect its secrets.

No sooner had he settled down with his tea and opened a report when a Flying Squad reserve officer appeared at the door. 'You'd better come, Guv'nor. There's been an incident at Nine Elms.'

Shatford was startled by the urgency in her voice. 'What do you mean "incident"?'

'It's either a terrorist explosion or a robbery,' she replied as they both rushed to the Flying Squad reserve room.

'All units proceed with caution,' a voice was crackling on the radio, 'suspects are armed.'

'What the hell is it?' asked Shatford.

The first panicked reports from commuters calling on mobile phones were suggesting a terrorist strike – bomb blasts, chaos, confusion.

More details came flashing in. 'First it sounded like an explosion,' she reported, 'but now it looks like the security depot at Nine Elms has been attacked.'

'God,' Shatford exclaimed, 'is anyone hurt?'

'I don't know, but the Bomb Squad have been called.'

'How much did they get away with?'

'Nothing, I don't think they got away with anything. They escaped by speedboat.'

Shatford ignored this bizarre detail for now, and concentrated on getting to the scene.

'Right, I had better get down there right away. Get me a squad car from Tower Bridge as quick as you can.'

'They won't get through. All the roads are totally blocked. The whole area is at a standstill.'

'Well get me a traffic car and tell them it's urgent!'

Minutes later, Shatford was standing on the pavement at Nine Elms Lane, absorbing the details of the crime. Beirut, that's what it looked like. A war scene in Beirut, not a London back street.

The BMW and white Ford transit van were still smouldering, and flames were flickering in the Ford Iveco lorry laden with Christmas trees. The power cutters were still running where the gang had dropped them, one of them spinning around on the street.

The pungent stink of burning paint and rubber was in the air, and amazed onlookers were stretching their necks to get a better view from behind police tape. A police dog named Charming Chas was straining on his leash, sniffing around for clues, while the Fire Brigade tackled the fires.

Echoing all around were the sounds: 'DRIVER UNDER ATTACK! SECURITY VEHICLE UNDER ATTACK!'

For no apparent reason, Shatford found himself softly singing, 'They'll be back . . . they'll be back!'

A thickset Flying Squad officer approached him, a Detective Constable named Fred Mellor*. He was clutching a clipboard and grinning.

'You won't believe this one, Guv'nor.'

'Try me.'

'There were ten or twelve of them,' said Mellor. 'Maybe more. They blocked off the whole of Nine Elms Lane in both directions by parking three trucks across the road.

'They cut the brake and transmission lines and then just pissed off. Nothing can get through. They had all the time they needed, knowing the Old Bill couldn't get through.'

Shatford asked, 'What went wrong then?'

'I'll show you,' said Mellor, walking his boss over to the lorry packed with Christmas trees.

'This is what went wrong. Underneath this is the biggest battering ram you've ever seen.'

He parted some trees to expose a giant, sharp metal conical spike. It was projecting over the back of the lorry like a huge cannon, ready to be fired into the back of the Securicor van.

Shatford looked with astonishment at its sharpened point, and pushed his finger against it to make sure it was real.

'Jesus Christ!' he muttered.

'This,' said Mellor, 'is embedded in concrete and welded into the chassis.'

Perplexed, Shatford asked, 'Why didn't it work?'

Mellor explained how the peeved commuter had stopped the robbery by taking the ignition keys away.

'Bloody hell . . . I wonder if he knows what he did?' said Shatford. 'Didn't he happen to see there was an armed robbery going on all around him?'

'Apparently not,' replied Mellor, still grinning widely at the audacity of the whole operation. 'Just as well too, with the sort of firepower this gang had.'

Shatford shook his head in disbelief.

They walked to the security van and inspected the abandoned disc and bolt-cutters scattered on the pavement. The tailgate of the truck was down and fluid was leaking from just beyond its rear axle.

'Any descriptions?' asked Shatford.

'No, just that they were all wearing dark clothing and had some sort of hats on, ones like mountaineers wear.'

'Mountaineers?'

'That's how they've been described,' said Mellor, who explained the gang's escape. 'One went to each vehicle and detonated some sort of device which exploded. They ran off towards the power station, down to the Thames and away on some sort of speedboat. The type that commandos use.'

'Like a military operation,' mused Shatford.

'Looks like it.'

'An inside job?'

'Too early to tell.'

'What do we know about the driver and his mate?'

'The driver has been with the firm for over thirty years,' Mellor explained. 'The mate was swapped with the regular one, but he has worked with the firm for about four years.'

'To be safe,' said Shatford, 'given the circumstances, let's check it out anyway. How much cash was in the truck?'

'I can't get an exact figure but it seems it was between ten and fifteen million.'

'What!' The numbers hit Shatford like a punch in the chest. This was a staggering amount of cash.

Shatford quietly speculated, 'Whoever this gang was, they knew exactly what they were after. Military precision, all this planning, the effort to recruit such a big gang . . . we've got a right little team here. We need to turn the driver and his mate inside out. And the one that swapped his shift.'

Shatford broke away from the officer and paced the crime scene alone.

A *speedboat*? he thought.

He was utterly amazed. He had spent over 25 years as a London policeman, had seen almost every kind of plot, but rarely did a criminal really impress him with creativity. Brutality, yes. Tenacity, yes. But intellect – not that often.

This is extremely clever, Shatford thought. So good it's almost brilliant. A sealed-off target area. A complex lightning strike planned with clockwork precision. Chain-cutters and a giant sharpened spike. Vehicles rigged to explode, blasting away much of the forensic evidence. And a high-speed getaway . . . by boat. He'd never heard of that before.

It took the gang just minutes to climb down rope ladders into the inflatable speedboat, shoot across the river, torch the boat, dash into an escape van and vanish in the rush-hour traffic. The entire operation took only a couple of minutes. A clean, perfect escape.

By an amazing stroke of bad luck, only one thing went wrong for them – the lost keys. £10 million in cash was still sitting safely in the Securicor van.

The power tools and the comic-opera touch of the lost keys reminded Shatford of a botched cash raid that occurred in Winchester in 1995. A gang of six men forced a security van driver into a wooded area, where they used industrial-strength, high-powered equipment to cut a rectangular hole in the vehicle.

The van contained £11.4 million in cash. But the gang accidentally set the money on fire. Their equipment raised the temperature inside the van to several thousand degrees centigrade, setting off a multi-million-pound bonfire.

'They managed to open up the van like a can of pilchards,' said prosecuting lawyer Guy Boney at the gang's trial, 'but they also produced a horrendously expensive bonfire.

'The van was on fire and things were going badly wrong,' Boney continued. 'By this time the whole operation was slipping out of control. A fortune in money was burning merrily away, sending smoke rising into the air. The gang panicked and ran away.'

In fact, 'smash and grab' assaults against security vans had decreased in London during the 1990s due to the increasingly sophisticated counter-measures deployed by police and security companies. It was a very difficult job to pull off. These days, the toughest criminals were much more likely to deal in drugs – a far simpler way to make money.

Shatford chewed over the possibilities in his mind.

What troubled him most was that he hadn't had as much as a whisper that the job was in the planning. Normally he would have expected a tip from a snout, especially with a job on this scale involving so many people.

What discipline, he thought, to abort the robbery the instant the plan went wrong.

Military precision. Professionalism. Like commandos. Soldiers, soldiers . . . maybe a renegade group of ex-soldiers setting themselves up for life? Perhaps they were serving soldiers? Or ex-SAS commandos? My God, he thought, they could even be policemen. Or the IRA.

The Irish Republican Army was observing a fragile cease-fire with the British government, but there was at least one ultra-violent splinter group still fighting, and robberies had been a prime source of capital for the IRA in its heyday in the 1970s and 1980s.

Shatford moved to the BMW, where police forensic experts were prodding through the boot.

'What sort of explosive device was used?' he asked.

'Some crude form of incendiary device that sparked into a petrol container, by the look of it. We'll have to send it to the lab. I've not seen anything like it before.'

Shatford asked, 'Not the IRA then?'

'Not their style,' replied the forensics man.

Shatford went off alone to a quiet spot and tried to detach himself and absorb all the details.

Clearly a new kind of gang was on the loose.

But who was the mastermind?

It was someone brilliant and careful, and extremely dangerous. Someone with a taste for brute force, obsessive planning and spectacular raids.

Whoever it was, Shatford felt damn sure of one thing: he was going to strike again.

Shatford spotted a bubble of TV cameras and reporters forming around Angie Evans, a Scotland Yard press officer. He was relieved to see her – on a job like this there was sure to be strong press interest, and Evans was highly skilled in dealing with reporters.

At a crime scene, a good press officer like Evans can take a lot of pressure off the SIO by carefully structuring all his statements to the media.

Evans broke away to confer with Shatford.

'I don't want to play this one up,' Shatford said quietly, surprising her.

'But you're usually the first to appeal to the public.'

'This gang is bound to lie low,' Shatford replied. 'The more they think we are putting into this inquiry, the longer they'll keep their heads down.'

'But they'll know the Flying Squad are going after them,' Evans pointed out.

'I know. I just don't want them to know how serious we will be treating it.'

Moving over to the gaggle of reporters, Shatford got to work 'talking down' the story as the press peppered him with questions.

'Mr Shatford, this must have been a meticulously planned robbery.'

Shatford: 'The gang got away with nothing.'

'But they used explosives to blow up their vehicles.'

'Well, they set them alight to destroy forensic evidence, the way car thieves do.'

'We can still see the smoke in the air now. Was anyone hurt?'

'No, I'm glad to say they were not.'

'Can you tell us about their escape? We understand it was rather dramatic on an inflatable raft across the Thames. That seems highly sophisticated.'

'Fairly innovative, yes,' Shatford acknowledged.

'Have you ever known a gang escape across the river before?'

He had to admit, 'No, I haven't.'

'How much money would they have got away with?'

'I'm sorry, but we don't discuss those sorts of details.'

'What will the Flying Squad's next move be?'

'I'm sorry, but it's not our policy to provide that sort of detail.'

'How do you rate this gang?'

'They are thugs with guns.'

'Do you give them any credit at all?'

'No,' Shatford declared, ending the press conference.

'They are thugs.'

On the drive back to the Yard, Shatford was so invigorated by the thought of taking on this gang that he felt like a boxer going into the ring. He could visualise the finely tuned investigative team of the Flying Squad kicking into gear.

At a set of traffic lights he took out his PDA and jotted notes for a 'to do' list.

Get a rundown on all cash depots within half a mile of a river, anywhere in southern England.

Plot them on a map, circling out from London.

Contact the cash delivery companies, review their contingency plans.

Put word out on the street to snouts and pub-crawlers – keep your ears open.

One last thing on the checklist – the gang might execute the member who mislaid the keys. Check for bodies floating in the Thames.

3. The Sweeney

There are a million crimes a year in London, and only 30,000 police to fight them.

The officers protect a population of 7.2 million people spread across 33 Borough Operational Command Units, and a total area of 620 square miles.

They face an invisible army of rapists, murderers, pickpockets, kidnappers, child molesters, mafia bosses, smugglers, drug traffickers, fraudsters, terrorists, thieves and blaggers.

By definition it is often the ultimate high-risk job, walking the razor's edge of violence and chaos. Since Sir Robert Peel formally organised the London police service in 1829, many thousands of officers have sustained serious injuries on the job and over 500 of them were killed in the line of duty.

The first name on the Roll of Honour was PC Joseph Grantham, who was beaten to death in 1830 while trying to subdue a drunken civilian at Somers Town, Euston. In the year 2000, the latest inscription was for 24-year-old PC Kulwant Singh Sidhu who, in 1999, fell to his death through a skylight while chasing suspects across a roof in Twickenham.

The London police have a vast array of tools at their disposal: hundreds of vehicles, boats and aircraft; state-of-the-art forensic laboratories, a network of computer databases and a support staff of over 11,000 civilians and technical experts. And to fight armed robberies, Scotland Yard has a high-precision blunt instrument called the Flying Squad.

They are the 'best of the best' of London Police. And their target is the 'worst of the worst' of London's most dangerous armed robbers.

To combat armed robberies like the spectacular aborted attack on the Securicor van at Nine Elms, the Flying Squad have over 150 officers divided into four offices across London. Barnes covers South-west and Central London, Finchley covers the North-west, Tower Bridge the South-east, and Rigg Approach, as it was in 2000, covered the East.

Each office has about forty officers, and investigates all armed robberies within its area. The offices work independently of one another under the charge of a Detective Chief Inspector but, when necessary, they combine their resources and utilise other specialised departments, like SO19 and SO11.

Established in 1919 as a 'Mobile Patrol Experiment' to deal with the post-war influx of criminals to London, the Flying Squad gained fame as a highly mobile strike force using fast cars, with fearless 'thief-taker' detectives specialising in the 'pavement ambush' – pouncing upon armed robbers in the act.

The pavement ambush is the perfect image for the Flying Squad – an image (illustrated by the squad's emblem of a swooping eagle) designed to strike fear in the robber.

In 1921 the *Daily Mail* christened the unit a 'flying squad of hand-picked detectives', while blaggers (armed robbers) gave the squad the rhyming-slang nicknames of 'the heavy mob' and 'Sweeney Todd', or 'The Sweeney'. (The squad was immortalised in the hugely popular ITV series of the 1970s *The Sweeney,* and featured a boozed-up, fictional Detective Inspector Jack Regan cruising around London in an MK1 Grenada, slamming suspects against the wall and barking 'Shut it!')

The Flying Squad covered robberies against banks, cash-in-transit vans, building societies, betting shops and commercial premises. Apart from the specialist firearms teams, they were the only other full-time firearms team in the UK, with 90 per cent of their officers trained to carry firearms, primarily the Glock 9 mm semi-automatic handgun. To deal with gunshot wounds, they received extra first-aid training.

'The biggest difficulty in combating armed robbery is that it happens so quickly,' said Flying Squad Detective Inspector Adrian Smales in a 2003 interview with the *Police Review* magazine. 'Invariably the robbers have got some form of mask or scarf hiding their face, which makes identity very difficult for witnesses who have been traumatised after having had firearms pointed at them.

'With officers carrying firearms when they respond to a job, there is no room for error,' explained Smales. 'What a Flying Squad officer needs is nerves of steel,' he added. 'A lot of the time you are watching and waiting to see whether a job will go down. You have to be totally calm with the ability to make the right decision.'

The Sweeney had a stellar eighty-year operational history, but it was punctuated by moments of utter public disgrace.

The successes include tracking down many of the 'Great Train Robbers' responsible for the commando-style robbery of £2.6 million in used bank notes in 1963, the 1990 pavement ambush of bank robber Kenny Baker (who was killed after opening fire on the police), and the arrests of the Knightsbridge security-deposit robber Valerio Viccei, and the Brixton bomber David Copeland.

More recently, the Sweeney pursued the armed robbers Matthew Missenden and Shivan Pillay, who conducted a string of raids on video shops and off-licences in London and the Home Counties in 1998. Through a painstaking analysis of CCTV footage, Flying Squad detectives arrested the suspects and secured their convictions on twenty counts of armed robbery. The mastermind, Missenden, was sentenced to sixteen life sentences.

But, in the 1970s, the Squad's reputation took a steep plunge when its commander, Kenneth Drury, was convicted and jailed on corruption charges, and Scotland Yard was infected by bribery and pornography scandals. The corruption involved only a small number of bent coppers, but the public and media damage was severe.

In the mid-1990s, it happened again – officers from Scotland Yard's CIB3 Anti-Corruption Command, or 'Ghost Squad', raided the Flying Squad office at Rigg Approach in East London. An undercover investigation revealed the existence of a small gang of Flying Squad officers who were suspected of helping themselves to hundreds of thousands of pounds of cash confiscated in anti-robbery operations.

Only five Flying Squad officers were convicted, but the scandal hurt morale and infuriated many police, especially the incoming Metropolitan Police Commissioner, John Stevens.

The towering six foot three Stevens was a highly decorated 35-year Scotland Yard veteran who had spearheaded a series of inquiries into security breaches in Northern Ireland. He faced a tough set of challenges when he took over as Commissioner on 1 February 2000, ten days before the attack at Nine Elms.

Besides the residual effects of the Flying Squad scandal, the Metropolitan Police Service was stinging from the charge of 'institutional racism' contained in the Macpherson report on the brutal murder of the black teenager, Stephen Lawrence, in 1993.

And the previous year, the Police Federation reported that bad press, low pay and sinking morale were triggering a recruitment crisis, and the force was undermanned by 700 officers.

That's why Commissioner Stevens was about to launch a campaign to match Scotland Yard's reputation to its reality – as the best police force in the world.

Jon Shatford had spent his entire career in the London police force. He had never served on the Flying Squad. And that, said his bosses, was one of the main reasons why they had appointed him as head of the day-to-day operations of the Squad in 1998, in the immediate wake of the Rigg Approach crisis.

They told him he had a reputation for being honest, tough and experienced, and he didn't suffer fools gladly. He had no previous connections with the Squad, and no misplaced loyalties. He was seen as someone who had the operational credibility to bring the Flying Squad back on track.

Shatford entered police training school when he was 21, and his first job was as a constable in the high-crime section of Brixton in South London. On his first day patrolling alone he arrested a gang of burglars in the act of looting a house. He quickly won a reputation as a 'thief-taker'.

Over the years, Shatford was involved in undercover drug operations, anti-organised-crime initiatives, murder and kidnapping investigations, and hostage rescues.

He didn't tolerate the bureaucratic tango of scripted meetings and back-scratching speeches. What turned him on was catching criminals. Good police officers, he believed, made their own luck. They are on the streets, on the look-out, following their instincts and refining them.

Shatford worked his way up as a plainclothes officer and undercover detective in the CID, and as a Detective Superintendent in the heart of London's East End.

In 1986 he was promoted to Scotland Yard's elite anti-drug division, the Central Drug Squad and, in 1989, was promoted to Detective Inspector. In 1991 Shatford oversaw Operation Bumblebee, the most successful anti-burglary initiative ever staged by UK Police, resulting in thousands of arrests.

One of the highest-profile Bumblebee cases was that of a sadistic burglar dubbed Lucifer by the media. For several years, Lucifer burgled his way across the capital, preying on the homes of London's wealthy elite. His specialty was tying up and terrorising victims in their homes. In 1994, Shatford launched an intense surveillance operation against Lucifer, resulting in his capture.

Like all London police officers, Shatford was furious at the bad press inflicted by the Rigg Approach scandal. His mission now was to restore the reputation of the Flying Squad, and he knew the only way to do it was through excellent police work. The Flying Squad needed a win. And the Nine Elms case might be it.

4. The Investigation

New Scotland Yard, 15 February 2000, 10.00 a.m.

Who the hell are they? wondered Shatford.

He was looking for a sophisticated and extremely dangerous gang – a gang of sufficient organisation and capability to carry off huge robberies. He was sure they'd strike again, but he had no idea where, when or how.

News of the Nine Elms job was circulating quickly on the police grapevine, and for serving and former Flying Squad officers it was electrifying. Detectives who were tired by internal politics, paperwork and court appearances were finding new vigour as they contemplated the bungled raid. A career of tracking armed robbers had given them insights into their way of thinking that no computerised Intelligence system could match.

It was at times like this, in the wake of a spectacular unsolved crime, when being a detective goes beyond a profession and becomes a consuming passion.

Each detective in the grapevine seemed to have a theory. They were a brand new gang. Or a gang that had re-grouped after a prison stretch. Judging from the tactics and the improvised matching combat outfits, maybe they were ex-British military, recently discharged? Or a team from overseas – French or American? Or East European mafia?

To Shatford, an overseas gang seemed unlikely. There were easier ways to get rich than mobilising a ten-man commando attack to blow open a near-impregnable Securicor van with split-second timing, seal off the area with blocking vehicles, load up £10 million in cash and escape by speedboat across the Thames.

There was something about the theatrical audacity of the Nine Elms attack that suggested a British gang. And the attack was so well-orchestrated that it suggested a team which had done this kind of thing before.

Now, as the investigation began, the most urgent priorities were to complete the forensic examination, interview witnesses, and trace the provenance of the boat and vehicles used in the attack.

Shatford pulled out the files and began building a photo chart of known top-tier robbers and faces, or criminal 'players', based in and around London, collecting scraps of data and profiles, plotting possible teams and combinations of bank robbers, hijackers and gunmen.

'An inside job?' Shatford asked.

'Probably not,' said Detective Inspector Steve de Burgh Thomas.

The aborted Nine Elms attack fell under the jurisdiction of the Flying Squad's busy Barnes office in South-west London, and the investigation was headed by Thomas and his deputy Detective Sergeant Grant Powell. In the days after the Nine Elms attack they had methodically analysed all angles of the crime.

As Shatford read through the witness statements and police reports, he was gripped by a growing sense of amazement. This gang had left behind no clues at all.

Detectives had interviewed both Securicor officers immediately after the attack, and it looked like they were in a state of genuine, total shock.

Still, the possibility of an inside man had to be explored. In fact, there was a major recent precedent for this theory. In July 1995, a gang of masked men attacked a fully loaded Securicor cash-delivery van in the Midland Bank cheque-clearing centre in Salford, near Manchester.

In a meticulously planned twelve-minute operation, using scaling ladders to enter the depot, tie up the driver and hijack it to a nearby location, the gang made off with 29 blue cash bags containing £6.6 million in cash and cheques.

It was billed as the biggest cash robbery in Europe to date, and the gang vanished.

But Manchester police quietly launched an international investigation code-named Operation Volga and, in August 1999, twelve people were arrested, including Graham Huckerby, the driver of the Securicor van and a former Manchester policeman. Huckerby was accused of taking a £1,000 bribe to let his bomb-proof van be hijacked and robbed.

One of the things that made the police suspect Huckerby was the 'inside man' was that he didn't activate the Datatrak Automatic Vehicle Location (AVL) device, located inside the cab, when he was attacked.

Datatrak was a highly sophisticated electronic-tracking system that was developed by Securicor company technicians to defend the company's cash-in-transit vehicles. It was so effective that it became widely adopted by security, police and emergency authorities across Britain and Europe.

A typical Datatrak-equipped vehicle was fitted with a multi-purpose antenna, an emergency power pack, a computer keypad and built-in sensors. Every two seconds, the sensors transmitted phase-locked signals to a control centre reporting the vehicle's speed, direction and temperature, the status of the doors, the load on the axles and, most important, the vehicle's location.

The sensors could even detect unplanned stops, variations from pre-designated routes, and find hijacked vehicles within a radius of 70 ft. The signals broadcast over a low-frequency network of fourteen terrestrial radio transmitters that covered 95 per cent of the UK mainland road system. For the other five per cent, it switched to GPS positioning satellite transmission.

In the Nine Elms attack, however, the Flying Squad discovered that, unlike the Manchester case in 1995, these two Securicor officers responded exactly the way they were supposed to. They had activated Datatrak as soon as they could, setting off the tracking alarms back at base just around the corner. One of the two even furtively dialled back to base on a mobile phone when the gang wasn't looking.

Still, the possibility of an inside man bothered Shatford.

'What about the last-minute switch of guard?' he asked Detective Inspector Thomas. But Thomas reckoned the man was innocent because he had only got the job because of a family illness.

The story checked out. This was no inside job.

'And the tail-lift?'

The armoured tail-lift system on the back of the van was expressly designed to lock up if the van was attacked, providing an extra blast-proof barrier of defence.

But the Nine Elms gang had figured out a way to force down the tail-lift and expose the thin metal shell of the back door to the giant ramming spike.

Was this breach the product of some inside information?

Thomas explained that an expert mechanic had thoroughly examined the van's wiring, and had come to two tentative conclusions. By slashing away at the back of the van the way they did, the gangsters either were so technically sophisticated that they figured out a design flaw that hadn't even occurred to the designers, a flaw that triggered the drop, or they just got lucky.

Another problem was the lack of clues. In the immediate aftermath of the raid, police had interviewed dozens of shaken witnesses on the scene including Securicor employees, pedestrians and motorists. But all the witnesses saw were men in black outfits in the pre-dawn gloom.

Black balaclavas hid their faces. Gloves hid their hands. No distinctive features of any kind were revealed. No blood or DNA was left behind.

One witness did spot an unmasked driver jumping out of one of the blocking lorries and running into an alley, but he couldn't make out any identifiable details. Other witnesses saw the gang sprinting down to the Thames, but only from a distance.

No witnesses could be found to the getaway on the other side of the river, when the gang entered a vehicle and seemed to instantly blend into early morning traffic.

A few of the witnesses did say that the masked men in charge of crowd control sounded like they had 'aggressive South London' accents, which lent support to the theory that it was a local gang. But almost to a person, the forty plus interviewed witnesses swore they couldn't identify anyone in the gang.

Intriguingly, some witnesses reported seeing shadowy figures in a white transit van, and an inflatable boat in the area as early as three months before the attack. It looked like the gang had the area around the Securicor depot under surveillance for some time, and perhaps conducted practice runs.

Specialist lab teams at the Scotland Yard Fingerprint Bureau pored over possible crime scene forensic evidence, but couldn't turn up anything useful. Fingerprint marks on the vehicles were either inconclusive, or didn't match anything in the fingerprint database of active criminals in London.

The detectives did manage to trace the registration numbers of all three blocking lorries to their point of sale, a trading company on the outskirts of London. But the vehicles, a used Leyland and two used Ford lorries, were sold for cash on the spot to two unidentified men eight weeks before the attempted robbery.

The dealer could remember nothing about the buyers other than one was in his mid-30s, white, about five foot ten with a heavy build, and spoke with an 'East End accent'. The other was a stocky, five foot eight 'Maltese or Eastern European', about 45 years old, who spoke with a foreign accent.

The other two vehicles used in the attack, the fire-damaged BMW and the white transit van, were both reported stolen. Forensic analysis of the sledgehammer, crowbar and holdalls found in the BMW boot were inconclusive, as were tests on a box of shotgun shells found on the river shore.

The Flying Squad fanned out across London and pumped informants for leads, but something unusual happened – absolutely nothing. Normally, the underworld would be abuzz with chatter about something as spectacular as Nine Elms, but nobody was talking about it.

To Shatford that pointed to two disturbing possibilities: either the gang were so brand new that nobody knew them, or whoever orchestrated the attack was so dangerous that no one dared speak.

In the back of Shatford's mind was a distant, lingering fear. It was a very remote possibility, but not totally impossible, given the handful of crooked cops in recent history.

What if the gang had a man inside Scotland Yard?

He had to get more irons in the fire, and fast.

And he had to do it covertly.

'Where are you starting?' asked Detective Inspector Gary Kibbey as he sat down in Shatford's office on the fifth floor of New Scotland Yard.

Shatford hooked a dilapidated 'Do Not Disturb' sign on the handle, and shut the door.

Kibbey was a specialist in one of the most secretive departments in Scotland Yard, SO11, the Intelligence branch.

SO11 gathers, organises and analyses Intelligence about criminal activity and crime networks, using tactics ranging from special operations to high-technology surveillance. When necessary, it teams up with other units like the Flying Squad on special operations.

Kibbey was tall and personable, but his highly calculating mind gave him an edge of intensity. Shatford and Kibbey knew each other fairly well, so the atmosphere was relaxed.

Shatford took Kibbey through all the details and dead ends of the Nine Elms investigation, and ended with a look of puzzlement. 'So there we have it.'

Kibbey asked Shatford if he had any preliminary guesses at all about the gang.

Shatford confessed that a few possible suspects were being put forward, but it was just bits, pieces and guesswork. At the Rigg Approach Flying Squad branch, for example, Detectives Bob Boughen and Gary Staples noticed similarities between Nine Elms and a 1996 armed raid at a cash-in-transit depot in Barking, on the east edge of London, in Essex, just inside the boundaries of the Metropolitan Police.

Details of the robbery, which was still unsolved, immediately gripped Shatford's interest. The raid happened on 27 August 1996, at the

Security Express Depot in Barking. The robbers lay in wait as two steel gates opened to allow in a large, armoured security vehicle.

As the van entered, the gang drove in behind it in a short Land Rover and a stolen blue Renault panel van. Half a mile up the road a stolen lorry was edged across the carriageway, blocking traffic from entering.

The robbers were masked and shouted orders and waved handguns. A security guard was taken hostage by having a gun pointed at his head. As they took control, the robbers pulled three wheelie bins from the back of the panel van.

The bins were pushed to the back of the security van and filled with cash and bonds totalling £3 million. When they were full they put them back into the van and sped off towards a Tesco's supermarket, about half a mile away.

The robbers escaped over a footbridge across the river Roding into an unknown getaway vehicle and escaped. This was a classic escape favoured by blaggers – a carefully chosen change-over point prevents vehicles chasing them from crossing, and buys valuable minutes.

The crime triggered a Flying Squad investigation called Operation Bury, but so far, nearly four years later, only a few tentative suspects had been identified, with no evidence to bring charges. To date, no one has been charged with this offence.

For the Nine Elms raid, however, Shatford told Detective Inspector Kibbey that he was now starting to suspect a gang that was on many detectives' minds, and was rising to the top of the pack of possible suspects.

The Brinks-Mat gang.

Brinks-Mat was the biggest robbery in British history to date. Not cash, but gold bullion. £26 million of it.

At 6.30 a.m. on 26 November, 1983, a team of six robbers in ski masks broke into the heavily defended Heathrow Airport warehouse of Brinks-Mat Ltd., one of England's top security firms.

Brandishing handguns, the gang penetrated an array of electronic security devices, tied up and pistol-whipped six terrified security guards, drenched two in petrol and threatened them with lighted matches to reveal the codes to open the safes.

Using the warehouse's own forklift trucks, the gang loaded 76 boxes containing 6,800 gold bars onto a getaway van.

By 8.15 a.m. they had vanished into morning traffic with £26 million in gold.

The Flying Squad soon discovered that the robbers had had an inside man, a security guard, who confessed that he gave the gang the plans of the warehouse.

By pumping its network of informants, the police were able to identify some of the gang members who had been recruiting for talent among the London underworld in the weeks before the crime.

Although three members of the gang were captured and imprisoned, several of the suspected robbers and most of the gold has never been found – a continuing thorn in Scotland Yard's side.

'What are the Brinks-Mat lot doing?' asked Shatford.

The question forced a smile on Kibbey's face that was speculative rather than amused. 'I'm not sure,' he said. 'I think McAvoy's in Spain. I'm not sure about the others, but they are all meant to have fallen out in any event.'

Mickey McAvoy, a former builder, was the notorious South London robber convicted of leading the Brinks-Mat raid.

Recently paroled, McAvoy was reportedly furious with his former gang members for spending his share of the loot while he was in prison. He would soon be spotted by the *Daily Mirror* wearing shorts and a baseball cap, driving a spiffy Volkswagen Golf, and living with a brunette in a house in suburban Kent.

One of McAvoy's fellow convicted gang members, Brian Robinson, was also free. Another Brinks-Mat player, the infamous Kenneth Noye, had served four years in prison for handling some of the stolen gold and was now back in prison, soon to be convicted and sentenced to life for the vicious 1996 road rage stabbing of 21-year-old Stephen Cameron on the M25.

Noye seemed unlikely to be connected to Nine Elms, but some Flying Squad detectives wondered if he might have some dotted-line connection, even in custody.

'They don't all have to be involved, do they?' asked Shatford. 'Perhaps one or the other have got another little team together.'

'Could be,' said Kibbey.

'Let's just put it this way,' said Shatford. 'I would like to know where they are and what they are doing, particularly if there are any whispers about them.'

'I'll see what I can find out. Have you looked at the Operation Bury team?'

'They seem good as well, but the trouble is we just don't know, and that worries me,' Shatford complained. 'I would have thought there had been a whisper at least.'

Kibbey agreed, saying, 'We've picked up nothing, and given how many were involved that's quite something. You would have thought one of them would have been bragging.'

'I know. That's why I just want to know where these players are for now. Whoever did Nine Elms must be looking to do somewhere else in the future. Having failed here they are bound to try again.'

'You're right, Guv'nor.'

'Just one other thing, Gary,' said Shatford, bringing the meeting to a close.

'This conversation must stay between us. We don't know how connected this team are, and I can't afford to have details of what we are doing leaking.'

'Understood.'

As Kibbey walked out of the office, the two men agreed to keep in daily touch.

Some of England's best-known criminals were soon placed under observation.

For lack of any other solid direction, Shatford and the Flying Squad focused on Brinks-Mat faces.

But as spring gave way to early summer, the Nine Elms investigation took the Flying Squad all across England, and turned up nothing.

No leads, no Intelligence, not even a whisper.

The Nine Elms attack was a job tailor-made for the Flying Squad.

But by the early summer of 2000 they could not turn up a single clue.

The investigation stalled for five months.

By July 2000 it was dead in the water.

5. Attack #2

Kent, 7 July 2000, 7.30 a.m.

'For fuck's sake, call the police!'

Securicor driver Kenneth Weller* was shouting into a hands-free phone to an operator at the depot less than a mile away.

Weller and his partner Bill White* were being surrounded by blocking vehicles and attacked by a criminal SWAT team of armed men in black combat-style outfits.

'We are under attack at the end of the road. Call the police.'

'All right, all right,' said the operator.

Their vehicle contained 733 sealed and bar-coded containers holding £8,796,000 in cash.

It was morning rush hour on the outskirts of Maidstone, in Kent, midway between London and the coast. It was broad daylight.

There were bystanders everywhere, commuters in vehicles, some slowing down to check things out.

White fumbled for the Datatrak button and triggered the alarm. Then, in horror, he spotted another button through his armoured windshield, being held high in the air just 5 ft in front in him.

The gang leader had his finger on the red switch of a remote control radio-detonator.

Earlier, at 6 a.m., the Securicor officers had arrived at the depot, drunk a cup of tea and had gone to the secure loading area to begin loading millions of pounds of cash into their armoured HGV van.

Weller checked the oil and water, and White tested the alarms before loading eight giant steel cages holding hundreds of cash containers through the tail-lift.

After completing a checklist of security procedures they were waved out of the depot, and drove a few blocks along Beddow Way, an industrial estate area on the outskirts of Maidstone. The van was going to drop off the cash to various banks and customer outlets through the area.

They were travelling at 25 mph approaching the junction with Forstal Road, when they noticed a 40-foot-long, white Volvo Arctic cab with an attached trailer blocking the lane, covered with strong blue plastic sheeting. It was parked diagonally across the road from the pavement to the yellow line. There were construction sites nearby, so it didn't seem unusual.

'You'd think he would have pulled over to the side,' said Weller.

'It's not a hold-up, is it?' said White jokingly.

Weller replied, 'No, I think he's broken down, he's trying to find his gears.'

'Go around him,' suggested White.

Weller slowed down, and pulled around the Arctic as the car in the opposite lane flashed to let him pass. Once around, a blue van up ahead approached the cash van from the opposite direction, suddenly pulled right into the lane and rolled to a stop, diagonally blocking the road with its hazard lights on.

The Securicor van was now boxed in between the two vehicles ahead and behind, and the oncoming traffic, so Weller slowed down to a stop.

They could hear the Arctic manoeuvring behind them, reversing and whining its gears.

'Fucking hell, Bill, what's going on here?'

'It's a bloody hold-up,' said White.

A black-masked man suddenly appeared standing in the road directly in front of them.

He was pointing a silver-barrelled gun at them.

'Drop the fucking tailboard,' he ordered with a rough London accent.

The voice was cool, aggressive and frightening.

'I can't!' said Weller.

'Operate the tail-lift,' the gunman commanded.

He was dressed like a police rapid-response officer, like something from an American action film you'd see on Sky. Everything he wore was brand new and black: the Army-style helmet, the woollen balaclava, combat overalls and multi-pocket trousers tucked into lace-up police boots.

He was almost six feet tall, and looked like he was wearing ammunition straps. A pair of handcuffs poked out from a pouch under his black bomber jacket.

His gloved hand had its finger on the trigger of a small silver gun with a square handle, and the gun reminded Weller of the kind James Bond used to carry.

'DROP THE FUCKING TAILBOARD,' said the gunman, pointing the weapon at shoulder level up at Weller, at which Weller simply threw up his hands.

The gunman produced a green ten-inch-wide object that looked like a small land mine and waved it at the Securicor drivers. That's when they became aware of two men at the back of the van grinding into the tail-lift with power tools, sending out showers of sparks.

'They're trying to cut the tailboard off,' said White.

'I can see a bloke's bare arse out in the road,' said Weller, checking his side-view mirror. 'His pants are riding low.'

Another gunman in black combat gear and a yellow reflective waist coat emerged from the blue van and trotted by the Securicor van, holding a large pistol in one hand and a pile of giant nylon bags in the other.

The lead gunman appeared at the passenger window and shouted, 'give us the key to the back.'

'We don't have a key,' said White.

The gunman vanished and White muttered to his partner, 'Have you done the Datatrak button, have you done the Datatrak – push the button.'

'I did, I did,' said Weller, who had quietly triggered the distress call to the control centre a few seconds earlier on one of the multiple buttons hidden in the cab. He had also locked the security bolts on the van in case the gang tried to lever the doors open.

On a hands-free mobile phone, White punched in 999 and got an emergency operator on the line.

'Attack, attack, attack!' he said, which seemed to confuse the operator.

'Who do you need?' she asked.

'Police,' he answered, but when she passed him through there was no answer.

'The police are not answering, I'll try again.'

In frustration, White disconnected and dialled the Securicor depot.

The gunman reappeared before them, held up the limpet mine for them to see and slammed it on the front of the cab with a magnetised clonk. He pulled two more mines from his pocket, and attached them to the driver and passenger doors.

He then produced a little black box with a red button and very purposefully pulled up a three-piece, twelve-inch aerial.

The message was clear.

'Drop the tail-lift,' he announced, 'or I will blow up the front of the vehicle.'

'We can't do it, it's locked up,' yelled White.

'GET OUT THE FUCKING CAB,' said the gunman, pointing both his gun and the remote control aerial at the Securicor men.

'We can't get out, we're locked in!' replied White.

He was, he now assumed, about to die.

I will never see my family again, he thought.

It was 7.30 a.m., and civilian bystanders were appearing from everywhere.

A construction worker stepped out of a portable toilet and found a pistol pointed at his head by a masked gunman.

'You fucking go away,' he growled.

The workman was too stunned to move, so the gunman shouted, 'Don't be stupid. Fuck off.'

He did as he was told, and was struck by how commanding the gunman's voice sounded.

An older woman slowed her car, trying to navigate around the obstructions.

A gunman strode up to her and in a firm, cool voice, said, 'Fuck off. Keep out of it.'

When she saw the gun aimed directly at her windscreen, she panicked and started scrambling out of her car.

He ordered her to get back into her car and back it up into a yard, shouting, 'Reverse it. Park it there.'

But she was in a full panic, crying hysterically.

The gunman lowered his weapon and walked up to the driver's window, saying calmly, 'Don't worry, you're not going to get hurt. You've got nothing to worry about as long as you do what you're told. Move back and you won't get hurt.'

He was so controlled and relaxed that, despite the circumstances, she calmed down and obeyed.

One nearby witness was impressed by how quickly the gangster's tone changed from rage to coolness.

'Reverse it back,' he said, and he walked with her as she reversed, backing the vehicle off the road so it was pinned up against another vehicle.

'The keys,' he said.

'I'm not going to hurt you, just give me the keys and I'll chuck them over there. You can get them later.'

He threw her keys over a fence.

'You see where they went,' he assured her. 'Stay there and you will be alright.'

He repeated the procedure with four other vehicles, grabbing the keys at gunpoint and chucking them over the fence.

Incredibly, normal commuting was proceeding around the attack-in-progress.

Some people were getting out of their cars and walking about, wondering what was going on. When they grasped the picture, many were dialling 999 on their mobile phones and unleashing a small torrent of emergency calls to police.

A Securicor employee on his way to the depot slowed down, noticed what was happening and gestured to the trapped officers that he would call the police.

'Look over there,' said an amazed Weller inside the Securicor van. Pointing to a nearby tourist with a camera, he exclaimed, 'There's a bloke taking photos!'

White replied, 'I can't believe all these people are driving past. Look at all those people driving past!'

The gang were using a fleet of at least five blocking and support vehicles in the attack: a Ford Transit panel van, a Nissan Urvan panel van, a Leyland Road Runner tipper lorry, a Volvo Arctic unit with an attached trailer and a Ford Transit van.

At the back of the Securicor van, a team of three gang members in goggles was struggling to cut into the tailgate with power cutters, bending over and leaning into it with force, concentrating on the bottom edges of the tail-lift by the hinges.

One raider was having trouble with his trousers, which were repeatedly slipping down to offer bystanders a view of his butt cheeks, forcing him to stop cutting and hitch them up.

On the other side, his partner was struggling to restart his power cutter, which was choking and seizing up.

The gang leader was patrolling up and down the scene, establishing a perimeter of operations.

When a large delivery lorry rumbled towards the scene, he ran towards it and levelled his weapon at the driver.

'Stop – fucking get back,' the gunman shouted, but the lorry kept coming until stopping nearly 5 m from him.

'Go back or I'll have to do you,' he exclaimed.

But the driver wasn't moving.

'MOVE YOUR FUCKING LORRY BACK OR ELSE I'M GOING TO SHOOT!'

The gunman fired one shot at the windscreen, expelling smoke and a cartridge.

The lorry lurched backwards.

The two Securicor officers were still in the cab and heard the noise of power tools abruptly cut off at the rear of the van. The security alarm was screeching 'DRIVER UNDER ATTACK – CALL POLICE.'

Then they heard a loud revving sound.

Witnesses saw a gang member loosen a blue tarpaulin from the trailer of the Arctic lorry, the back of which was now facing the rear door of the Securicor van from 300 ft away.

It revealed the sharp tip of a massive metal spike welded into the chassis.

The Arctic reversed and charged towards the Securicor van, rapidly picking up speed.

The impact rocked the locked-up Securicor van with such force that it briefly flipped up on its front wheels and slammed back down on the pavement. Both vehicles rocked violently with the impact.

After being knocked around inside the cabin, one of the Securicor officers shouted, 'They're going to ram us again!' He frantically groped to fasten his seat belt while his partner leaned forward to brace himself.

Four gang members gathered around to inspect the damage, wrestling with the tailgate, forcing it up and down with their hands. It was loose but still attached to the door.

Police sirens wailed in the distance.

Almost £9 million in cash was inches away, ready for the taking.

The Arctic lorry repositioned itself for another strike, but it launched too quickly.

The gang members were still fiddling with the tailgate when the Arctic charged directly at them.

The two men manhandling the tailgate had to jump out of the way as the Arctic hurtled at them, missing them by inches.

One of them hit the pavement in a parachutists' roll as his pants dropped halfway down his backside.

The blare of two-toned police sirens was growing louder, and a Kent Police Range Rover appeared cautiously at the nearby junction.

A gang member swung around, pointed his revolver at the Range Rover with both hands at shoulder level and, from 5 ft away, fired a round over the vehicle and shouted 'Go on, go, go back, back off!'

The police vehicle rapidly reversed a few dozen yards as the gunman kept steady pace, and the officers inside were amazed by how cool, calm and collected the gang appeared.

One more ramming might blow open the door, but by now the gangsters realised they'd run out of time. They'd been at it for over twenty minutes.

'Fucking leave it,' screamed the gang leader, 'forget it. AWAY!'

The attackers dropped their bags and tools to the ground.

One of the support vehicles, the blue transit van, swerved over and swallowed up most of the gang members while another one, evidently older, jogged behind it with difficulty, trying to catch up.

He made it alongside and was pulled in through the sliding side door. To avoid parked vehicles, the van raced onto the pavement parallel to Forstal Road and headed towards Aylesford village.

The police took off in hot pursuit, cutting across flower beds and front gardens at speeds of over 50 mph. A second police vehicle joined the chase, but the escape van peeled ahead, eventually pulling off into a public park and down to the bank of the River Medway.

There, an escape speedboat and pilot were waiting.

As the gang transferred to the boat, the first police Range Rover pulled up and unloaded two officers.

A gang member charged towards the police and fired a round at them, forcing them to take cover before racing back and joining his mates in the boat.

On seeing the gunfire, the second police vehicle reversed out of the line of sight.

The speedboat raced down the river and vanished from view.

6. The Call

New Scotland Yard, 7 July 2000, 9.30 a.m.

The voice on the phone was sharp and excited.

'There's been another one.'

Shatford was flipping through a book of robbery statistics when the phone rang.

'Another what?' he asked.

'A Securicor cash-in-transit job,' said Flying Squad Detective Inspector Steve De Burgh Thomas.

'Where?' asked Shatford, riveted.

'Aylesford, in Kent, not far from Maidstone.'

'What happened? How much did they get away with?'

'They didn't get anything,' said Thomas. 'It failed, but it looks just like ours, blocking vehicles, a rammer, but the police turned up and they escaped along the river Medway.'

'Where are you now?'

'At Barnes, we've just had a call from their Intelligence unit.'

'Get straight down there,' said Shatford. 'I want to know exactly what happened, and who's in charge. Get back to me as quick as you can.'

In minutes, Thomas and Detective Sergeant Grant Powell were racing east in a squad car to the scene of the crime. Within two hours, they had met local police officers, quickly surveyed the scene and were calling in a preliminary report.

'No doubt about it, it's the same team,' said Thomas.

'Talk me through it,' said Shatford.

'They blocked off the roads around, just like on ours,' the Detective Inspector reported.

'They've got an identical conical spike as a battering ram, which they actually did charge into the security van, twice, but this time the police got through. The robbers let one off at them, piled in the back of a van and sped off to the Medway about a mile away and escaped on a waiting speedboat.'

'Bloody hell,' muttered Shatford. The similarities were overwhelming. 'It's identical.'

'The vehicles were rigged to explode,' said the detective, 'but they didn't have time to set them off.' Petrol bombs had been taped inside each of the abandoned vehicles, except the Arctic and trailer.

Then Thomas added, on the spike, someone had scrawled a message: 'PERSISTENT, AREN'T WE?'

Just what we need, thought Shatford. An armed gang with a sense of humour.

Army bomb disposal experts were called in to examine the three limpet mines attached to the outside of the Securicor van's cab. They turned out to be *Fray Bentos* Steak and Kidney pie tins, painted camouflage green and fitted with magnets and flashing red lights.

'Another thing,' added Thomas. 'They've got spare ignition keys taped in the cab of the ramming lorry.'

Shatford had to chuckle, 'Well, it looks like they've learned their lesson from Nine Elms.'

'Looks like it.'

'OK, Steve, who's in charge?'

'The Detective Chief Inspector is Lee Catling, but overall it's Detective Superintendent Douldon.'

'Right. Well, I'll speak to him but keep on top of them; make sure they know what our interests are and, if they need any help, give it.'

'OK, boss.'

Now there was a political complication.

Shatford wanted the Flying Squad to take full charge of the job. The Metropolitan Police were the only force in the country with a Flying Squad expressly dedicated to catching top-tier armed robbers, but this attack happened outside the Met's jurisdiction, so Scotland Yard had to work alongside Kent police. They'd ask if they could co-operate with Kent, but would they let them?

Shatford knew he'd have to navigate the Flying Squad as close to the investigation as possible, giving Kent what support he could, while avoiding the impression that the Sweeney was muscling in on a very high-profile police operation. Over the years, local and provincial forces had sometimes looked on the Flying Squad as a 'heavy mob'.

Some provincial forces regard the Metropolitan Police with great scepticism, thinking that London officers consider themselves superior. No other unit epitomises this perception more than the Flying Squad, with its particularly robust profile. Add this to the fear that the Flying Squad might be looking to muscle in on their investigation and the suspicion could grow. But, ironically, when police officers work together for any length of time a mutual trust develops.

Shatford had assumed this day would come. Ever since the Nine Elms job, the gang had been on the loose, and presumably highly pissed off over the botched raid. They would have been hungry and looking for a fresh target, having absorbed the lessons of Nine Elms. It would have taken them a few months to re-deploy, and fully plan and finance a new operation. It might have taken the gang weeks of intense surveillance and over £100,000 in operating expenses to stage a new attack.

At Aylesford, once again they came within seconds of becoming multi-millionaires. This time, they opened fire, both at police and at a civilian. With each botched raid, the danger level of the gang was increasing, perhaps exponentially.

The man from Scotland Yard was jealous. This detective had a much bigger office than he had.

It was 10 July 2000, and Jon Shatford was at Maidstone Police Headquarters, in the office of Detective Superintendent Andy Douldon. Compared to Shatford's chaotic, cramped workspace at the Yard, Douldon's tidy office was huge. It was almost tranquil, with windows looking out to green fields.

Shatford suppressed his envy and said, 'Well this is a job and a half, isn't it, Andy?'

Douldon smiled, saying, 'It sure is.'

The two detectives got on well. Their departments had worked together in recent months on a kidnap operation, so there was some familiarity.

Shatford was careful not to appear to want to take over, which was what he really wanted to do. His main concern was to try to discover who the robbers were, so they could be tracked and captured on their next job.

'We've got some hopes with forensic,' Douldon said, 'given that they didn't set fire to the vehicles like the Nine Elms job.'

The Aylesford gang abandoned four vehicles and a speedboat after the aborted attack, and they did not have time to detonate the explosive devices to eliminate forensic evidence.

Kent police discovered that of the four vehicles, three were stolen and had false number plates: the two transit vans and the 1987 Volvo Arctic cab and lorry used to block traffic on Beddow Way. The history of the 1988 Leyland Road Runner tipper lorry used to ram the cash van was unclear.

'Let's hope something turns up,' Shatford said. 'What about the River

Medway, Andy? Can we give you any help there?' The gang might have disposed of some of their weapons as they fled. Kent did not have its own dedicated Marine unit and divers, while the Metropolitan Police did.

'I do want to drag it,' replied Douldon, 'in case they dumped their firearms there.'

'I can help you with that,' offered Shatford, 'I'll get our Marine Support Unit involved.'

'That would be a help, thanks.'

'What about Flying Squad officers,' said Shatford, 'can I assist with staff?'

'If we can call on you when we need you,' said Douldon, 'it would be helpful.'

In the minutes after the aborted raid at Aylesford, a pair of sharp-eyed Kent police officers in an unmarked car spotted a suspect walking along a towpath close to the Malta Inn public house, near where the gang abandoned their speedboat. He was out of breath and appeared very nervous. The suspect was a South London criminal, Gary Durning*. When questioned by officers, he initially refused to answer but then claimed he was having an affair with a woman in the area.

Two days after the Aylesford attack, Durning was taken to Brixton police station in South London for an identification parade. He was picked out by one witness who placed him on the speedboat at Aylesford an hour before the robbery.

Durning made no admissions, and if he was involved, he was probably only a minion. There was no other evidence and the case against him was not strong, so he was released. As of now, there were no other suspects identified.

'I do think it's important that we stay linked on this case,' Shatford told Douldon. 'We have some Intelligence from our job so you can certainly have access to that.' Douldon eagerly accepted, and the two detectives agreed to work closely together as the investigation unfolded.

Back at the Yard, Shatford thought about a loose end from the Nine Elms job. The Flying Squad investigation into the Nine Elms attack had uncovered a witness who remembered seeing a speedboat being pulled from the river and hooked to a car three months prior to the attack. For some reason it had seemed suspicious to him, so the witness took down the registration number of the vehicle that towed it away. He thought it was being stolen.

Police traced the registration number of the vehicle and arrested the driver. He admitted that he had towed the craft, but said he was a minicab driver and didn't know who had hired him. His story was that he was asked to meet a customer at a slipway to the Thames, near the Star and Garter public house in Putney. When he arrived, the minicab driver claimed, he met two men who hitched the boat to the towing bar of his cab. He then followed them to a place off the Walworth Road, near the Elephant and Castle. He said he was paid £50.

Shatford always found this story implausible, but there was not very much he could do about it. His suspicions were raised further when he discovered that the cab driver had a tenuous connection with an old-time armed robber who was well known to the Flying Squad. This blagger was an associate of Mickey McAvoy, the Brinks-Mat robbery gang leader, and had, in fact, married McEvoy's ex-wife.

If the cab driver was linked to this robber, then a connection between key faces in the Brinks-Mat and Nine Elms gangs might be established. On top of this, a surveillance request from the Flying Squad's Tower Bridge office had just arrived on Shatford's desk reporting that the associate of the cab driver had been spotted in the company of suspected armed robber Timothy Spurlock*.

Spurlock associated with some of South London's most formidable robbers, and Tower Bridge Flying Squad detectives wanted to initiate surveillance on him to gather evidence on a 1999 bank robbery. But the police were severely restricted in what they were allowed to do. The Human Rights Act of 1998 had introduced a number of changes to British law enforcement including stricter codes of practice on how police conduct surveillance – later to come into legislation as the Regulatory of Investigative Powers Act.

The Act meant that detectives could no longer follow anyone at will, as this could be regarded as an invasion of human rights. A senior officer of at least superintendent rank was now required to approve every application for surveillance. The officer has to consider whether surveillance is proportionate to the offence under investigation, whether there are other less intrusive means of getting the information, and whether it is likely to intrude into the lives of any innocent bystander. It is an elaborate bureaucratic process with many forms to be filled in and reviews.

To Shatford, the surveillance request on Spurlock already looked fully justified based on the available evidence relating to the 1999 bank job, and it offered a possible bonus – information on the Nine Elms and Aylesford attacks could turn up as well. A long shot, perhaps, but it was worth a go.

After signing off on the paperwork, Shatford called Tower Bridge and left a message with the office manager summoning the detectives who were investigating Spurlock to come to his office.

7. The Team

New Scotland Yard, 10 July 2000, 3 p.m.

Five men squeezed into Shatford's office.

They were Detective Inspector John Swinfield, also known as 'Swinni', Detective Sergeant Mark Drew and Detective Constable Sean Allen, all from the Flying Squad Tower Bridge office. Joining them was Detective Inspector Gary Kibbey, the specialist from SO11, Scotland Yard's Intelligence branch.

Shatford hung the tattered 'Do Not Disturb' sign on his door, and closed it.

Shatford had not worked directly with the Tower Bridge men before, but he knew them by their reputation, which was excellent.

Swinfield, for example, was a former Royal Navy Engineer Officer with a distinguished service record. During his time on the Flying Squad he had been commended twice for bravery.

The first time was in 1993, when Swinfield was one of four officers in a Flying Squad gun ship that was chasing suspects who had just carried out a raid in Blackfen, South London.

As the suspects Anthony Pendrigh and Steven Farrer were cornered, they opened fire on the police with a Scorpion sub-machine-gun and two Magnum revolvers.

The gun ship was riddled with 26 bullets and the driver, PC Mick Stubbs, took one in the head and somehow managed to keep driving. Fortunately, he survived.

The robbers sped off, firing from the rear window, with the gun ship still chasing them. It only stopped when one of the robber's bullets pierced the wiring loom, causing them to crash. Pendrigh and Farrer were convicted of attempted murder.

Swinfield received a High Commissioner's Commendation and a Queen's bravery award for his part in the capture. His second commendation was for an operation in December 1995 in Bermondsey High Street, South London, when an armed robbery was committed on a security van. The guard was shot in the abdomen with a sawn-off shot gun, and the robbers sped off just before the Flying Squad arrived on scene. This triggered a rapid search of the surrounding streets.

The detectives in Swinfield's car were the first to spot the robbers and, as they approached, the robbers opened fire. With a lightning-quick reaction, the driver of the gun ship rammed the robbers' vehicle, causing it to crash beside theirs into a wall. Unfortunately, the crash activated the door locks in Swinfield's 820 Rover, locking them inside.

All the desperate Flying Squad officers could do was to wind down their windows and point their guns at the robbers, ordering them to put their hands in the air. Meanwhile, the driver escaped through his window and managed to release them.

Swinfield was commended by the Commissioner for his part in this case, and received a Bow Street Bravery Award. Today, in Jon Shatford's office, Swinfield and the Tower Bridge detectives were visibly curious about why they had been summoned, and looked on with great expectancy.

'I want to make it quite clear,' said Shatford, carefully looking each man in the eye, 'that what we discuss in this room this afternoon stays here.' Nods of agreement. He then described in detail the jobs at Nine Elms and Aylesford, stopping to answer questions that only a detective would ask.

'It worries me,' said Shatford, 'that we have a tasty firm like this operating in and around London, but we have not picked up so much as a whisper as to who might be responsible.'

'Could be any of a few,' said Swinni, wondering whether the lack of Intelligence was an implied criticism of his team.

'I know, but if we cut out the cowboys it should be a narrow list,' said Shatford. 'We are looking for someone who is highly organised, well-financed and with enough clout or savvy to stop word getting out,' said Shatford.

'Do you fancy anyone in particular?' asked Swinni.

'The team that most comes to mind is Brinks-Mat,' said Shatford.

Detective Sergeant Drew observed, 'I thought the Brinks-Mat lot all fell out because each thought the other had ripped them off.'

'They have,' said Shatford, 'but that doesn't mean that one of them can't get another firm together. They've got the pedigree.'

'What about the Operation Bury lot,' asked Swinni, referring to the shadowy faces that the Flying Squad's Rigg Approach branch had unsuccessfully investigated for the 1996 armed raid at Barking. 'Are Rigg still working on them?'

'Not actively, no,' Shatford replied. 'The trouble is that after Aylesford, they've probably gone to ground for a while. What we need is a way of getting into them.'

'Have you plotted up the Brinks-Mat gang?' asked Swinfield.

'We don't know where they are right now,' reported Kibbey. 'McAvoy seems to share his time between here and Spain.'

'Given the locations of the two offences,' said Drew, 'there's a good chance that whoever pulled this off is from South London.'

'Probably Bermondsey boys,' agreed Allen. That wasn't hard to believe. This inner London area just south of Tower Bridge has a reputation for breeding some of London's most prolific armed robbers.

'Exactly what I thought when I saw your surveillance application for Timothy Spurlock,' said Shatford.

'Well, he's capable enough,' speculated Swinfield, 'but I wouldn't think he was the brains.'

'It's not just Spurlock I'm interested in,' continued Shatford, 'but anyone he associates with.'

'He's connected to a few faces,' said Allen. 'We know most of them, so we've got a head start.'

'Good,' said Shatford, 'but the one who interests me most is the blagger known to the cab driver who towed the speedboat. He knows McAvoy and Spurlock and many others.'

'Spurlock certainly could be one of them,' said Drew. 'We know he's active.'

'The only way we are going to get into this firm is by making ourselves busy around them,' guessed Shatford.

'Well, Spurlock's a good start,' said Drew.

'Exactly, and you never know if you take him and his cronies out on the pavement one of them might roll,' said Shatford. (The Flying Squad had developed the expertise over the years of ambushing armed robbers as they crossed over the pavement.)

'Be nice to catch him going across the pavement,' said Drew.

'Do you want us to do anything on the Brinks-Mat players?' Swinfield asked.

'Not specifically no,' replied Shatford. 'I hope the minicab driver's mate or Spurlock might take us to him. We just need to see what develops.'

He continued, 'As the Aylesford investigation progresses, there could be a bit of work in Kent. I intend to use you as the operational team, so be ready to scramble at any time.'

'We're already linked in to Dick Lennon down there,' said Allen. 'He's a good bloke in charge of their Intel unit.'

'Good,' said Shatford, 'because we need to stick really close to Kent on this one.'

'How tight do you want us to keep this in the office?' asked Swinfield.

'Very!' said Shatford emphatically. 'I don't trust this firm not to have connections within the police.'

'That's why Spurlock is such a good start,' he said. 'The rest of your team only need to know that you are working on him.'

That was fine with them, agreed the three Tower Bridge detectives.

'From now on,' said Shatford, 'I want you to report directly to me on this. Don't trust anyone. I want you to assume that whoever this gang is they've got bent police on board.

'I want to know of anyone who makes themselves busy by asking one over the normal question. Understood?'

They all nodded in agreement. They all knew there was at least a slight risk of being compromised from the inside, and there are few things more repulsive to hard-working police officers than a bent copper.

The meeting broke up with Kibbey agreeing to give everyone a full briefing on the Brinks-Mat and Aylesford jobs. Shatford was impressed by all four detectives.

With a team like this, he thought, we may actually get somewhere.

8. The Breakthroughs

Kent, July 2000

In many detective stories, it is the tiniest, most routine piece of police work that can lead to a breakthrough. That's exactly what happened in Kent.

Earlier that year, on 25 April 2000, Detective Constable Andrew Bean of the Kent Constabulary went to an isolated compound called Tong Farm Packhouse, some twenty miles from Aylesford. He suspected that stolen vehicles were being hidden there.

Tong Farm was in a remote area of Brenchley, Kent, and incorporated a modern packing-house covering 28,500 sq ft, surrounded by fifty acres of orchards. Bean surveyed the scene and noted details of a caravan in an orchard beside the packing-house, a white Ford transit van and a heavy goods vehicle cab that had been cut from its chassis.

When he returned to the police station he entered details of the vehicles onto the computerised force Intelligence system. After a few simple checks he discovered that the registration number of the white Ford transit van actually matched to a blue Rover 416. They were stolen number plates.

After logging in the information, the detective made it his mission to make secret observations of Tong Farm at periodic intervals, to note the registration numbers of any vehicles on the site and build an investigative file.

On 18 May he paid another visit and took photos of the buildings, the caravan and several other vehicles. They included two blue transit vans, one of which had a letter missing from its registration number. Back at the station he passed all these details to Detective Constable Nicky Lennon at the FIB, the Kent police Intelligence unit.

In July, after the botched Securicor attack at Aylesford, one of the routine checks performed by Detective Constable Lennon was to feed the registration numbers of all the vehicles involved through the FIB computer. Incredibly, the search threw up an instant match. Two transit vans used at Aylesford were the same ones that had been spotted by Detective Constable Bean on Tong Farm.

'We had to make a decision,' recalled Detective Superintendent Andy

Douldon of Kent Police. He could have made arrests for stolen vehicles at Tong Farm, Douldon later told a reporter, 'but the chances are they would have claimed to have bought them at an auction, not knowing their background.' Douldon decided to wait.

At Scotland Yard, when Jon Shatford heard the news of the Kent Police's computer-match breakthrough, he was ecstatic. There was an excellent chance that the Nine Elms–Aylesford gang were using Tong Farm as a safe house.

Shatford raced down to Kent to see Douldon.

His biggest fear was that Douldon might decide to raid the farm prematurely, and scare off the gang when they were somewhere else. It was unlikely the gang would return to the farm immediately, but they might eventually return if they thought the police had not discovered it.

Shatford was convinced the gang would simply bide their time before striking at another target.

If they came back to Tong Farm then there was a chance the Flying Squad could identify them. It was time to hold off, dig in around the farm and watch.

Shatford was relieved to learn that Douldon had exactly the same plan.

In late July 2000, the Kent Police, in co-operation with Scotland Yard's Flying Squad, launched a full-scale surveillance operation on Tong Farm.

Tong Farm was owned by a family called the Wenhams, a cash-rich group of scrap metal dealers who owned at least four properties in the area worth a total of over £500,000.

Shatford quickly developed the working theory that although the Wenham property had to be linked to the Aylesford crime, the Wenhams were probably not the masterminds.

31-year-old Lee Wenham, for example, seemed to Shatford to be a nuisance, but not very smart. He had some street cunning, but he seemed unlikely to organise an operation on the scale of Aylesford.

Shatford arranged for the deployment of SO11 'crops' officers around Tong Farm. Armed with camouflage, telescopes and long-range cameras, they dug in for extended periods in the most inaccessible locations. Within 24 hours the ditches and hedgerows around the farm were occupied by some of the hardiest officers in SO11. Detective Inspector Barry Waterman led the team.

Over the next weeks, the SO11 unit endured one of the wettest summers in memory. The coast, Kent in particular, was hit by a torrent of continual rain. Streams and rivers burst their banks and became lakes, and roads were flooded. News broadcasts were dominated by pictures of people being rescued from houses by firemen in boats.

The area around Tong Farm was typical of the conditions. Deep in the muck and mire of nearby ditches, trees and hedges, unknown to anyone, lay scores of surveillance experts from Scotland Yard. Sometimes they could barely keep their heads above water, but they waited and watched.

They worked in shifts, taking elaborate steps to make sure they were not seen. This meant crawling for long distances through the undergrowth on their bellies. Even simple bodily functions had to take place where they lay. At times they were in floating quagmires of neck-deep water and mud. They could barely function, but still they had to watch.

On 2 August, a JCB digger was spotted entering Tong Farm in convoy with a white transit van. It didn't seem significant. It was assumed at the time that it was probably stolen and was going to be resold.

As August progressed, anyone who entered the farm was given a code name for recognition purposes. Each sighting was recorded on a surveillance sheet using their nominated code name. Lee Wenham was given the name 'Oak'. He was sometimes seen talking to unknown visitors at the farm, but the conditions prevented police from getting close enough to see who they were.

One man in his 50s became a regular visitor, and he was given the code-name 'Beech'. He drove a white van, which was often parked overnight at Tong Farm, and it looked like he lived in the vehicle. He spoke regularly to the Wenhams but, while he was seen to come and go, nothing was known about him.

The surveillance officers logged his registration number.

One interesting feature of the Nine Elms and Aylesford jobs was that they both occurred on a Friday. The significance of this was unknown but, as a precaution, every Friday after Aylesford the Flying Squad were on special alert, positioned near cash-in-transit depots in and around London.

If there was to be another robbery attempt, Shatford wanted to be ready to try to launch a 'pavement ambush'.

The second breakthrough came in the early morning of 17 August. It came from a lead foot and a bottle of booze.

At 1.35 a.m., the local police received a call to The Halfway public house in Brenchley, Kent. The driver of a white Ford transit van had reversed into the pub fence and fallen asleep at the wheel. He was breathalysed and found to be over the limit.

When the suspect was taken to Tonbridge police station, officers discovered that his vehicle was of interest to the Serious Crime Unit in Kent and to the Flying Squad. The van was displaying false registration plates, and a check of the chassis number confirmed that it was stolen.

Detective Inspector Gary Kibbey of SO11 was told about the arrest that night and he dispatched Detective Constable Bob Lawrence to

Tonbridge. Lawrence met up with Detective Constable Rouse from Kent, and they confirmed that the man in custody was the character identified at Tong Farm who was code-named 'Beech'.

'Beech' was soon identified as Terrence Millman, a cadaverous-looking, 56-year-old London man who had served long periods of imprisonment for armed robbery.

Police found a mattress and some bedding in the back of Millman's van, which confirmed that he had been living in the vehicle. They also found clothing, binoculars, a sports bag and a mobile phone.

One piece of the clothing, a reflective tabard, was similar in description to that worn by one of the robbers who fired at the police during the Aylesford attack. It was later sent to the laboratory to check for traces of firearms residue, but none was found.

Millman was interviewed about his possession of a small amount of cannabis, charged with the drink drive offence and released on bail. Before he left the police station most of his property was restored to him except the van and items submitted to the lab.

As he made his way back to London, Millman did not notice the SO11 surveillance team behind him tailing his every move. Soon they would tail him all the way back to Tong Farm.

The identification of Millman was a big leap forward in the investigation. His career as an armed robber made him the obvious suspect to be the link between the Wenham property and the London gang behind the Nine Elms and Aylesford attacks, whoever they were.

Days later, a forensic report revealed a match.

Millman's finger marks were detected on several contact points in the vehicles used in the Aylesford robbery – on plastic bags, a paint bucket and a copy of the *Sunday Mirror*.

The surveillance operation on Tong Farm and on Terrence Millman was stepped up.

The next breakthrough came from a bunch of police officers sitting around a table.

On 24 August, Shatford called a special meeting at Kent Police Headquarters in Maidstone. He wanted to bring together all the officers involved in the investigation, to see if there were any new leads, big or small.

Twenty-five detectives crowded into the first floor conference room, and took seats around a shiny, oval table. In keeping with the precise way that the Kent police seemed to handle everything, ink blotters separated each place.

The room was well lit with four large windows down each side; the walls were decorated with pictures of ceremonial police events. Some were of senior officers from a bygone time, while others appeared more recent.

The drone of chatter dominated the room as officers found their seats. They were a mixed bunch. Some were dressed in overalls and looked downright scruffy (these were the 'crops', the surveillance specialists from Kent and SO11). Some detectives wore suits, while others wore casual attire with open-necked shirts.

There wasn't room for all the officers, so some sat on the windowsills.

Detective Inspectors Barry Waterman and Paul Chapman headed the Scotland Yard SO11 team, and Detective Sergeant Jools Lloyd led the operational surveillance team. Gary Kibbey led the Intelligence input from SO11, while Dick Lennon headed Kent's Intel unit.

Representing the Flying Squad were Shatford, Detective Inspector John Swinfield, Detective Sergeant Mark Drew and Detective Constable Sean Allen.

After weeks of 'digging in' together, the Scotland Yard and Kent police teams had meshed together effectively. The feeling Shatford got from them was like brothers and sisters fighting a common cause, closing ranks against a common enemy.

'Right everyone,' said Shatford, bringing the chatter to a close. 'My name is Jon Shatford. For those who don't know me I am the operational head of the Flying Squad. The purpose of this meeting is to pool our thoughts together to make sure we're not missing anything.

'We have linked Tong Farm to the Aylesford robbery from the vehicles,' he continued. 'We now know that Millman, a convicted armed robber, is going there, and his prints match some found on the Aylesford job. Millman must be in the gang. We also know there have been some unknowns at the farm – any ideas who they are?' He looked around the room for inspiration.

'The conditions out there are terrible, Guv,' said one of the crops officers. 'We're just not getting close enough.'

The surveillance officers had briefly spotted unknown figures at the farm, but they were too dark, distant and fleeting to get a fix on. The farm was a perfect hideout – the occupants could see anyone coming and going in a wide-open area. They patrolled the estate with dogs, and police suspected that they were using untraceable 'throw-away' mobile phones, and monitoring police radio frequencies with scanners.

'Are these unknowns our team?' asked Shatford.

'Too early to say,' said another crops man. 'They could just be buying nicked plant equipment off the Wenhams.'

'Well, coming to the Wenhams,' Shatford said, 'Lee has been heard talking about mixing with some faces from London. Any clues who they are?' asked Shatford.

'He may be referring to Millman,' said Drew.

'Possible, I suppose,' agreed Shatford.

After three hours the room had thinned to a few officers from Kent, SO11 and the Flying Squad.

'What is happening here?' asked Shatford in frustration.

By now, after two weeks of surveillance, he was fairly well baffled by the lack of solid Intelligence on the gang, other than the ID of Wenham and Millman.

It wasn't for lack of trying.

The Kent Constabulary even brought in a forensic tacographic consultant to analyse the records of the vehicles abandoned at Aylesford. A tacograph is a small instrument inside a vehicle that records the speed of the vehicle, and the distance and time travelled in the last 24 hours. By analysing the data, a specialist can provide educated guesses as to what route a vehicle took. When multiple tacograph records are available, routes can be plotted on a map, and theoretically tracked back to a common destination. Unfortunately, the analysis can be obscured by congestion and stop-and-start driving, and the Aylesford tacograph data was inconclusive.

One piece of Intelligence, did, however, reinforce the theory of a link to the Brinks-Mat gang – an associate of a Brinks-Mat 'face' was seen parked up near the Aylesford Securicor depot on several occasions in May.

'We've missed them twice now. We've got to get them next time,' Shatford declared. 'Where's it going to be?'

Turning to Detective Sergeant Lloyd, Shatford said, 'Jools, let's go through again where Lee has been going.'

'Nowhere really special,' replied Lloyd, 'mainly he goes to see to his girlfriend or thereabouts. Visited the Millennium Dome, been in pubs, speaks to various people. Apart from that, Tong Farm.'

Turning to Dick Lennon, Shatford asked, 'Can you talk us through the splattering of Intelligence we have on him?'

'Word is he's got an interest in a building site,' said the Intelligence specialist. 'He's talking about some guys from London. Looks like he might be doing some work for them. Little more really.'

'What about this building site?' asked Swinfield.

'We don't know,' replied Lennon. 'But it sounds like he's going there tomorrow, so we might find out.'

'Are you on him tomorrow, Jools?' Shatford asked Lloyd, the surveillance man.

'We can be if you want, Guv'nor.'

'Just as well then,' said Shatford. 'You never know, he might meet up with someone.'

Shuffling some papers, Dick Lennon offered one more nugget of Intelligence data. 'The other thing, for what it's worth, is that he has talked about getting some tickets to something. A family ticket cost £57 and a single cost £20. He's getting the family one.'

'A family ticket . . . Perhaps it's a day at Butlin's?' quipped Shatford.

'Could be anywhere,' replied Lennon.

'So he's visited the Dome, he's interested in a building site, visits his girlfriend, goes on the piss, wants to buy some tickets and frequents Tong Farm. Could be any one of you at the moment,' Shatford muttered cynically to the sound of muffled laughter.

'Except we wouldn't visit the Dome,' said Drew to more chuckles.

'That should be enough to get nicked for,' said Swinfield, deciding to trade in on the laughter.

The very mention of the Millennium Dome struck everyone in the room, and most everyone in England for that matter, as a joke.

Now in its eighth month of operation, the lonely Millennium Dome at Greenwich had become a national disaster, plagued by financial misjudgements, dreary exhibits, chronic mechanical troubles and low attendance.

One of the officers cracked a throwaway line, 'Maybe they're going to hit the Dome.'

He was quickly shouted down by quips: 'Come on, no one goes to the Dome. 'Why would anyone go there?'

On the wall was a map with coloured pins indicating that Wenham had been to the Dome twice.

Barry Waterman said, 'there's always the Millennium Jewels.'

This brought a few laughs, although no one knew what he was referring to.

'What are they?' asked Drew.

'They're on display at the Dome,' said Waterman. 'Meant to be priceless; millions of pounds. I only know because I used to be the Detective Inspector at Greenwich and was involved a bit with the initial security.'

A voice piped up, 'Maybe they're going to steal the Millennium Jewels!'

'Well, that would be a turn up,' said Shatford, looking to move on to other items. Suddenly his thoughts caught up with him and he stopped cold.

'Wait a minute,' Shatford said.

'The Dome . . . is right on . . . the river.'

The entire room froze, like a scene from a cartoon.

'Christ, that's it!' blurted an officer.

Sean Allen stood up abruptly and left the room as though he was on a mission.

John Swinfield speculated, 'Every day the news reports are full of the fact that people are staying away from the Dome. Yet Lee Wenham, a reprobate from Tong Farm, has been there twice. Is it possible he's the eyeball for the London firm?'

'That would make sense,' said Mark Drew. 'There must be a lot of CCTV up there, so those boys wouldn't want their mugs all over them.'

The room began filling up with energised, chattering police officers.

'It can't possibly be,' said Shatford, standing up and starting to pace around, absorbing the excitement.

The idea seemed too incredible for words, like someone was planning to steal the Crown Jewels.

'It's the shape of that river that worries me,' said Shatford, pointing to a map. 'The Dome is on a peninsula. The Thames wraps right round that curve with the Dome right in the middle. It would be ideal for them.'

At this point of the Thames, the river provided not one, but three possible fast getaway routes by speedboat – west to Preston's Road on the Isle of Dogs, north to Lower Lea Crossing or east to Woolwich Road.

'Who owns the diamonds, Barry?' he asked.

'De Beers,' replied Waterman. 'Biggest diamond company in the world, I think.'

'Where are they based?' asked Shatford.

'In the City,' Waterman responded. 'Charterhouse.'

Sean Allen came back in the room.

'Guess what?' he said, smiling and looking quite pleased with himself. 'I've just checked on the Internet. The cost of tickets for the Dome is £57 for a family ticket, and £20 for a single.'

'Well done, Sean,' said Shatford. 'I wonder if that means his code for the Dome is a building site?'

'Makes sense,' declared Swinfield. 'Not long ago that's all it was.'

'Right! We must cover this,' Shatford said emphatically. 'Sean, can you get into the Dome? Give them some cock and bull story about being from the locals and you're interested in drugs or dippers or something. If you can control the cameras, we can get him and anyone he meets on CCTV.'

'Will do, boss,' said Allen.

'Jools, you'll be with him anyway,' said Shatford, 'but can you get some staff in the Dome as well?'

'Can do,' said Lloyd.

'Whatever you do, don't let on you're from the Flying Squad. We don't want to set any hares running.'

The investigation now had a name: Operation Magician.

9. The Temple of Diamonds

The Millennium Dome, Greenwich, 25 August 2000

On Friday 25 August 2000, plain clothes surveillance teams from Scotland Yard's SO11 surveillance branch followed Lee Wenham as he drove from Tong Farm in Kent towards Greenwich and onto the grounds of the Millennium Dome.

At 10.45 a.m., Wenham entered the De Beers Millennium Jewels exhibit, armed with a camcorder and accompanied by a woman and a little girl.

His every move was being watched. Walking a few feet behind him was a female SO11 officer, disguised as a tourist, one of dozens of surveillance officers scattered around the Dome grounds. Following him into the diamond display area, she saw Wenham look all around the room and cabinets, top to bottom.

After a few minutes inside the exhibit, Wenham came out and made a call on his mobile phone. At 1.23 p.m., he took up a position directly opposite the entrance and watched people moving in and out. After wandering around the Dome, he returned to the jewel exhibit at 1.30 and videoed the entrance area.

At 1.47 p.m., Wenham walked out of the Dome to the edge of the Thames, taking a very good look in all directions, across and up and down the river, paying close attention to the north and Bow Creek. A few minutes later, joined by the woman and child, he drove off.

The gang was planning to hit the Millennium Jewels – Shatford was sure of that now. What he didn't know was when, or how, or even who the gang were, outside of Wenham, who was probably just a spotter, and Millman, who was clearly a soldier and not the brains.

Shatford had never been to the Dome, and he immediately wanted to get a close look at the target. Together with his deputy, Detective Inspector John Swinfield, Shatford paid a reconnaissance visit to the site, dressed as a tourist.

Like most Londoners, he'd seen the Dome from a distance, and from the opening credits of *EastEnders*, but had never really focused on it.

Now, as he drove up close, he was amazed.

When approached from any direction, the exterior of the 1,050-foot-wide building seemed bizarre and gigantic, looking like a beached mother ship from *Close Encounters of the Third Kind* or a fairy-tale city from the distant future.

'If you were looking for metaphors,' wrote Adam Nicolson in his 1999 book *Regeneration: The Story of the Dome,* 'the buried history of the site could scarcely have been more articulate. It had, in its time, been both a bleaching field and a vitriol factory, a rhubarb farm and a giant gasworks, a marsh over which the highest tides effortlessly washed and a place where the more celebrated criminals, once hanged, were shut in iron cages and left, quite literally, to twist in the wind.'

Nicolson described the clean-up of the poisoned, polluted former British Gas site, which began in 1996, as creating a 'broken, post-Armageddon landscape' that 'looked like the aftermath of some terrible nuclear accident.'

Today, the metallic mushroom-shaped Dome roof was stabbed by twelve gigantic yellow pylons, in a kind of techno-organic crucifixion. In a strange way, Shatford thought, it was absolutely stunning.

But the exhibits inside the Dome, however, were hideous.

Some of them looked like rejected Monty Python sketches designed by inept government bureaucrats. In one of the exhibits, the 'Body Zone', a walkway led visitors through a giant wrap-around colour replica of the inside of a human intestine. You were walking into someone's bowels.

In tribute to British humour, another exhibit featured a speaking toilet, but it was closed after repeatedly catching fire.

The Scotland Yard men paced all around the Dome property, eyeing every entrance, alcove and escape route.

They approached the 'Money Zone' exhibit housing the public vault for the De Beers Millennium Star and the Millennium Jewels.

Diamond companies are understandably very reluctant to announce the value of the jewels they put on public display, but Shatford had learned from confidential sources that the total value of all twelve jewels on display in the Dome was almost beyond belief. The most conservative estimate was a bare minimum of £200 million, but experts thought the number could be much higher. One consensus figure was a staggering £250 million.

£250 million. Shatford still couldn't believe that figure. It was ten times the value of the 1983 Brinks-Mat heist of £26 million in gold and valuables. It would dwarf the world's biggest safety deposit robbery, the

1987 raid at the Knightsbridge safety deposit centre in London that yielded £20–40 million in valuables.

If the Millennium Jewels were stolen, it would be the largest theft of all time, exceeding every other robbery of diamonds, cash, gold, valuables, artwork, financial instruments or anything else.

According to the *Guinness Book of World Records*, the highest-value bank robbery on record happened in 1976 when PLO-affiliated guerrillas used plastic explosives to blast open the vaults of the British Bank of the Middle East in Beirut, and got away with valuables worth £19 million.

The world's biggest diamond robbery occurred in Cannes in 1994, when three thieves ran into the Carlton Hotel jewellery shop firing machine guns and made off with £18.5 million in jewels.

In 1990, two men used fake police uniforms and moustaches to bluff their way into Boston's Isabella Stewart Gardner Museum and take away thirteen paintings by Rembrandt, Vermeer, Manet and Degas. The total value was a breathtaking £180 million.

To a Scotland Yard detective, all of these cases except Brinks-Mat and Knightsbridge had a glaring, depressing fact in common – the thieves got away with the loot scot-free and were never captured.

There were at least two other historical cases that were in the ballpark of the Millennium Jewels, but didn't really qualify as robberies in the traditional sense.

In 1990, £292 million in Treasury bills and bonds was stolen from a City courier, but they were impossible to cash as soon as they were stolen. And in 1945, in the closing days of World War II, hundreds of millions of pounds worth of cash, gold and valuables stolen by the Nazis from Jews and conquered nations went missing. But this wasn't a single traditional robbery; it was a series of lootings, confiscations and disappearances by Nazi officials and others (including a few Allied soldiers).

The De Beers Millennium Star was the Holy Grail of diamonds.

The reason for its stratospheric value was the fact that it was, quite simply, the world's largest flawless diamond. The weight of it alone, over 200 carats, placed it in the absolute top tier of finished diamonds, the value of which rises exponentially with weight. On top of this, it was completely colourless, one of the rarest marks of a diamond.

Finally, it was 'full flawless' (flawless both internally and externally, a testament to the genius of how it was cut and polished). There were two bigger internally flawless diamonds, the Centenary, at 273.85

carats, and the Incomparable, at 407 carats, but they were not flawless externally.

As Shatford and Swinfield approached the De Beers exhibit, which doubled as a diamond vault, there was – in keeping with English tradition – a visible lack of armed security in the area.

Shatford slipped through the narrow black entrance hall into the Millennium Jewels exhibit.

It felt like being in a temple. It was a darkened circular chamber, and its walls held cases displaying the eleven priceless blue De Beers Millennium diamonds, including the 27.64-carat Heart of Eternity, the largest vivid blue diamond in the world.

And there, in the centre of the room, suspended in pinpoint spotlights and floating in space in a dreamlike trance, was the crowning achievement of the greatest diamond empire in history.

He walked up to the De Beers Millennium Star display case, and gazed upon the largest perfect diamond the world had ever seen.

10. The Colour of Magic

The Republic of Zaire, 1992

The digger wrapped his fingers around the stone and pulled it up from the ancient riverbed.

He was a poor diamond prospector from a mud village, and he scratched a living out of the dirt with a shovel and sifting pan, searching for precious stones. It was almost a hopeless quest; the stones were rarely of gem quality, and almost never bigger than a few carats in weight.

But right now the digger held in his hand a clump of prehistoric crystallised carbon, formed a hundred miles underground and forced up towards the Earth's surface by eons of heat and pressure on a journey to its first glimpse of sunlight in 3,000,000,000 years.

It glittered in the digger's hand like a piece of solid ice.

And was enormous.

He scrutinised the object, carefully wrapped it up in a cloth and headed for the village, which would soon swirl into a frenzy of excitement and disbelief.

Night was falling on the steamy African diamond-trading city of Mbuji-Mayi when the Englishman heard a knock on his window.

In the front yard of his fenced-in, home-office compound, there stood a tribal elder and eleven of his villagers.

The elder was holding something in his hand, wrapped in tissue paper. He had a smile on his face. When he unwrapped the paper to reveal the object, the Englishman felt his pulse jump.

It seemed far too big to be a rough diamond; it was a slab almost the size of a cigarette pack.

In the diamond world, this would be a behemoth. Diamonds rarely exceeded a few carats in weight. If it were real, this one could be many hundreds of carats.

The Englishman pressed his fingers against the object.

It was cold to the touch.

At the age of 28, Andrew Churcher was the De Beers mining company's field man in this teeming, lawless city 600 miles east of Kinshasa, capital of the collapsed African kleptocracy once known as Democratic Republic of Congo, now called Zaire.

For two days he had heard rumours swirling out of the jungle of a giant stone being discovered somewhere in the vicinity of a village forty miles from here.

He'd heard such rumours before. They never panned out. Now he was looking at an unusually large hunk of sparkling stone, shaped like a blunted spear tip. The colour was bright and clear. He'd never seen anything like it.

Instantly, Churcher realised he might be looking at something that, in his business, could fly beyond the limits of beauty and into the realm of magic.

He beckoned the delegation into his little office, locked the door and fastened on his jeweller's eyepiece.

Amazed, he could not find a single flaw.

It was a freak of nature.

The villagers circled around as he placed the gem on his desk scale. The scale registered a number that was both gigantic and lucky: 777. This is a once-in-a-lifetime stone, Churcher thought. I cannot let it out of the office.

As the local buyer for De Beers, the world's leading diamond company, Churcher was authorised to make dozens of deals every month that totalled, on average, about £2 million per month. But on this deal he wanted back-up.

Churcher switched on his short-wave radio, his only link to the outside world, and called his boss John Wenham[2] in Kinshasa, the capital of Zaire.

'It's in the office,' Churcher declared. 'It's fantastic, but I need a second opinion.' Wenham told him to try to hold onto the diamond until he flew up the next morning.

But Churcher's guests wanted to return to their village that night, and they insisted on taking the diamond with them.

That could be a disaster, Churcher realised.

The streets of Mbuji-Mayi were thick with criminal gangs, rebels, smugglers, corrupt government officials and dozens of competing diamond buyers. Many of them had already heard the rumours and some would kill to get their hands on a gem like this.

[2] Note: No relation to Lee Wenham or the Wenham family at Tong Farm.

Churcher persuaded the villagers and their chief to sleep overnight in the compound. The diamond was locked in the office safe. In the morning, curious onlookers were already gathering at the entrance when John Wenham arrived from the capital.

The negotiations ground on all day, with the villagers holding out for their first and only offer price.

As twilight approached, the deal was done.

The price: a reported £4.2 million, a world record for a rough diamond. The Englishmen gathered all the cash they had on hand to give the villagers as a deposit, and signed a credit slip for the balance.

A De Beers jet was waiting at the airstrip on the edge of town.

But by now the crowd outside was swelling, and a team of armed soldiers was sealing off the front of the property. They weren't there for crowd control. The troops had been bribed by a Middle Eastern diamond company to block the villagers from leaving until they could fly a planeload of cash into town with a competing offer.

The Englishmen decided their only chance to escape was to try to sneak out the back of the compound, and make a run for the airstrip. As their driver approached an adjacent alley, Wenham placed the diamond box in a satchel, draped it on his shoulder and quietly slipped through the garden.

He clambered over the back wall, dropped into the alley and into the waiting vehicle.

Minutes later, as the De Beers plane was taxiing for take off with Wenham and the diamond inside, another plane touched down from Kinshasa, containing the representatives of the Middle Eastern company.

According to eyewitnesses, they were shaking their fists at the De Beers jet as it vanished into the darkening sky.

11. The Heart of an Empire

17 Charterhouse Street, London, 28 August 2000

Deep inside a nondescript six-storey building on a quiet London street east of Hatton Garden, was a vault that contained £2,000,000,000 in diamonds.

70 per cent of the world's wholesale diamond market was controlled directly from this building, the headquarters of De Beers, the world's leading trader of rough diamonds. Hidden cameras and security sensors covered every square inch of the property.

The vault at 17 Charterhouse Street was in the most secure building in Europe, and it represented the heart of a global empire that stretched from diamond mines in Russia and Africa to the trading houses of New York, Antwerp and Tel Aviv.

It was never photographed or publicised, but the diamond vault evoked the kind of mythic wonder conjured up by F Scott Fitzgerald in his story, *The Diamond as Big as the Ritz.*

'There was a room,' wrote Fitzgerald, 'that was like a platonic conception of the ultimate prism – ceiling, floor, and all, it was lined with an unbroken mass of diamonds, diamonds of every size and shape, until, lit with tall violet lamps in the corners, it dazzled the eyes with a whiteness that could be compared only with itself, beyond human wish or dream.'

Every five weeks, over 150 diamond dealers from around the world flocked into this building to partake in a pre-scripted ritual – a ceremony that was conducted by the omnipotent-sounding De Beers 'Central Selling Organisation'. One by one, the diamond dealers were ushered through the brass-handled front door, led to a room on the second floor, and presented with a box containing their fixed allotment of uncut diamonds to re-sell into the world's wholesale and retail markets.

The quantity, and the price, was non-negotiable.

De Beers was accused of being a cartel, but the company preferred to call the process 'single channel marketing'. The process was highly effective, as it sustained the high stable prices of a world diamond market that was based on an illusion. It was De Beers' own chairman Nicky Oppenheimer who once observed that 'diamonds are intrinsically worthless, except for the deep psychological need they fill.'

On a sunny day at the end of August 2000, Scotland Yard detectives Jon Shatford and John Swinfield walked into 17 Charterhouse Street to meet Tim Thorn, the head of security for De Beers.

The façade of the building consisted of stone that was blackened in places, and it was divided in the middle by an arch with big metal gates leading to the door. The policemen were led by a security guard through narrow corridors into a large outer office, and then escorted across a courtyard to meet Tim Thorn.

When Lee Wenham was spotted inside the De Beers display at the Millennium Dome, the detectives debated how and when they should inform De Beers. The one thing they worried about was the chance, however remote, of an inside agent or an inadvertent leak that could compromise their investigation.

Thorn's opulent office was illuminated through glass panels in the ceiling, and its window was covered with vertical slatted blinds. A brass reading lamp and leather ink blotter adorned an immaculate oak desk.

The most impressive features were two large photographs on Thorn's wall, mementoes of his Royal Air Force days. One photo showed three Jaguar fighter jets at low level in an arrow formation over open countryside. The handwritten inscription in the corner read, 'To Squadron Leader Tim Thorn from his colleagues'. The other photograph was of the tall, distinguished-looking Thorn dressed in a flying suit and standing between two Jaguars with his helmet under his arm.

Shatford and Swinfield were impressed, thinking that this was a man they could do business with.

The three men sat in the leather chairs.

As the detectives talked him through the threat to the Millennium Jewels, Thorn was visibly stunned.

Thorn described how the diamond exhibit at the Dome was in fact a heavily reinforced vault built inside a highly complex security system.

De Beers Company had spent over £750,000 on building the exhibit, a combination display-vault that its designers promised was impregnable. It featured time-locks, steel doors, 20mm-thick reinforced glass cabinets and 4-foot-thick concrete walls built to withstand a 60-ton ramraid.

The designers calculated that the jewel case would take at least thirty minutes to drill into, using any known drilling instrument.

The exhibit was monitored 24 hours a day on CCTV at De Beers' headquarters. Additionally, around the twenty-acre Dome site, 170 high tech TV cameras kept watch on all entrances and exhibits, while radio-equipped Dome security guards were on patrol.

'But do you mean the diamonds are not taken out every night?' asked Shatford in disbelief. In diamond shops around the world, gems were usually taken off display every night when the buildings closed and put in vaults for safe keeping.

'No,' replied Thorn. 'The exhibit itself is a reinforced vault. The diamonds are as safe in there as any other vault.'

'But are they ever taken out?' asked Shatford.

'Occasionally, yes,' said Thorn, 'for special shows.'

'When are they being moved next?' asked Swinfield.

Thorn went to check a diary on his desk.

'Now let me see, yes, it looks like the 31st, this Thursday,' he said.

The Star was flying to Japan.

The detectives were stunned to learn that the De Beers Millennium Star was scheduled to be moved out of the Dome in a high-security convoy and shipped to Tokyo for a two-week exhibition.

Shatford and Swinfield exchanged knowing glances. That must be it, they thought. This must be when the next attack would happen.

Shatford asked, 'How will it be moved?'

'Two Brinks-Mat security vans will arrive at the Dome just before it opens,' the De Beers security official explained. 'Each driver will be handed a case. One will contain the diamond. The other will be empty. Only my staff will know which is the real one.'

'Does that mean the display will close down?' asked Shatford.

'No. Two of my staff will go into the jewel house before the vans arrive and replace the genuine diamond with a convincing replica,' replied Thorn.

'So for the time that the real De Beers Millennium Star is in Tokyo the one on display at the Dome will be a worthless copy?'

'Yes, although it's still worth about £6,000.'

'Then if there's going to be a robbery it would need to be an inside job, either here or at Brinks-Mat,' said Swinfield.

'What?' said Thorn, visibly exasperated.

'We've got to face the possibility,' said Shatford. 'If this is a robbery, the gang must know which van to hit. And how else would they know the diamond was going to be moved in the first place?'

'But my staff are well paid, of the highest quality,' argued Thorn. 'I find it incredible that any of them would be involved.'

'Well, we are talking a lot of money,' said Swinfield.

'I know,' said Thorn, 'but how can they hope to get away with it?'

'Perhaps they don't have a choice,' said Shatford. 'It could be that they or their families are under some sort of threat. We will have to cover the transfer on 31 August.'

'What do you want me to do?' asked Thorn.

'Just carry on as though everything is normal,' said Shatford. 'This may never happen. If it does, then I will make sure we are ready to deal with it.'

'In the meantime it's better that we don't come here again in case we arouse suspicion,' said Swinfield. 'Is there any other place we can meet you if we need to?'

'How about Snow Hill Police Station?' replied Thorn.

The policemen agreed to keep Thorn updated on any developments and Thorn, in turn, agreed to get them the names of his staff who would be at the Dome doing the handover.

Now the police had both a probable target and a likely date for the next attack.

The police reckoned that the so-far unidentified London gang must be planning to hit the diamond in transit, on the road, as the convoy moved between the Dome and the De Beers vault in central London. In other words, a ramped-up spectacle adapted from the Nine Elms and Aylesford attacks.

Such an attack would run a much higher risk of bloodshed and civilian casualties.

In response, the Flying Squad would now have to stage the biggest and most high-risk 'pavement ambush' it had ever attempted.

When Shatford returned to the Yard he made a call to SO19, Scotland Yard's firearms branch.

It was time to bring in the heavy firepower.

12. The Plan

New Scotland Yard, 29 August 2000

Shatford was hunched over a street map of London, surveying the probable routes of the De Beers convoy scheduled for Thursday 31 August.

It was all bad news.

The convoy was scheduled for the morning rush hour.

The route would take the Millennium Star out of the Dome, through the Blackwall Tunnel, then due west through the heart of the densely populated East End towards the financial capital of Europe, the City of London.

There were dozens of possible ambush points for the gang.

The De Beers convoy would pass close by residential neighbourhoods, schools, hospitals and markets, and packed, narrow streets. The vehicle and pedestrian traffic on a week day morning would be heavy.

So far, the gang responsible for the Nine Elms and Aylesford attacks had used firearms, explosives, boats and small fleets of lorries and vans in their strikes, with teams of up to a dozen men.

If the gangsters hoped to stop the convoy and break into the Brinks-Mat van, they would sharply need to escalate their weaponry and manpower, and launch a small war.

They might deploy a team of twenty spotters, soldiers and getaway drivers. They would need more guns, more vehicles and more powerful explosives, like Semtex or rocket-propelled grenades. And if the gang lost control of the attack and things fell apart, scores of civilian bystanders could be injured. Downtown London would be a war zone, the site of a historic massacre.

To Shatford, the only effective response seemed to be overwhelming force – an invisible, mass deployment of hundreds of police, all along the route.

On a job of this magnitude, Shatford had to brief his superiors. The stakes were huge, but if he overstated the risks, the operation would never be approved.

Shatford had already discussed the job with his immediate superior, Detective Chief Superintendent John Coles. Now he went another level up, to see Commander Alan Brown.

'Sir, I need to discuss a quick job with you,' said Shatford, knowing he would be anything but quick.

'OK, come in and take a seat,' said Brown.

He had known Alan Brown for several years. They were both career detectives, and he knew he could talk openly to him. They got on well together, but mention of the Dome was bound to be political dynamite. Brown would need to be absolutely certain that Shatford's plan was sound if he was to allow him to deploy armed officers in such numbers. If he was not satisfied, he might insist that the operation was aborted.

'It's about the Nine Elms and Aylesford robbers,' said Shatford.

'Have we identified them yet?' asked Brown.

'Not yet, no, but I think we are closer. We might have their safe house down in Kent.'

'Good. Sounds promising.'

'Well it might be,' said Shatford. 'I think I know where their next job might be.'

'Where?' Brown asked, his eyes wide with obvious excitement.

'Millennium Dome.'

'What!'

'Well, when I say the Millennium Dome, I don't mean inside.'

'Thank God for that!'

'No,' Shatford explained. 'There's a diamond, called the De Beers Millennium Star. It's worth hundreds of millions, and it's being moved from the Dome on Thursday. We know that Lee Wenham, that's one of the blokes who owns the safe house, is going there and it might be to meet the gang.'

Shatford was not entirely happy with the way he had summarised the situation. He suddenly realised how little they knew about the gang.

'Well, they're not likely to do it today are they?' asked Brown.

'No, it's being moved on Thursday. It's actually displayed in a vault at the Dome, so they would not be able to get at it there.'

Brown intently absorbed the details as Shatford talked him through the entire investigation, interrupting with probing questions.

As Shatford prepared to leave Brown's office, he promised to keep him updated. He was secretly pleased that Brown had not raised any objections to his plan.

Shatford's mobile phone rang just as they were wrapping up. It was John Swinfield, with amazing news.

'What!' Shatford exclaimed. 'Excellent. OK, we will talk later.'

Shatford stared at Brown as he ended the call.

'When we saw Tim Thorn, the head of security for De Beers, he told us that the diamond was being moved on Thursday. He has just discovered it was put in the register wrong, and it will actually move on 1 September.'

'What's the significance of that?' asked Brown, slightly puzzled.

'It's a Friday. Both Nine Elms and Aylesford were carried out on a Friday,' said Shatford.

'It looks like the game's on.'

'We are going to need very good control of the area,' said SO19 firearms specialist Inspector Vincent Esposito as he pointed at the map, 'so I can get my people in the right positions.'

In a small office on the top floor of the Flying Squad's Tower Bridge office, six policemen were gathered around a big map of the Dome, which they could see through their office window in the eastern distance.

The policemen were worrying about their snipers – where to put them and how to hide them. Most important, they were worrying about how to keep members of the public out of harm's way.

Everything the police did was governed by the strategy of risk control, reducing to the maximum extent possible any risks that the gang posed to civilian bystanders.

'Every police officer has got to be able to demonstrate that he used minimum force at all times,' wrote former London police officer Keith Lloyd Webb in 1997. 'He is not fit to be an officer of the law unless that doctrine is uppermost in his mind at all times.'

The identities of most of the gang were still unknown, but if the gang contained veterans of the Nine Elms and Aylesford jobs, they showed little compunction about using violence.

Those criminals were volatile and unpredictable, combining paramilitary ruthlessness and determination with flourishes of incompetence, hence the lost keys at Nine Elms and the falling trousers at Aylesford.

During both attacks, the gang showed no hesitation to threaten violence or unleash lethal force. They pointed weapons point-blank at the heads of members of the public and security officers, set off explosive devices that incinerated vehicles, conducted an extremely dangerous high-speed ramming operation involving two large vehicles, and opened fire on police after a high-speed chase.

The existence of such a gang posed a threat to public safety, and there was a chance that if they struck again they would injure or kill members of the public and police officers.

If a new attack occurred, the challenge for Scotland Yard was to protect the public at all costs, capture the criminals, and get enough evidence to convict them and get them off the streets.

On 29 August 2000, the Flying Squad office was a buzz of excitement, with Squad officers coming and going. The core officers joining Shatford around the table were Detective Inspector John Swinfield, Detective Sergeant Mark Drew and Detective Constable Sean Allen. Their qualities were the polar opposite of the fictional TV images of John Thaw's bone-crushing Detective Inspector Jack Regan in *The Sweeney*, or the cop-on-the-edge archetype of Hollywood detectives.

These officers were exemplary in illustrating how, in the real world, the most powerful weapons in a detective's arsenal include diplomacy and charm – the ability to build relationships of trust with witnesses and suspects, and to work smoothly with other police officers as part of a team.

Swinfield, for example, the number two man on Operation Magician, combined good humour and a soft voice with razor-sharp instincts concerning criminal psychology. He was a superb operational detective who worked amazingly long hours when on a job, and never seemed to tire.

Similarly, Mark Drew was a detective with an ideal personality for the job – warm, polite and respectful. He undertook every task with enthusiasm and total commitment, and was very good at preparing case papers after an investigation, a crucial talent for a detective. Drew was a close friend of Sean Allen, an engaging and methodical officer who was also superb at organising paperwork. He had a near-photographic memory for villains and never forgot a face.

The Millenium Dome covered a 180-acre site on the North Greenwich peninsula, and was surrounded on three sides by the Thames. The meridian time line cut across the north of the site, which was about two miles from historic Greenwich. In policing terms, it was a potential battlefield.

The introduction of SO19 into Operation Magician automatically increased the odds in favour of police and the public. SO19 is the firearms force of the Metropolitan Police Service, just one step down from the SAS in defending against an organised threat of violence.

The Specialist Firearms Officers of SO19 are highly trained, highly mobile tactical experts who provide weapons support to the rest of the force when needed, enabling the vast majority of police work in London to be performed by unarmed officers.

As the SO19 advisor to Operation Magician, Inspector Vince Esposito was reviewing the details of the mass defensive deployment planned for 1 September.

The convoy of two unloaded Brinks-Mat security vans would approach the Millennium Dome from the Blackwall Tunnel northern approach, and proceed to Gate 4 of the Dome. This area around the entrance, the police agreed, was the point where the diamond would be most vulnerable.

The Brinks-Mat security officers inside the vans were to have no knowledge of the increased police presence to avoid the risk of compromising the operation in the event, however unlikely, of an inside agent.

'What we will have to prepare for is the possibility of an attack on the De Beers staff before they get to the security vans,' said Shatford.

'And when the jewel is about to be loaded,' added Esposito.

It was only an educated guess, but based on the split-second getaways of the Nine Elms and Aylesford attacks, the detectives had concluded that the gang had been monitoring police radio frequencies prior to the raids to estimate police locations and response times. Such high-tech equipment was illegal in Britain, but the gang could have bought it abroad.

'We are pretty certain,' said Shatford, 'that this gang has the ability to scan and intercept our radio communications. We will need a complete radio blackout.'

The police would be able to communicate only on their mobile phones and pagers.

'We have good eyeball from the south side,' said Swinfield, tapping positions on the map. 'We've got a lookout position on the top of Canary Wharf, and another spot south of the Dome down here.

'Then I thought we might be able to bury crops officers in here,' Swinfield continued, pointing to spots near Millennium Way, 'which puts us very close to the vans.'

'Does that give us any blind spots in this larger area?' asked Shatford, circling his hand around the map.

'Yes it does,' Swinfield replied, 'but there are two cranes in the middle. If we could get into one of those we could cover the whole area.'

'That would be excellent,' said Shatford. 'We must be able to do that, mustn't we?'

One police officer in the room looked a bit sceptical.

'Well,' said Detective Inspector Adrian Smales in a slow, deliberate voice, 'you will have to be careful who you put up there.'

'Why's that?' asked Shatford.

'Because they will need to have a real head for heights, if the forecast is anything to go by. It's going to be very windy, and those things bend and sway in the wind like they're toppling over.'

'Well, I'm sure there'll be some hardy Flying Squad officer who can stomach it,' guessed Shatford.

'No,' said Smales, 'I'm telling you, it won't be easy. You also have to make sure the cab is properly secure, or it could be worse. The cab can actually swing round.'

'How do you know all this, Adrian?' asked Shatford.

'Well, I used to be a crane driver,' replied Smales.

A beaming smile appeared on Shatford's face that was replicated on all the other officers' faces, as together they looked Smales up and down.

'Oh, come on!' said Smales, suddenly realising he'd just nominated himself. 'Why did I have to open my big mouth?'

'What you will need to look out for is their third eye,' said Shatford. 'You will have to see what security is about. I think there might be a night watchman.'

A 'third eye' is a gang member who watches for watchers. They observe the gang and see if there is any activity around them that could be hostile, meaning police in most cases. If they see anyone out of place or taking an interest in any of the gang they will warn them off. Smales had to sneak into the property and on up to the top of the crane without alerting anyone.

'I will have a look tonight and do a trial run,' said Smales, resigned to his fate. 'And I will have to get some special wind-proof clothing and waterproofs.'

'OK,' said Shatford, still smiling at Smales's inadvertent initiative.

'But make sure I see the receipts.'

Later that day Shatford met with De Beers' security director Tim Thorn in an interview room at the Snow Hill Police Station, in the City of London.

Thorn handed him the names of the two De Beers employees who would package the diamond at the Dome on the day of the transfer.

The plan was for both employees to go to the De Beers exhibit early, each carrying a case. One of the cases would contain a replica of the De

Beers Millennium Star – an almost identical copy made of Zircon and plastic. After cleaning the diamond, they would swap the real Millennium Star for the fake. When the security vans arrived, a case would be handed to each driver. Neither driver would know which case contained the diamond and which one was empty.

The plan sounded good to Shatford, since in theory it immediately cut the odds of a successful robbery by 50 per cent. But it also gave him an opportunity to cut the odds to zero, by secretly arranging an extra deception: a 'double swap'. He could arrange for one of the De Beers employees to leave the original diamond on display and pass the replica to the Brinks-Mat van in its place.

'We are putting the finishing touches to our operation around the Dome,' the detective told Thorn. 'I will have close to 300 police officers covering the area and the route.'

'Are you confident the robbery is going to take place?' asked Thorn.

'There are few certainties in this game, but the Intelligence looks reasonable,' said Shatford. 'We must plan for it.'

'Well, I'm sure you know what you are doing,' Thorn replied.

'There's one other thing,' said Shatford. 'When the two De Beers men exchange the diamond for the fake, can we somehow arrange to swap it back again without the other one knowing?'

'Well that might be tricky,' Thorn speculated, 'but I daresay it would be possible.'

'Which of the men do you trust the most?'

'Both are good, but Jonathan Marsh* is responsible for it so he would be the obvious choice.'

'OK,' said Shatford, 'but you must make sure he does not breathe a word to anyone. Not even the person he's with.'

'I am sure I can trust him to be totally discreet,' said Thorn.

13. The Convoy

The Millennium Dome, 1 September 2000

It was 12.30 a.m. The convoy was going to move in eight hours, carrying what everyone except a select few thought to be the priceless diamond. The tactical plan called for the heaviest deployment of police to be dug in and hidden in spots immediately around the Dome, but Shatford was worried about the rest of the journey, through the East End and into the City.

To reinforce the officers covering the route, he arranged with the Ministry of Defence to borrow two Royal Air Force Wessex helicopters and pilots. They contained a strike team of heavily armed SO19 officers who could descend rapidly from the sky at any given location.

To cover the river, the Metropolitan Police Marine Support Unit had positioned high-speed launches covering both ends of the Thames, each craft containing more SO19 sharpshooters.

On the opposite side of the river, at East India Dock on the Isle of Dogs, armed Flying Squad officers lay in wait, ready to cover the North Side of the Thames the minute an attack took place.

As a precaution, an ambulance crew was placed on standby to rush casualties to hospital. Two hospitals were nominated, Woolwich and Greenwich.

At 12.30 a.m., Detective Inspector Adrian Smales was picked up from his home by Chris Bishop, a Flying Squad driver. Already in the car were two other hefty squad officers who would act as minders. Smales was dressed all in black.

He was dropped off with his two minders at Peninsula Place, very close to the Dome. He was carrying a small holdall which contained bolt croppers, and a few other essential items. It was a burglar's kit.

The only sign of activity was at a building ballast depot on the river about 700 yds away, where a ship was being unloaded.

He walked towards his target, a construction crane, which was in an area surrounded by 8-foot-high hoardings. The weather had turned much of the surrounding area into a lake. He said goodbye to his minders and scrambled over the hoardings.

On the other side he hid in some nearby bushes. There were sounds of life coming from a Portakabin that was lit up close by.

A few minutes later a security guard came out, got in a car and drove off.

It was time to move. Smales left the cover of the bushes and climbed a 3-foot-high fence to move nearer the crane.

It was pitch black as there was no moon, though the sky was clear with fast travelling clouds from east to west.

When Smales arrived at the base of the crane the only light he could see was from the Portakabin and distant street lighting. He climbed the ladder to the first platform of the crane above the large concrete ballast weights at the bottom.

Access to the tower of the crane was prevented by plywood around its four sides intended to stop trespassers. It had a trap door in the middle that was bolted down.

Smales took the bolt cutters from his holdall and went to work on the lock. It snapped easily. As he climbed higher it seemed like the crane was swaying from side to side.

Eventually he arrived at the area under the cab that holds the slewing cogs which allow the crane to swing around at the top while the tower remains still. He was 150 ft high, and stopped to get his breath.

Despite the darkness he had a good view over London.

The breeze was exaggerated because of the height, and it was bitterly cold for the time of the year. The main jib was pointing west in line with the wind and, by following its length, he looked out towards the big HSBC building that was illuminated in big red letters. The Dome stood in the middle. And the river was fast-running to the right – in places, the lights of pathways followed its shoreline.

A padlock secured the cab door as he tried to enter. It was time for the bolt cutters again. The Commissioner would settle the bill later.

At 3.30 a.m., officers were taking up their positions and digging in for the long wait.

Shatford, Swinfield, Allen and Drew were with eight other gun ships parked behind a supermarket off the Millennium Way.

Crops officers were dug into a gully near the spot where the security vans were expected to stop.

It was a windy, drizzly night, and a chief topic of conversation was Adrian Smales, high up in the crane.

The more the wind blew, the more intense the covert laughing and joking became.

At about 4.30 a.m., the police were alerted when a white van drove into the area around the Millennium Dome, but it left without incident.

Miles away, armed Flying Squad officers were watching the homes of the two De Beers employees who were scheduled to move the diamond. It was possible that their families could be kidnapped or put under duress by the gang.

As dawn broke, the wind and drizzle continued. At 7 a.m., SO19 firearms officers dozing in their cars came alive and tooled up with their body armour and standard-issue weapons, the Heckler and Koch MP5 carbine, and the Glock 17 9 mm SLP (self-loading pistol).

At 8 a.m., the De Beers men arrived at the Dome.

As they were let inside, Shatford was receiving a commentary by mobile phone from Tim Thorn, who was monitoring the situation on CCTV at his headquarters.

At 8.30 a.m., the two Brinks-Mat vans arrived.

This was the signal for the two military helicopters positioned a mile away at Woolwich Arsenal to start their massive rotating blades. The pilots were ready, having plotted their route to the Dome.

The tension had now built to an incredible pitch.

The Blackwall Tunnel entrance and exit was an obvious choice for the gang to place blocking vehicles and strike. The Flying Squad were prepared for this, and had squad cars positioned on each side.

From atop the crane, Adrian Smales was reporting in by mobile phone.

The Brinks-Mat drivers entered the Dome, but lingered awhile as the De Beers men were not yet ready.

Suddenly Shatford's mobile rang. It was Tim Thorn, with startling news. One of the drivers had breached procedure. He had jokingly asked which vehicle the real diamond was going in. Did this mean there was an inside agent?

At 9.30 a.m., the De Beers men handed a case to each of the drivers. The drivers got in their vehicles, pulled out, and headed towards the Blackwall Tunnel.

Atop the Canary Wharf building, a Flying Squad officer followed the action through his binoculars. At a height of 800 ft, it was the tallest building in Britain, giving an excellent view for miles.

'Heading out towards Millennium Way,' he announced on his mobile phone, shivering from the fierce breeze spiralling around the rooftop, 'towards Central Bravo Nine 5.'

Central Bravo Nine 5 was the call sign for the closest Flying Squad gun ship. In the rear were two SO19 officers. If they were anxious, it didn't show on their faces.

Phase II of the operation began, an 'invisible shield' designed by John Swinfield.

The plan was for eight unmarked Flying Squad gun ships and two SO11 surveillance vehicles to fall in, and travel in front and behind the Brinks-Mat vans, providing a hidden escort for the rest of the trip.

Falling into position ahead of the security vans was Mark Drew, in command of another gun ship. He would enter the tunnel before the vans arrived in case blocking vehicles were being put in place.

Separating the gun ships from the security vans was a van carrying an SO11 surveillance team. At the first sign of an ambush they would break radio silence and call in the gun ships.

The Brinks-Mat vans drove along Millennium Way to the roundabout. The roads were busy with rush-hour traffic making its weary way into London.

The vans pulled away from the Dome grounds without any problems.

At this, an advance party of two Squad cars peeled off towards the De Beers headquarters in the City of London to prepare for the possibility of an attack at the end of the route.

The next possibility was for the vans to be attacked inside the tunnel, where police would be out of mobile phone contact. It was the ideal place for it to happen, and Shatford was almost convinced it would occur here.

The first security van eased away at the roundabout onto the A102 Tunnel Approach.

As the second van pulled out, it had to slow down for a white transit van that approached at speed.

Suddenly, the van was in between the two security vehicles as they made their way towards the tunnel.

Four vehicles behind them was a gun ship driven by Grant Johnson, a burly Flying Squad officer.

'Don't like the look of this,' said Johnson to the SO19 firearms officers in his car. 'That van's driving like a nutter.' His passengers instinctively moved their fingers to cover the trigger of their weapons.

'Entering the tunnel now, boss,' said Drew, taking the last opportunity to report back to Shatford by mobile phone before losing the signal in the tunnel.

The white van was really worrying Johnson.

It kept changing pace, slowing so the rear security van had to brake, then racing to catch up with the one in front.

'He's driving like a lunatic,' said Chris Bishop from the wheel of another gun ship. 'Just doesn't look right to me.'

Johnson wanted to warn Drew what was happening behind, but knew he would be out of signal range.

The vans were getting closer to the tunnel.

A series of deep breaths later, Johnson's car was in. The security van in front was barely visible, then disappeared altogether when it turned a corner.

'At least the traffic is still moving,' mused Bishop.

Slowly now in the heavy traffic, the gun ship turned one corner then another until daylight at the other end could be seen.

'So far so good,' said Bishop.

'There's a long way to go yet,' Johnson countered.

They emerged into the daylight on the north side of the Thames and could see the security vans ahead. The white van was still between them. Traffic began to move faster as the road widened.

Police spotters and marksmen were hidden in positions all along the route to the De Beers headquarters.

There was some guesswork here, since the Brinks-Mat drivers had no idea of the police presence and had some flexibility about what route they would take, depending on the traffic.

The first Brinks-Mat van's left indicator switched on.

'He must be going into East India Dock Road,' said Johnson. It was the route the police expected. They were now travelling through the heart of London's East End.

The security vans continued with their invisible shield past Bow Police Station and Thames Magistrates Court.

'I still don't like the look of that van,' said Bishop. The SO19 officers peered forwards to get a better look through the front windscreen.

They were envisaging exactly what they would do if a gang of armed men jumped out of the van at the traffic lights.

The vans were approaching Mile End underground station. They slowed for the red traffic lights which then went green. They moved off slowly as traffic on the left tried to merge into their lane to avoid the bus lane. A lorry suddenly pulled out from a side road on the right and pushed its way behind the last security van, causing traffic coming in the opposite direction to brake.

'What do you make of that?' asked Johnson.

'Don't know,' said Bishop, 'for a minute I thought . . . '

'Me too,' said Johnson.

Their vision was now mostly obscured by the rear of the lorry.

They passed the Rotherhithe Tunnel entrance, passed Sidney Street and headed into the one-way system at Aldgate.

It still seemed that both the white van and lorry were closely shadowing the Brinks-Mat vans.

But here, the white van pulled away.

The convoy moved into Commercial Street, past Spitalfields Market and into Great Eastern Street.

Now the lorry pulled away into Shoreditch High Street and vanished, giving everyone in Grant Johnson's gun ship a better view of the tailing security van.

'They could hit it at the entrance of De Beers,' Johnson speculated.

'Could be anywhere,' replied an SO19 officer.

The invisible fleet of gun ships and support vehicles tightened up their formation, circling around the security vans.

The line of traffic filtered to the left into Old Street roundabout.

They were now in the City of London. These were narrow streets, made all the more difficult by parked delivery vehicles.

The vans turned left into Aldersgate Street and moved slowly down towards Charterhouse Street, the home of De Beers. Mark Drew was already there, his gun ship positioned in a small entrance near Smithfield central markets.

'Towards you now, Mark,' said Johnson on the mobile phone.

'We've got eyeball,' announced Drew.

'Approaching now . . . indicating . . . held for traffic . . . careful, no he's turning . . . number one in . . . number two indicating . . . he's blocked . . . no, he's turning . . . number two in.'

The Millennium Star (albeit the fake) disappeared into the secure bubble of the De Beers complex.

Across London, some 300 police officers were standing down.

There was no attack.

'What in the fuck just happened?' exclaimed Shatford.

'How could we have misread this?'

Swinfield, Drew and Allen were standing with him in the supermarket car park near the Dome. They were all mystified.

'I don't know, I was sure it was going down,' said Drew. 'We all were.'

Was there a leak? Had an inside agent tipped off the gang? Had they misread everything?

The officers had been up all night, and were totally dejected. Every emotion was exaggerated because of sleep deprivation.

It was back to square one.

Detective Constable Allen, still keyed up from the action, decided to go into the Dome and spot-check the CCTV security room.

When he returned to his office at New Scotland Yard, Shatford shut the door and buried his head in his hands.

He had staged a huge, expensive police operation on a bad hunch.

'What a fool I am,' he thought.

'How could I ever have believed for a minute they were going to do that? What an idiot I am!'

As if on cue, his phone rang.

It was Sean Allen, calling from the Dome.

'We've got them on the plot!'

'What?'

'They're here – they're *inside the Dome!*'

14. The Shadow General

**The Millennium Dome, Bronze Control Room,
1 September 2000, 10.45 a.m.**

Detective Constable Sean Allen was looking at a ghost.

The man on the closed-circuit TV screen was about as close as one can come to being invisible in a modern society.

He was not known to have a job, pay his taxes, possess a National Insurance number or have a legal bank account. His name rarely appeared on official documents.

The policeman leaned closer to the television monitor and intently studied the image.

'I know who that is,' Allen suddenly realised.

He was in the Millennium Dome Bronze Control Security Room, studying dozens of flickering, remote-controlled images.

After the morning's operation had fizzled out, Allen decided to return to the Dome and resume what he'd been doing for the last week – familiarising himself with the security systems. He was getting to know how everything worked so, in case of an emergency, police could throw security personnel out of the room and seize the TV controls.

Fearing that the gang might have an inside man on the Dome staff even here, in the extra secure TV control room, Allen had a cover story: police were investigating possible drug dealing on the Dome property.

Police had kept the details of today's operation secret even from Dome security guards. Private security guards were sometimes unreliable – older men or guys who flunked the police exam and gossiped about their work in pubs. One extra pint down their throat and news of the police operation could leak across London in a flash.

On one of the screens, a dark-haired man in his late 30s, wearing a baseball cap and sunglasses, was strolling nonchalantly through the Dome, accompanied by a stocky man in his 40s and a woman pushing a baby stroller.

In a completely random fluke, at exactly 10.45a.m., Sean Allen's eyes had rested on the monitor at the moment the face was clearly discernible.

He recognised the face behind the sunglasses – it belonged to a shadowy 39-year-old man he had seen before.

'It's Ray Betson,' Allen declared furtively into his mobile phone.

'Who?' asked Jon Shatford from his office at New Scotland Yard.

'Betson, Raymond. B – E – T – S – O – N.'

In minutes, police surveillance officers in plain clothes were scurrying into the Dome and surrounding the targets from a safe distance, shadowing their movements and recording them on videotape.

Allen remembered Betson's face from an earlier investigation. Flying Squad officers had heard of Ray Betson, but other than a list of previous convictions, they didn't know much.

Betson's name had surfaced as a player in a lucrative illegal cigarette operation, but police could not gather evidence on the man and almost never got near him. Allen did once manage to catch a glimpse of Betson, and he never forgot that face.

Ray Betson was a divorced father of two who was raised in South-east London. Despite having no legitimate source of income, he had recently bought a £500,000 house in rural Kent.

Betson's current girlfriend was a brunette named Susan Foster. She resembled a fashion model, and was so glamorous that a few years earlier was featured in a photo spread in the *Sun* about beautiful women.

In fact, over the years, Ray Betson had been a burglar, thief, fraudster and smuggler – he was a career criminal. Outside of a few stints in construction, he was never known to make an honest living.

In recent years, he had become, in his own words, a 'very successful' criminal, and for the last seven years had almost completely evaded the police.

Betson's lawbreaking career started at the age of fourteen, when he was convicted of burglary. He was convicted again, two years later, for theft and burglary. He was convicted yet again in 1979, this time for purse snatching and, at the age of seventeen, was sentenced to a detention centre for three months.

In March 1980, Betson was convicted of theft and loitering and was sent to borstal. It was supposed to be the last step before prison.

For Betson, it didn't work.

In July 1980 he was convicted for attempted theft. In December he was again sentenced for attempted theft, and went back to borstal. A year and a half later he was convicted of theft from a car.

It was at this point, in his early 20s, that Betson graduated to more serious crimes like cheque-card fraud.

In October 1983, he was given an eighteen-month sentence for deception and handling stolen goods, the result of his involvement in an illegal, traveller's cheques cashing scheme. After he was released from prison he was fined for excess alcohol (drink driving) and possession of cocaine, and was disqualified from driving.

In 1985 he was sent to prison for eighteen months for handling stolen goods. In 1992 and 1993 he was fined for taking a car and motorcycle, and was again barred from driving. In his late 20s, Betson got involved in high-level smuggling – a vocation that continued right through to 2000. He smuggled counterfeit designer clothes, alcohol and large amounts of tobacco. Betson found the booze and cigarette operations to be very profitable, and he virtually doubled his money with each shipment, less a bit of expenses.

Cigarette smuggling, while profitable, was a highly dangerous game, and increasingly populated by violent Eastern European gangs vying for control with British and Italian crime families. £2.5 billion per year in customs revenue was lost to highly organised smuggling networks that shipped duty-free bootleg cigarettes across the Channel and recycled them into the black market, where they wound up in pubs, offices and corner stores across the country.

By the 1990s, Betson's activities had come to the attention of police when he was seen associating with other criminals. When police had tried to observe him, Betson seemed to demonstrate the awareness of a person who had learned from the system. Having been repeatedly caught by the police in his formative years, he apparently put the experience to good use. He used public telephone boxes to make calls and seemed to practise anti-surveillance methods when driving. He could have been on the look out for the 'Old Bill' all the time.

Betson was so difficult to track that police wondered if he might have had access to sophisticated technical equipment. Ironically, the brother-in-law of Betson's girlfriend, Susan Foster, was a serving police officer who sometimes saw Betson at family get-togethers. The officer was frightened of Betson, who, he later testified in court, he suspected was a dangerous character.

By the late 1990s Betson had developed an extremely low profile. He was careful not to put his name on any kind of document – for a house, a car or anything else. By 1999 it was as if he did not exist. In late 1999 and 2000, he suffered massive financial blows when he invested tens of thousands of pounds of his own money in illegal tobacco container shipments that were intercepted by Customs. Betson's fellow conspirators were captured and his money was lost.

Betson had never been charged with any firearms offence or any act of violence, nor was he ever charged with either the Nine Elms or Aylesford crimes. But this sometimes unlucky career criminal now had a chance for a big haul. Now it looked like he was involved in the emerging plot surrounding the diamonds in the Dome. The police would soon have a nickname for Betson. They would call him 'The General'.

At Betson's side that day was his long-time crony – a chunky 47-year-old man from Catford named William Cockram. They'd known each other for twenty years and, for a while, had lived in the same neighbourhood, near the Elephant and Castle. They both knew Terry Millman, the convicted bank robber whom police had linked to the failed Aylesford attack.

Bill Cockram was responsible for a string of crimes dating back to 1970, when he was convicted for taking a scooter. In 1973, he was convicted of wounding with intent, the result of an argument in a pub, when Cockram swung an iron tube at a man who assaulted him while police were questioning the other man.

For a 1985 burglary at a woollen shop in Seven Oaks, Cockram was sentenced to nine months in prison. For TDA he got another three months.

In 1987, Cockram was convicted of trying to shoplift £370 of goods from Marks & Spencer, and sentenced to six months. In 1988, for some reason, he went right back to Marks & Spencer, tried to shoplift £260 of goods and was sentenced to community service and fined.

He was fined again in July 1989 for taking a vehicle without the owner's permission, and in 1992 he was sentenced to fifteen months in prison for ramming a vehicle through the front window of a shop and handling £40,000 in stolen goods.

Between convictions, Cockram periodically pursued legal employment as a builder and plumber. Like Betson, Cockram was never accused of or charged with any firearms offence or any act of violence (other than the 1973 wounding conviction), nor was he ever charged with either the Nine Elms or Aylesford crimes.

The two friends, Betson and Cockram, knew how to party. On the night of 31 December 1999, the Millennium Eve, when the Queen was holding her celebration for 10,000 guests in the Dome, Betson and Cockram were celebrating at The Plaza Hotel on Fifth Avenue in New York with Cockram's wife Pauline and Betson's companion Susan Foster.

According to Pauline, money was no object on the trip, despite

Betson's recent business setbacks. She didn't ask where the money came from. She knew better.

Located on the wealthiest street in the world, the opulent Plaza Hotel had a rich history. Over the years, in addition to kings, movie stars and tycoons, the Plaza had hosted a raucous parade of crooks, scoundrels and mob-connected celebrities. According to former mobster Henry Hill – the inspiration for the movie *Goodfellas* – 'this famous hotel has put up (and put up with) every high-rolling gambler, politician, Trump, and high-end-wiseguy to come through New York City.' 'If these walls could talk,' he added, 'you'd cover your ears.'

For New York's Mafia families, the Plaza was a favourite spot for parties and weddings, and they sometimes paid from satchels of cash to avoid paperwork.

Frank Sinatra held court there in the late 1940s, and one night was spotted chasing Lana Turner down the cavernous sixth floor hallway.

A visitor to a private party in one of the Plaza's suites in 1958 was confronted by the stunning sight of FBI Director J Edgar Hoover sternly sitting in a chair wearing a black ladies wig, a fluffy black dress, lace stockings, make-up and high heels. Or, at least, so it was claimed by the 'eyewitness' – a story so vivid that it entered American pop consciousness as gospel truth.

During the 1960 election campaign, John F Kennedy chose the Plaza's suite 1651 to consummate his affair with Mafia moll Judith Campbell, impressing her with a dozen red roses in the morning. The following summer, according to Campbell, the now-president was so delighted with their more spacious accommodation in the plush suite 1529–31 that he bounced on the bed and happily nibbled on *hors d' oeuvres*.

And in the 1990 movie *King of New York*, the mob boss (played by Christopher Walken) launched a crime war to conquer the city from his Plaza Hotel headquarters.

Ray Betson and Bill Cockram could hardly have chosen a more cinematic place to usher in the new millennium, and perhaps raise a toast to dreams of riches to come.

Exactly nine months later, police were excitedly communicating by mobile phone and recording Betson and Cockram's movements as they paced around the Millennium Dome.

At 10.49 a.m., Cockram stopped directly opposite the entrance to the Money Zone and began taping it with a Canon video recorder. A few minutes later, he entered the De Beers Millennium Jewels exhibition vault and videotaped the diamonds on display. The planned movement of the jewel to Japan had not yet been publicly announced.

For weeks, the two men had been developing and refining a plot to steal the Millennium Jewels.

Now, as he stood inside the semi-darkness of the vault, soon joined by Betson, Cockram was stunned.

He couldn't believe how close he could get to the diamonds.

He couldn't believe the apparent lightness of security.

He couldn't believe there were no guards inside the vault.

And he couldn't believe how vulnerable the cabinets looked.

When he thought no one was looking, he even discreetly tapped on the display case to determine the thickness of the glass.

He knew how to get his hands on the diamond.

After leaving the De Beers vault at 10.55a.m., Cockram lingered near the entrance and held an intense conversation with Betson.

Later, joined by a woman pushing a pram, Betson and Cockram spent the next four hours walking around the Dome property inside and out, videoing the layout, going near the riverbank, and pausing to check their watches and make mobile phone calls.

At one point, Betson and Cockram shared a quick laugh at the sight of an elderly-looking Dome security guard.

Plain-clothes police officers tailed the two men as they left the Dome grounds at 3.02 p.m., walked to the North Greenwich station and took the underground to Surrey Quays Shopping Centre in Rotherhithe.

Police officers watched through high-powered field glasses as Betson and Cockram sat down on a bench and studied a Millennium Dome brochure. At 3.32 p.m., a young, dark-haired man in sunglasses joined them. All three shook hands and proceeded to review Cockram's map and video, make mobile phone calls and point at the Dome looming in the east, across the Isle of Dogs. At one point, Cockram pumped his fists out in front of him, a gesture that the police couldn't figure out.

This third member of the gang, police soon learned, was a 31-year-old 'ladies' man' with a thick cockney accent, Aldo Ciarrocchi. Ciarrocchi was raised in Bermondsey, South London, by an Italian father and British mother, worked variously as a bricklayer and video machine vendor, and had pleaded guilty to a shoplifting charge in 1992. He had never been accused or charged with any firearms offence, nor any act of violence, nor was he ever charged with any connection to the Nine Elms or Aylesford crimes.

He had known Betson for eight years, and Cockram for ten. Cockram, in fact, was a father figure for Ciarrocchi, who once dated his daughter. Ciarrocchi spent most Sunday lunches and every Christmas with Cockram's family. Despite his seemingly modest income, Ciarrocchi drove a SAAB convertible and lived in a fine apartment in London's Docklands. His live-in girlfriend was a stunning American fashion model in her early twenties, Elisabeth Kirsch, who had a degree in English Literature from New York University and a passion for Shakespeare, especially *Romeo and Juliet*.

Her romantic chords were struck by her very first glimpse of Ciarrocchi at Tower Hill station in the summer of 1998. 'He had really dark hair,' she recalled wistfully to journalist Angela Levin, 'and was wearing dark sunglasses, a black shirt and black trousers. He looked like a movie star.'

'He made no bones about the fact that he had four other girlfriends and didn't want to get involved,' she added. 'That was fine by me, as I was only interested in a summer romance. I can see he is attractive to other women. When we were out they were always making eyes at him.'

After Kirsch moved in with Ciarrocchi a year later, she told Levin, he demonstrated his affections by giving her a Cartier timepiece and surprising her with treats of expensive chocolates and strawberries and cream. And right now Ciarrocchi was taking in the emerging details of a complex, totally audacious plot to steal the Millennium diamonds as described by Betson and Cockram, two men he trusted.

'How do we get in the cabinets?' he asked Cockram.

'Don't worry about that,' said Cockram, 'leave it to me, I'll get in there.'

Ciarrocchi was impressed. The whole plan was making sense. He thought about Elisabeth Kirsch, about paying off his mortgage and financial freedom.

If they were talking about any place other than the Millennium Dome, Ciarrocchi might have asked more questions. But there seemed to be something crazy happening at the Dome every week. Besides, he thought, you've got to have a bit of courage to get somewhere in life.

Just after 4 p.m., the gang split up and blended into afternoon traffic.

He'd been following the wrong gang.

Until now, Detective Superintendent Jon Shatford thought that faces from the 1983 Brinks-Mat heist may be key players behind the emerging Dome plot. There was no evidence to link any of those guys to the investigation. He'd been on the wrong track.

At 4.30 p.m., he walked out the front door of New Scotland Yard, took the District line at St James's Park and travelled the eight stops to Tower Hill.

It had been a day of wildly oscillating peaks and troughs, beginning with the defence of the De Beers convoy and the apparently unrelated and totally coincidental sighting of the gang at the Dome.

Now on a high, all Shatford wanted to do was to meet up with John Swinfield and discuss what had happened. He hadn't slept for 36 hours and was running on pure adrenalin.

He had arranged to meet Swinfield halfway between the station and Tower Bridge Flying Squad Office. He walked through the underpass towards the Tower of London, and then turned left towards Tower Bridge when he saw Swinfield striding towards him.

They acknowledged each other with an amazed smile, and sat on a bench opposite the Tower of London.

'This is unbelievable,' said Shatford in a welcoming handshake.

'I know,' said Swinfield, both men looking pleased with themselves.

'So much for the Brinks-Mat gang,' said Shatford.

Swinfield noted, 'At least we know the enemy now.'

'I know,' Shatford replied, 'but Raymond Betson – it's incredible.'

'Definitely an A team,' marvelled Swinfield.

'This is dynamite,' Shatford predicted, 'as it can only mean they are planning to do the robbery inside the Dome itself.'

There was no evidence to link Betson, Cockram or Ciarrocchi to either the Nine Elms or Aylesford jobs, but a plot to strike the Dome was now coming into view.

'It's the only thing that makes sense now,' said Swinfield, 'but just how they are going to pull it off, I don't know.'

'I'm pleased we know who we are dealing with,' said Shatford, 'but we've got to figure out the how and the when.'

Swinfield responded, 'Hopefully we will get that from the Intel, but it's a bit quiet at the moment. Not much coming back from Tong Farm.'

'Our biggest danger is that they do the job when we're not ready for them,' Shatford mused. 'We need to put something in place around the Dome just in case.'

'Well, Sean (Allen) is ensconced in there so we've got control of the CCTV,' Swinfield noted. 'Trouble is if they strike with no warning, when we're not there.'

'Exactly,' Shatford agreed. 'We are going to have to do something to frustrate them, even if we have to stage an accident and put our blokes out in uniform to frighten them off with Old Bill activity.'

'We might be able to do that,' speculated Swinfield, 'but it depends on where they intend getting into the Dome. They might not even see our lot.'

'There's always that risk, but at least we can shut the doors to the Jewel House. I can arrange that with De Beers.'

'Good idea,' said Swinfield.

'I'll speak to Tim Thorn tonight and see what he can arrange,' Shatford said, making notes in his PDA. 'I'm sure we can put a sign up outside saying they are being cleaned or something. We're going to have to play this very much by ear.'

Swinfield agreed, wondering, 'What about approaching security at the Dome? Sean is well in with them now.'

'Let's give it a couple of days so things can settle down,' Shatford recommended. 'We might get a clearer picture. The fact that those vans weren't hit this morning means that there must be no inside agent. That would have been the optimum time for them to hit it.'

'OK, boss. How much of this do I pass on to the team?'

'Keep it tight for now,' Shatford said, 'just Mark Drew and Sean Allen. We need to see how things pan out first.'

'I'll speak to them and see if we can cover the Dome between us tomorrow. Saturday's a busy day.'

Shatford made his way back to the District line and called Tim Thorn. He agreed to put his staff on alert, and was prepared to shut the door to the diamond vault within seconds of getting a phone call.

At closing time, the diamond vault received its last visitors of the day.

An official from De Beers removed the genuine diamond from the display and replaced it with the replica that was meant to take its place that morning.

That night, the real Millennium Star was raced to De Beers' HQ in the City of London in the back of a Flying Squad gun ship.

15. The Collector

He was a total mystery.

On 1 September 2000, Scotland Yard had identified the core members of the gang, but the ultimate buyer of the diamonds was unknown.

He could, however, be glimpsed through shifting fragments of pure speculation.

After consulting secretly with experts in the field, Jon Shatford came to the conclusion that the De Beers Millennium Jewels were being stolen to order.

'Things like this,' gang leader Ray Betson later explained, 'are done in compartments.' Betson was the field commander of the plot, but he was probably working for someone at a higher level.

Diamonds like these were impossible to sell on the open market, as their size and beauty would make them instantly identifiable.

The De Beers Millennium Star diamond, noted Youri Stevelynck, an official of the Diamond Council in Antwerp, 'is unique and immediately recognisable, there's no way you could hold it for a few years and then sell it'. He compared the idea of robbing the Star with 'going to the Louvre and stealing the *Mona Lisa*'.

Although the Millennium diamonds did not have any special imprinted coding or trace marks, all diamonds over 1 carat had to be sold with a certificate of ownership and grading report, documents that were traceable by law enforcement agencies. Whenever a diamond is reported stolen, the FBI in Washington flashes a warning to diamond laboratories around the world to be on alert for it.

Cutting the diamonds down into smaller pieces and trying to re-sell them wouldn't work, either. First, there were only a handful of professional diamond cutters in the world who could cut down a 203-carat gem without shattering it.

These master cutters worked for reputable diamond companies and would report the crime. Also, the process of cutting the gems would destroy most of their 'street' value, and even small pieces of such extremely high quality would trigger alarm bells as soon as they hit the market.

De Beers' executive Andrew Lamont later explained, 'Cutting up the Millennium Star would be like cutting up a van Gogh or Monet. It would only be worth a tiny fraction of the whole.'

That left only a few possibilities. The mastermind could be a gangster, drug dealer or terrorist who planned to hold the diamonds hostage in the hopes of negotiating a ransom payment from De Beers and its insurance companies.

There were recent precedents for this in the art world. In 1994, for example, in a daring 50-second raid, the famous Edvard Munch painting *The Scream* was stolen from the National Art Museum in Oslo by robbers who demanded a ransom (they left behind a note: 'thanks for the poor security'). It had a £35,000,000 market value. Three months later, in an undercover sting operation that included Scotland Yard's art theft squad, the painting was recovered and arrests made.

The still-unsolved 1990 robbery of £180 million worth of paintings from Boston's Isabella Stewart Gardner Museum was believed to be a ransom plot gone wrong. Other art kidnapping plots unfolded through the 1990s, some involving Russian and Balkan mafia gangs, but the details were murky, as owners and insurance firms didn't want to publicise the deals made to return the works.

One spectacular art robbery came in the early hours of Millennium Day, 1 January 2000, when a thief broke into the Ashmolean Museum in Oxford, and made off with Paul Cézanne's landscape painting, *Auvers-sur-Oise*, worth £3 million.

It was a Hollywood-style, ten-minute heist, with the thief climbing up scaffolding onto the roof, breaking through the skylight and setting off smoke bombs to cloak his face from security cameras. He vanished with the painting into crowds of thousands of New Year's revellers.

Police investigating the crime came to suspect that the painting might have been stolen to order, possibly for a private collector. It has never been found.

'Perhaps the most romantic notion,' speculated David Shillingford of the Art Loss Register to a journalist on the Cézanne heist, 'which no doubt has been brought to the fore recently by films such as *The Thomas Crown Affair* and *Entrapment*, is that there are people who have such a passion for art that they are prepared, probably not to steal these things themselves... but employ people [to do this] for them." And that's the last time they'd be seen.

This was a possibility that intrigued Shatford. The De Beers Millennium Star was, after all, not just a diamond, but a priceless work of art. The diamond might be coveted by a super-rich mastermind with unlimited wealth and an unbridled passion for collecting masterpieces. In other words, a real-life 'Thomas Crown'.

Although many experts doubt the existence of such collectors, the possibility of their existence sometimes floated on the periphery of conjecture on unsolved art crimes. No such collector had ever been identified, but perhaps that was the whole point – they'd got away with it.

An operation on the scale of a raid on the Millennium Dome might require an up-front investment of half a million pounds for equipment, manpower and a wide range of expenses. Vehicles, scanners, explosives, weapons, safe houses and payrolls for up to a dozen gang members cost money, and lots of it. The Collector might be funding this.

Shatford wondered about what kind of person it was, and envisaged one profile based on real criminal characters he'd come across in his work: the Gangster-Collector.

He would be British. His net worth would be well into the tens or hundreds of millions. He would have started off as an armed robber, moved into drugs, and branched into stolen property. He'd have legitimate businesses, would launder money through scrap dealers or tanning shops, building up off-shore accounts in the Bahamas and Switzerland, fuelled in turn by VAT fiddles and tax scams.

Over the years, he would build up protective layers of 'shell' companies, loyal henchmen and trusted intermediaries, increasingly distancing himself from the crimes. Despite his position and wealth, his humble beginnings would haunt him. He would want to forget he was really just a blagger.

He would organise society functions, donate to charities and political parties and love to be photographed with celebrities. His houses would be enormous, and his mistresses would be even sexier than his wives.

In time, through influence and fear, he would float above the law. He would be a corrupter and user of people, and he would be responsible for a string of unsolved murders committed by henchmen and contract killers, over matters of 'respect' and 'honour'.

Although he wouldn't know the difference between a Rembrandt and a Jackson Pollock, he would buy fine art because someone had told him it was good. And one day, in late 1999, he would have read the news about the De Beers Millennium Star.

It would be the ultimate prize, and he would have to have it.

But there was one final personality type Shatford considered, and, in some ways, he was the most dangerous. He would be a true 'Super-Collector', the wealthiest of the super-wealthy. Though he might be European, Russian, or an Arab, he would have achieved such wealth and mobility as to be essentially stateless.

His personal fortune would be so well hidden and liquid as to be invisible, but it would exceed the many hundreds of millions. Armies of lawyers in different lands would manage discrete pieces of the puzzle, governments would be hard-pressed to track him, and only he would have an overall picture of the staggering magnitude of his wealth.

Like the Thomas Crown movie character played by Steve McQueen in 1968 and Pierce Brosnan in 1999, the Super-Collector would have made the bulk of his fortune in legitimate businesses and investments.

If he existed, the Super-Collector would roam the world in an aircraft like the new $40 million ultra-long-range Gulfstream GV, which would enable him to travel in non-stop bursts of up to 6,500 nautical miles from New York to Tokyo, from London to Singapore, and from the ski slopes of Gstaad and Val d'Isère to the beaches of St Barthelemy and the Seychelles.

He would shop on Avenue Montaigne in Paris, and Bahnhofstrasse in Zurich and Omotesando-dori in Tokyo, and he would have tailors on call in Hong Kong and Milan.

The state rooms and cellars of his custom-made 165 ft Feadship yacht would be stocked with Mouton Rothschild, Padrón cigars, Glenfiddich fifty-year-old Scotch, white truffles and white Beluga caviar. He would collect the rarest automobiles; mainly classic Ferraris, Bugatti Royales and Alfa Romeos, but he would almost always make his bids anonymously.

But all his toys and trophies would pale in the light of his passion for art.

The Super-Collector's interests would be eclectic and wide-ranging: portrait miniatures, landscapes, sculptures and paintings, from Old Masters and Impressionists to Modernists and American Conceptualists.

In one of his many libraries would be a collection of every book ever printed on the architecture of Frank Lloyd Wright. For as long as he could remember he would have been intoxicated by the beauty of Wright's visions, and amused by his contempt for human comfort. Every time he visited Fallingwater, Wright's ultimate masterpiece of a home suspended over a waterfall in the woods of Pennsylvania, he would weep.

The idea of commissioning the theft of the De Beers Millennium Star would occur to him almost as a joke, as an intellectual lark. But the more he thought of it, the more he could visualise the diamond in a secret gallery he would build for it.

'There are some very rich people who collect this kind of thing,' speculated Diamond Council official Youri Stevelynck.

Another diamond authority, Nir Livnat of The Steinmetz Group, agreed, saying, 'I'm sure there are enough people who would say that they'll buy the De Beers Millennium Star for ten per cent of its value. They'll keep it and enjoy it themselves. They'll keep it in their bedroom, and not show it to anyone.'

It was a fanciful portrait, thought Shatford, but a Super-Collector might exist somewhere. After 25 years in the London police force, Shatford always kept an open mind.

He was ready to believe almost anything was possible.

16. The Diamond Plot

The Gang's Own Story

To recap: the plot to steal the Millennium diamonds took shape early in the summer of 2000. As of 1 September of that year, police were hot on the trail of the gang. The leader was Raymond Betson. The core members were William Cockram, Aldo Ciarrocchi and Terry Millman, with others, including Lee Wenham, moving into supporting and peripheral roles.

Later, at their trial, the key gang members revealed pieces of how the plot came together. It was an incomplete picture with gaps and contradictions, and included accusations by the gang that were not supported by evidence.

Betson's testimony, for example, must be viewed in the context of his own admission in the witness box that he was a very successful professional criminal, a vocation, he agreed, that was based on dishonesty. But it was sworn testimony provided under oath and under penalty of perjury, and though it was sometimes hard to follow and harder to believe, it does offer some major outlines of the plot.

The operation, Betson revealed, was indeed a 'pre-order'. A buyer for the diamonds was already lined up.

Under oath, he claimed that the plot came to his attention through a London policeman, the one married to the sister of Betson's live-in companion, Susan Foster. The policeman, it turned out, had for a time coincidentally been posted to security detail at the Millennium Dome.

On 27 May 2000, Betson testified, he met him at the Strand. The policeman, Betson alleged, offered to introduce him to a friend named Tony – a character who had a plan to commission a theft of the De Beers Millennium jewels at the Dome.

'Tony', Betson's story went, had been working around the Dome area for some time and had been in a position to see plans of the building. Betson said that Tony, according to the policeman, was 'cute and caked'. ('Caked', Betson explained, was slang for someone who has 'got a few quid'.) 'And he's got a backer,' the policeman had allegedly added. 'He's got someone to sell the diamonds to.'

Tony was putting a detailed plan together – a plan to snatch the diamonds.

'I did want to meet Tony,' Betson remembered, 'and find out more about this.'

There are two important points regarding the gang's description of the plot. Under oath, the policeman named by Betson categorically denied that he ever knew anything about the plot, and denied knowing anyone of the description of the so-called Tony character. No evidence ever appeared in support of the gang's allegation of the policeman's involvement.

Additionally, no evidence ever appeared to support the gang's description of the Tony character as working around the Dome. In fact, no evidence ever appeared to support any allegation that any Dome staff were ever involved in the plot in any way.

But, according to Betson's testimony, a meeting was set up between Betson and Tony for a week or two later, in early or mid-June, at a pie and mash shop near the Walworth Road, just south of the Elephant and Castle.

Before the meeting, however, Betson went to see his old friend and criminal partner Terry Millman. According to Betson, he and Millman had a history of doing criminal business together.

Betson wanted Millman to review the Millennium diamond job because of his skills in complex criminal jobs, and his talent for disguise.

'I knew that he was experienced with larger scale thefts,' Betson said, 'in the sense that when I was doing the travel cheques [fraud] he was actually supplying me with travellers' cheques, and the way he used to get them is he used to go into Thomas Cook travel agencies posing as a telephone engineer, and he'd actually steal them out of the cabinet, so they were unsigned.'

Terry Millman was an experienced criminal, but he had a big operational liability. He was a walking dead man. He had cancer of both the stomach and lungs.

'No disrespect to Terry, God rest him,' recalled Betson, 'but Terry couldn't knock the skin off a rice pudding. He was like a skeletal man at that time. He was in the advanced stages of cancer. I think he suspected he had cancer. Certainly everyone else did. No one spoke about it. He was getting weaker by the day.'

According to Betson, Millman didn't want to talk about it either. 'It was an unspoken thing really, I think,' said Betson, 'because he drastically lost weight and a lot of strength over a comparatively short period of time, and he was one of those guys who I think didn't really want to know. He didn't go to the doctor's.'

Despite his impending doom, Millman was very interested in the Dome plot, and in Betson's briefing session with Tony.

'Let's meet the guy and see what he's got to say,' he told Betson.

According to Betson, on 27 May, the two crooks sat down with Tony.

'I thought you were going to be by yourself,' said Tony, taken aback at the sight of Terry Millman.

Ray Betson saw this as a good sign: Tony was a cautious character.

'You can trust Terry,' Betson assured Tony, 'and speak openly in front of him as much as you can in front of me.'

After chit-chatting over mouthfuls of pie and mash, the three men decided that the hard wooden bench seats and other diners sitting within earshot weren't conducive to strategic criminal discussions, so they adjourned to nearby Burgess Park.

Tony had lined up, claimed Betson, four or five inside men from the Millennium Dome staff who would escort them into the diamond exhibit with radio signals.

A back-up plan, said Betson, involved 'going in there with the staff, dressed up as staff.' Tony, he recalled, said he would provide the gang with overalls, uniforms, fake ID cards and possibly keys to open up the De Beers diamond cabinets.

'I'm not getting involved in anything heavy,' Betson testified he told Tony. 'I'm not carrying any weapons, and I'm only entering on the basis that what you say you can provide, and that these people can let us in when the coast is clear so that we can steal the stones.'

Betson was worried about the 'bird' for using guns on this kind of crime. If he was caught with weapons, he thought, the prison sentence would be, in his words, 'outrageous'.

Then Betson and Millman agreed. They wanted in. They wanted more details and a comprehensive plan of attack.

The three men met again a week later, in early June, at a library on Walworth Road. 'Tony' spread out a detailed architect's-type map of the Millennium Dome area, Betson testified, and they discussed in detail the logistics of breaking in, getting the diamonds and getting away.

Tony confirmed that the buyer for the diamonds was lined up, and he gave them pre-programmed mobile phones to stay in touch. Betson then took Millman to the Millennium Dome for their first personal reconnaissance of the target. He wanted to check the plan on paper against the reality.

When he walked into the De Beers diamond vault, Ray Betson was so excited he felt butterflies in his belly. Absorbing the details of the layout, Betson thought, 'This looks ridiculously easy.'

The two men walked around the Dome property to survey a possible getaway route. 'My main motivation,' Betson remembered, 'was trying to get the stones as quickly and as smoothly as possible.'

The two criminals decided, Betson recalled, that the plan 'was spot on, one hundred per cent.'

Betson's own base payment for the job, he said, was going to be £450,000. More cash would be divvied out to the rest of the gang. 'We thought it was an opportunity of a lifetime, really,' he recalled. He was 100 per cent confident they could get away with it.

A few weeks later, Betson called his crony William Cockram and said he had a proposition for him. They met in a South London cafe.

His first reaction, Cockram testified, was to laugh. He thought Betson was joking. It sounded like 'pie in the sky'. But when Betson described the evolving plans of attack, Cockram was shocked, then intrigued.

One day in early July, the whole group – Betson, Cockram, Millman and the mysterious Tony – convened for a planning session. They met in Millman's council flat in Bermondsey.

Tony briefed the gang in detail on the security set-up in the Dome. 'There's no one there ever until 12 o'clock,' he reported. 'That's why the place is going skint. That's why it's lost all the Lottery money.' It will be 'a piece of cake', he said, as long as they struck early in the day.

The plan that Betson and Tony were working out was elaborate, involving split-second timing, high-tech surveillance, disguises and multiple vehicles.

'There's the cameras in the Dome that go with the BT land line,' said Tony, 'to Hatton Garden to the headquarters of De Beers. They've their own security room there with a bank of monitors and everything, and they're in control of the cameras in the Dome. If the alarm system is tripped, then the message goes down the lines and goes to De Beers, and they notify the police and the Dome.'

Betson wanted to add smoke sticks to the plan, to create extra confusion and delay the response time of Dome security staff.

He assumed they'd have no problems getting close to the diamonds without detection. They would be visible on Dome CCTV, but so what.

'People don't sit there looking at a bank of monitors hour in and hour out,' recalled Betson. Security officers 'have a cup of tea, they write things down, whatever,' Betson reasoned.

He figured they had to breach the diamond cabinets in 45 to 50 seconds and get out of the area. He doubted that Dome security officers could respond in force to that spot in that short a period of time.

The plan was starting to look so good, Bill Cockram recalled, 'I had complete faith in the guy who had organised it. It was a gift.'

'Given all the information and all the help we was supposed to have had,' Cockram testified, 'I didn't really think there was anything that could go wrong.'

When he visited the Dome with Betson on 1 September, Cockram simply couldn't believe the security was so light.

'I just couldn't believe how simple it was,' he recalled. 'I couldn't sleep at nights. I just used to think about it and I thought: this can't be true.'

Cockram testified that he was to be paid a flat £100,000 for the job, and that his goal was to pay off his mortgage and get a new car.

His wife of 29 years, Pauline, later told journalist Lucy Panton of the *Sunday People* that Cockram wasted large sums of money on high living and bad investments. 'I was working three days a week in a department store, and had four cleaning jobs. I kept begging him to get a job but he just brushed me off saying he was working on something.' She added, he said he was working on a scheme that would set them up for the rest of their lives.

It was mid-August when Aldo Ciarrocchi joined the plot, as he was having a cup of tea in Bill Cockram's kitchen overlooking a garden.

'I was working me backside off, trying to build up some money,' Ciarrocchi remembered, explaining how he was running around London trying to keep his business going and taking his model girlfriend on casting calls.

'We've got something,' Cockram announced to his young protégé. 'It's really good. It's like winning the Lottery. Big, big money. It's diamonds.'

Cockram told him about the Dome and the jewels, explaining they were 'going to go in there and steal all the diamonds'. He couldn't give him any more details at the moment. Was Ciarrocchi interested?

At that point, Ciarrocchi testified, he wasn't ready to fully commit. He wanted more details. And, he remembered, 'I wasn't one hundred per cent sure if he was being deadly serious, you know, or testing me out or something.'

'Do you need a decision right away?' asked Ciarrocchi, 'because I don't know.'

'No, no,' replied Cockram, who said he would go back to the gang and report that he had Ciarrocchi in mind for the job.

On 31 August, Cockram telephoned Ciarrocchi to close the deal.

'Are you still interested in going to the party?' Cockram asked, using code for the Dome job.

'Yeah,' said Ciarrocchi, 'I'm interested, but I need to know more.'

'Do you want to meet me tomorrow at Surrey Quays by the windmill, at 3 o'clock?'

Ciarrocchi agreed, and met with Betson and Cockram the next day, 1 September. As the Millennium Dome loomed in the east, Betson outlined the plan.

'I was apprehensive and nervous, obviously, and a bit scared,' Ciarrocchi remembered. In fact, he was initially shocked at the audacity of the plan, as Cockram had been, but he quickly saw its merits.

It would be a lightning smash-and-grab raid. The plan was built on shock, force and speed. It used technical insight, high-tech communications and, above all, a massive amount of audacity.

The plan allowed for a total of only five minutes to enter the Dome, penetrate the vault, seize the diamonds, escape to the river, cross it and get away on the other side.

The plan allowed fifteen more minutes for the gang to rendezvous with their unnamed paymaster and intermediary at the Mayflower pub a few miles away in Rotherhithe by the Thames, pick up their pay-off and then split up, presumably into crime history.

'There's no way anyone will get hurt,' said Betson, 'including us.

'My brother-in-law's a copper,' Betson claimed, according to Ciarrocchi's testimony. 'He works down there and he's got all the inside game sorted out.'

The plan was so good, Betson announced, 'it's going to be a piece of piss.' He later boasted, 'We will never be caught.'

His fellow gangster Terry Millman was more philosophical about their chances. 'We will either come back rich and famous,' he predicted, 'or we'll be dead.'

17. The Gangster's Paradise

The Costa del Sol, Spain, Summer 2000

The sun was everywhere.

It smothered the foothills of the Sierra Blanca mountains, the palm trees in the Andalusian valleys, and the soft beaches of Marbella.

It drenched the luxury yachts that floated lazily in the marina at Puerto Banus, while music echoed off the marble of the old town square, and sweet wine and cappuccino flowed in an endless stream in the open-air cafés.

The sun blasted the white terraced villas facing the Mediterranean and their lush, fragrant gardens overflowing with purple, red and white bougainvillea.

And it roasted the pink skin of the fugitive British gangsters into a buttery, saddle-leather brown, blending over the years with sun-creams and tobacco smoke into a reptilian death mask.

They had flocked here to the Spanish Costa del Sol ever since 1978, when the extradition treaty with the UK collapsed and opened up a utopian criminal refuge less than three hours by air from London. They could buy secluded estates, play golf, start up new families and new criminal empires or just retire on their millions and luxuriate in the infinite summer.

Police believe that key parts of the Millennium Dome plot probably took shape here in the summer of 2000, in this dazzling global crime capital which, over the years, had hosted frolicking notables from Sean Connery, Frank Sinatra, Mick Jagger and Jackie Onassis to the Duke of Windsor, Antonio Banderas and the Saudi royal family.

If Raymond Betson dreamed at night, the Costa del Sol would be a lovely place to linger. It was a Hollywood-style Walk of Fame of celebrity British criminals.

They generally kept to themselves, but you could sometimes spot them on a side street parking their tinted-windowed Mercedes or Ferraris, sporting a Rolex and gold medallion, ducking in for a late breakfast at a mock English pub, complete with Union Jacks and sausages.

One of the first gangsters to come here was England's most wanted man, the armed robber and suspected drug dealer Mickey Greene, former boss of the notorious 'Wembley Mob' gang of London blaggers.

At least two of the Great Train Robbers from 1963 settled here, Gordon Goody and Charlie Wilson, though Wilson's stay in Marbella was fatally abbreviated by a hit man's bullet in 1990.

The 'Famous Five' were here, too: the suspects believed to be responsible for the 1983 Security Express robbery; at £6.25 million pounds the then biggest cash heist in British history. They included the flamboyant Ronnie Knight, ex-husband of the actress Barbara Windsor, former Kray Brothers' gang-enforcer Freddie Foreman, and the elderly alleged mastermind of the job, Clifford Saxe.

The extradition loophole was closed in 1985, but the new agreement wasn't retroactive, and scores of known British crooks walked the streets as free men. British police knew where many of them were, but couldn't touch them.

In the 1990s, a United Nations of international gangster networks blossomed on the 'Costa del Crime', based on drug trafficking and money laundering. With the collapse of European borders and Soviet communism, Russian and Eastern Europe gangs moved in, and the area became a continental switching point for the drugs trade, linking together buyers and markets in Europe, the UK, Africa and Latin America.

The Russians came in strength and they came with cash. As early as 1995, the Spanish secret service warned in an internal report, 'Marbella is an important centre for wealthy Russians who use it to rest from their illegal activities. Their time in Marbella allows them to contact other European Mafiosos.'

Gangs started ripping off and attacking each other and worried Spaniards began calling it La Costa del Plomo, or The Lead Bullet Coast. 'They're heavy, very heavy,' reported one British ex-pat about the Eastern Europeans. 'When they kill people down here they really kill them – you know, nine bullets in the head sort of thing – and then set fire to the body.'

At the centre of this criminal landscape, in a luxury villa near the city of Marbella, with British, Russian and continental gangsters within arm's reach, there lived a lean, tanned Englishman in his 40s named Brian Mitchell* – a man British police would soon nickname The Boatman.

He came from South London. Police knew very little else about him except that he was good with boats.

In the summer of 2000, The Boatman was in touch with members of the Betson gang as they plotted the robbery of the De Beers Millennium Jewels.

Around the end of August, The Boatman was on a flight from Spain to the UK. And in early September, he was spotted in London, standing beside Ray Betson and his gang, taking surveillance pictures of the Millennium Dome.

De Beers Millennium Star, the world's largest perfect diamond and centrepiece of an ibition valued at a staggering £250,000,000.

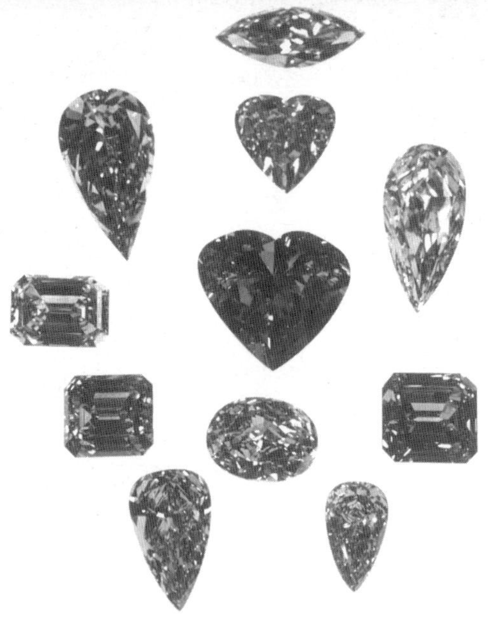

Above The De Beers Millennium Jewels featuring The Heart of Eternity (27.64 carats).

Below Model of the De Beers Millennium Star in the rough. Weight: 777 carats.

Above The De Beers Millennium Star is unveiled in September 1999 by Sophie Marceau – co-star of the James Bond mov *The World is Not Enough*.

Below Harry Oppenheimer holds the De Beers Millennium Star, 203.04 carats, D colour, internally and externally flawless, pear-shaped diamond.

right and centre right ack at Nine Elms, South ıdon, February 2000: a stery gang launches a nmando raid on a urity van loaded with ,000,000 in cash, using a nt ramming spike hidden ı lorry laden with ristmas trees.

tom right The gang uses cking vehicles to seal off attack zone.

Career criminal Ray Betson (*right*) and his lieutenant on the Dome Raid, William Cockram.

Aldo Ciarrocchi, key player in the Millennium Dome heist.

Happier times: Aldo Ciarrocchi with American model Elisabeth Kirsch.

Elisabeth Kirsch: Ciarrocchi surprised her with sweets, strawberries and cream – and the biggest diamond plot in history.

e Millennium Dome in London's Docklands and the site of the De Beers Millennium
els exhibition.

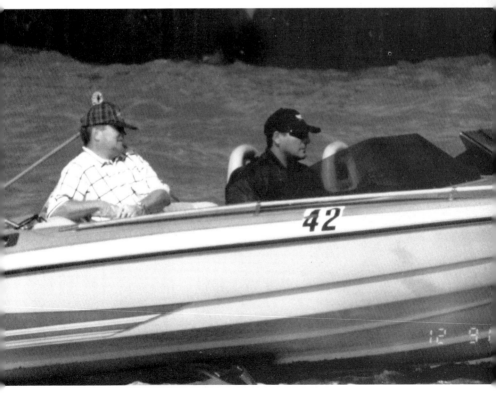

kram and Betson testing their getaway speedboat at Whitstable Harbour, Kent.

The Dome attack begins: 7 November, 2000. JCB and support van launch from Plumstead coal yard (*top*), enter morning traffic (*bottom left*) and make final charge toward the Dome

ught on tape: CCTV ages of the robbery in gress.

:son crashes the JCB ough the locked Dome urity gate. Three more ders are crammed inside specially modified nicle.

o the vault: Robert ams, wearing gas mask, netrates the heavily-ended De Beers llennium Star case, ding glass fragments into display.

tland Yard counterattack: ice officers swoop into vault.

abush: SO19 sharp-ooters cut off the JCB as gang's smoke device onates at far right.

Above Entrance to the De Beers vault at the Millennium Dome, built to withstand a 60-ton ram-raid.

Below left Designers promised that the armoured-glass display case was nearly impregnable The Betson gang blew it open in 27 seconds flat.

Below right Close-up of smashed diamond vault: the pedestal is inches away.

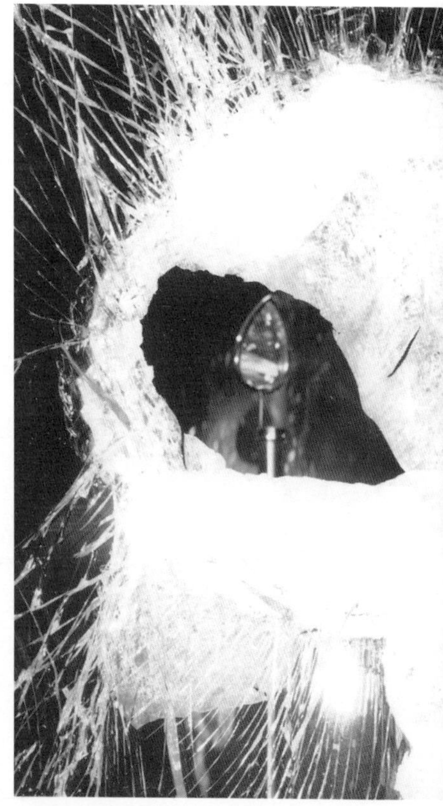

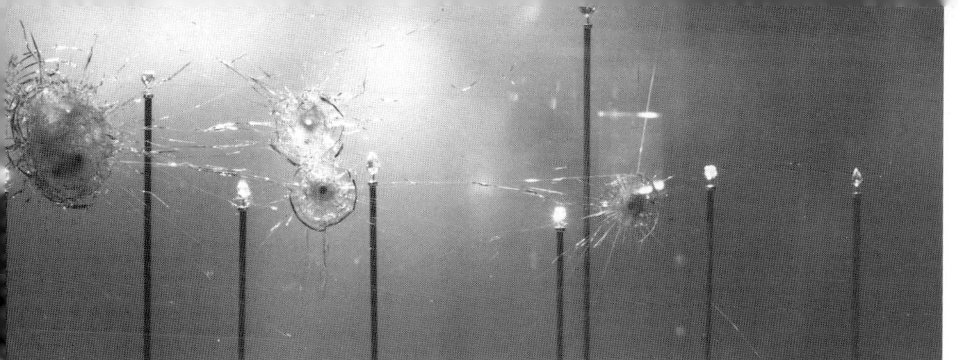

ove Smashed cabinets of
: blue Millennium Jewels.

ht JCB inside the
llennium Dome.

'ow left Ciarrocchi
ptured.

'ow right Getaway boat
ot Kevin Meredith on
at he thought could be
last day on earth. SO19
icer Clive Rew (*obscured*)
tanding guard.

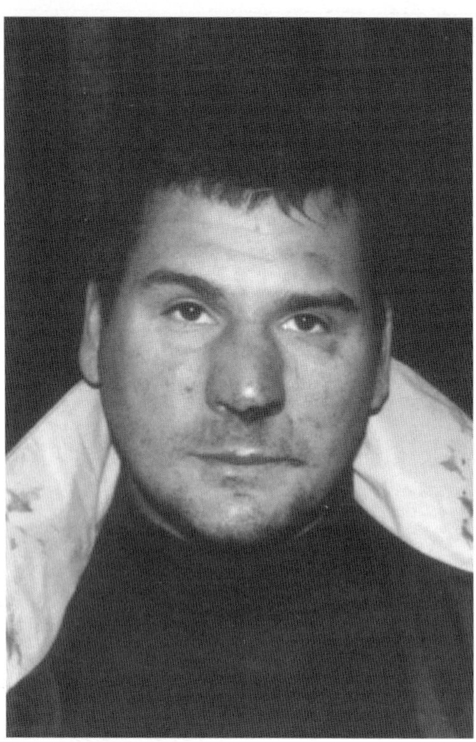

The would-be Greatest Robber of All Time: Ray Betson is captured.

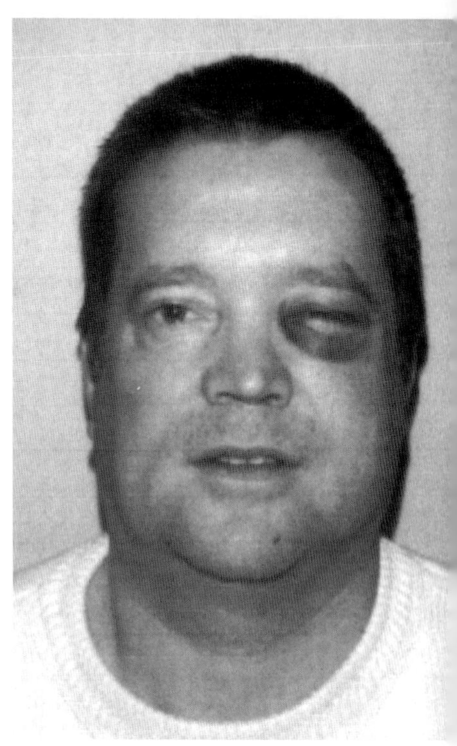

William Cockram captured.

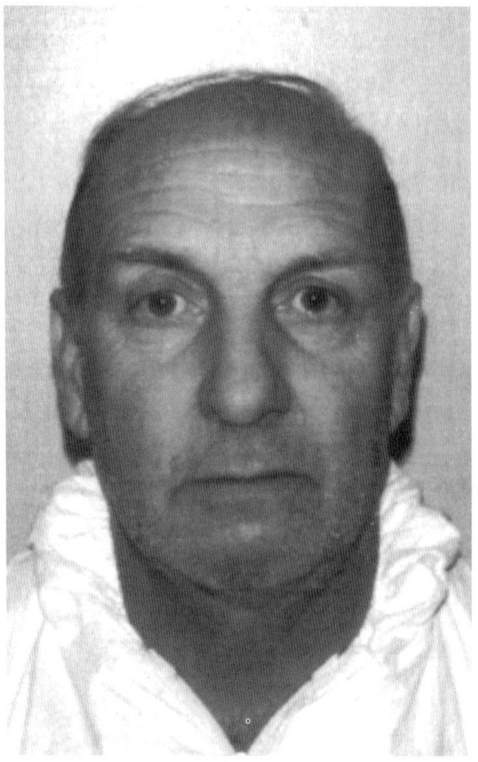

Robert Adams captured.

Kevin Meredith captured.

y, November 8, 2000 30p www.the-sun.co.uk

AMERICA DECIDES

Gore . . early wins

By TREVOR KAVANAGH and PAUL THOMPSON

BOTH sides were claiming victory early today in the neck-and-neck race to be America's next President.

The fortunes of Republican George W Bush and Democrat Al Gore see-sawed in the closest contest for 40 years.

Exit polls at first showed Gore, 52, forging ahead when he won the battleground states of Michigan and Pennsylvania. But Florida — which Gore thought he'd won — was later declared too close to call and edging towards his rival. Bush, 53, scooped many of the smaller states. By 3am our

Continued on Page Nine

SUN PICTURE EXCLUSIVE

M ONLY HERE
OR DE BEERS

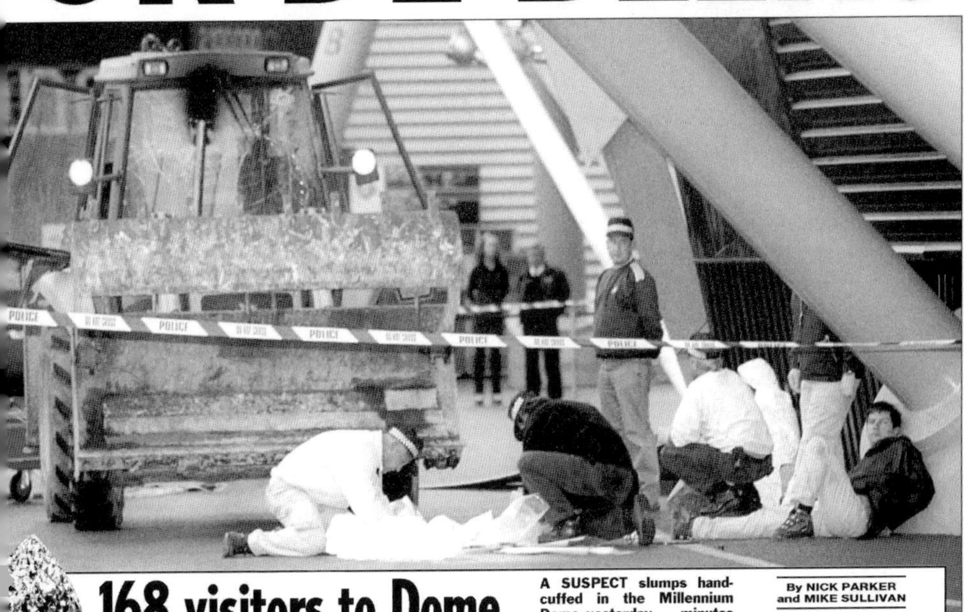

g . . egg-sized Star

168 visitors to Dome..
4 were gem thieves

By NICK PARKER and MIKE SULLIVAN

A SUSPECT slumps handcuffed in the Millennium Dome yesterday — minutes after police foiled the world's biggest robbery.

Four men smashed their way inside with a huge JCB digger, planning to snatch £350million worth of De Beers diamonds.

Their main target was the dazzling 203-carat Millennium Star. The men were held by police hiding among 168 visitors at the beleaguered Dome. Another was arrested trying to flee down the Thames.

Around 100 cops were lying in wait at the attraction in Greenwich, South East London, having tailed the gang for weeks.

FULL STORY: PAGES 2,3,4,5,6 and 7

crime triggered headlines around the world. This one, from the *Sun*, won an award. front page features a photo taken minutes after the attack showing a shocked, handcuffed o Ciarrocchi at far right.

Detective Superintendent Shatford reacts to conviction of the Dome Raiders outside the O Bailey, flanked by Detective Constable Sean Allen (*left*), Detective Sergeant Mark Drew (*hidden behind Shatford*) and Press Officer Angie Evans (*right*), 18 February 2002.

Metropolitan Police Service Commissioner Sir John Stevens (*centre*), honours officers who participated in Operation Magician with a commendation ceremony at Scotland Yard, Febru 2003. Jon Shatford is to the left of Stevens, holding a replica of the De Beers Millennium St

18. The Guns of September

**Snow Hill Police Station, The City of London,
4 September 2000, 11 a.m.**

'It looks like the attack will take place *inside the Dome.*'

Shatford sprang the news to De Beers security chief Tim Thorn just as they were sitting down in their secret, borrowed rendezvous room.

'But it's impossible!' exclaimed Thorn, his face illuminated in shock.

'They won't be able to do it,' he continued. 'We have spent three quarters of a million pounds on the security. We have been assured.'

'Well,' said Shatford, 'the gang think they can do it.'

'But how?'

'We have no idea.'

'They will be in for a shock,' Thorn predicted. 'There's no way they will get through. The whole vault is made up of thirty tons of concrete and tempered steel. They just cannot do it.'

'I am confident they cannot break into the vault,' said Shatford, 'which is why I think they must be planning to strike when it's open.'

'But even then,' Thorn continued, 'the glass cabinets that surround the Millennium Star are 20 mm thick. We are assured that it can withstand up to thirty minutes of any type of pressure.'

'I can't explain it, Tim,' said Shatford, 'I just know that they are going to have a try for it. Quite what they have up their sleeve I don't know.'

'This really is remarkable,' marvelled Thorn.

'I know,' Shatford agreed, 'but one thing I know about this gang is that they are pros. They would not embark on this unless they were sure they could pull it off.'

Thorn asked, 'Where do we go from here?'

'Well, needless to say I really need your continued support . . .'

'You've got it,' interrupted Thorn, 'let me know whatever help you need.'

'Well, thanks for that,' said the detective, his confidence boosted. 'I will make sure we allow for every contingency we can. Our Intelligence will improve as things move on. Until then we have the farm under surveillance, so we should know, I hope, when we are game on.'

Shatford returned to the Yard and reviewed the latest Intelligence reports.

When the gang were spotted at the Dome on 1 September, Shatford had cranked up police surveillance on Tong Farm, the gang's 'slaughter' and the nearby Starfields Farm, also owned by the Wenham family.

A speedboat that was first seen at Tong Farm on 25 August had not moved since. Various other cars, transit vans and lorries were seen going in and out of the farms. This was not unusual as over a dozen vehicles were at the farms at any given time, some legal, some stolen. But one vehicle was puzzling – a vintage 1992 JCB '3CX Sitemaster Backhoe Loader'.

It was an excavating machine complete with a high-powered shovel-bucket connected by a hinged boom-arm. It was built for moving around earth and other materials on construction sites.

The appearance of a JCB digger at a rural farm was not in itself unusual. But this one, it turned out, had been stolen to order in Tunbridge Wells and given a false number plate.

And a number of alterations had been made – the mounted forks had been removed from the front shovel, the rear scooper had been cut off, and the logos and company names removed.

What the hell is all *this* for, Shatford wondered. For now, he decided to adopt a strategy of wait and see.

At the Dome, the Flying Squad's Detective Constable Sean Allen was working in the Bronze Control Room among the CCTV operators, under the cover story of a drug investigation. At times the operators even brought to his attention people they thought might be taking drugs. Allen recorded the action diligently, never disclosing his true reasons for being there.

With scarce Intelligence to go on, Shatford decided that the speedboat had to be a key component. If it moved from the farm, it could be a signal that the job was on. And if that happened, he would authorise a full deployment of police around the Millennium Dome. But he would not deploy inside the Dome unless he was absolutely sure that an attack on the diamonds was about to take place.

Shatford figured he would only ever get a single crack at this since a big police deployment would spark a lot of interest, be the talking point for miles around and probably alert the gang to the fact that the police were on to them.

Protecting the public. That was everything. It was why he got up in the morning and it was why, like so many other policemen, he worked around the clock a lot of days and weekends and why in the middle of a tough case he sometimes slept on the office couch, living on adrenalin and stale scones.

Now he feared that a volatile and unpredictable gang were going to strike, possibly putting the public at risk. All he needed was a plan to catch the gang in the act and take them down, while having no idea how or when they would strike.

Worst of all, the Dome was a public place, and there was no way of knowing what kind of firepower and explosives the gang would carry in, how many gangsters were coming and, if the gang were armed, how many people would be in the crossfire.

In the whole of England, there was one man who might be able to figure this out. Shatford grabbed his telephone and punched in the number for a tactical firearms advisor in Scotland Yard's SO19 branch.

On the morning of Wednesday 6 September, Inspector Mark Williams stepped into Shatford's office.

He was a consummate professional in an extremely dangerous job.

Among Williams's many strengths was a methodical management style. He meticulously kept track of any changes in circumstances that could impact on an armed response, and briefed his weapons' officers and superiors accordingly.

'You already know about this job, Mark, because of the deployment around the Dome last Friday,' Shatford began, 'but now things have become clearer.'

'Is it still going to happen then?' asked Williams, who was accustomed to criminal gangs switching their tactics at the last minute.

'Well, it is, but there will be a variation,' Shatford replied.

'What's that, sir?'

'They're going to do it inside the Dome.'

'Oh,' said Williams, sounding almost underwhelmed as he jotted notes in his portfolio. 'What exactly does that mean?'

'The truth is I don't exactly know. The diamonds are displayed in a Jewel House which has all the security of a vault. They are encased behind special reinforced cabinets, so the gang must think they have a way to penetrate them.'

'Do you know when?' asked Williams.

'No. We have their safe house down in Kent under control. We know there is a boat in there, so the minute that moves we think the job will be game on. Apart from that, there's a JCB and a number of other vehicles down there but anything could go.

'Possibly,' Shatford went on, 'the JCB is for the gang to gain access to the site purporting to be workmen. Another possibility is that it's going to be used to knock out the Dome power supply to cause confusion.'

Williams let out a deep breath and said, 'Well, I will need to go down there and have a good look for myself.'

'Good,' said Shatford, 'but I ask that until we have agreed a plan between us, you keep this to yourself.'

A quizzical look appeared on Williams's face, but he readily agreed and left the office, still jotting down notes.

He was back the next morning, hunched over a schematic plan of the Dome sprawled out on Shatford's desk. 'I've been right through the plot and it's not all bad news,' Williams announced. But it does depend how you want to play it.' He added, 'Do you intend taking them out en route to the Dome?'

'It's not an option,' Shatford declared. 'We need to catch them dirty. And the only way to do that is to take them out when they make a move for the diamonds. Otherwise all we can do them for is possession of a stolen vehicle.

'If we move too soon,' Shatford concluded, 'chances are we will never prove a conspiracy and they will end up walking at court. If they ever get that far.'

'OK,' said the Inspector, 'I will advise on the options, it's for you to decide.'

Pointing at the De Beers 'Money Zone' exhibition, Williams explained, 'The diamond vault itself is quite easy to manage, because if we do it right we should be able to trap them inside.'

'Trap them inside.'

The words hit Shatford like breath of fresh air.

The diamond vault was an enclosed, confined space with only one way in and one way out: a narrow, dark passageway.

Williams had identified a critical irony – the gang's focus of maximum interest was also their point of most extreme vulnerability. In theory, it was the perfect place to spring a trap.

But with a worried look Williams continued, 'The danger you will have to face is what happens to punters who are visiting at the time. They could be trapped in there with the robbers, and you will end up with a hostage situation.'

He also explained that if they tried arresting the gang before they got to the diamond vault, it could turn into a shooting match across the Dome, again putting the public at risk. If they moved in too soon, they would not have sufficient evidence to convict the gang. And if they simply tried to prevent the robbery from taking place, then the gang would probably commit an equally dangerous crime somewhere else, when the police wouldn't be there to arrest them and protect people.

'Hostages,' Shatford agreed, 'are our biggest problem. The only thing I can say is that we should get some notice of when they are going to pull it off. I think it's unlikely it will be at a peak time, so we should be able to keep people back. We will have good vision from the CCTV so I am optimistic we can control it.'

Williams responded by suggesting a secret deployment point for his SO19 sharpshooters, a point near the Money Zone but largely out of view. 'The best place for us is opposite in the Harrison Building. We should be able to swoop around them and trap them. To be honest, I think this is probably the safest place because it restricts their escape routes and allows us tight control.'

'I was thinking that myself,' said Shatford, 'which is another reason it has to be inside the Dome. For one thing we don't know how they will get in there in the first place. It might be they all come in from different angles. We could never control that from outside. There are just too many variations of what they might attempt. The only thing we know for certain is that at some stage they will end up at that Jewel House.'

'If you can't find out how they're coming in,' said Williams, 'then my advice to you is that the diamond vault is the safest place, as long as you can keep members of the public away.'

'OK,' agreed the detective, 'let's work towards that. I don't think I will get away with deploying inside the Dome more than once, so your people will need to be ready. We know where the boat is, so the most notice we will have is the travelling time from Kent to Greenwich.'

'I will write some strategies around that,' Williams said, 'but I will need to review it with you every day, just in case there are any changes.'

'Don't worry,' promised Shatford, 'I will keep you fully briefed.'

Shatford pondered the paradox. The only way to stop the crime of the Millennium . . . was to *let it happen.*

19. The Commander

Fourth Floor, New Scotland Yard,
7 September 2000, 3 p.m.

'Would you like a cup, Mr Shatford?'

He was walking into Commander Alan Brown's office when the secretary greeted him.

'Why not?' he replied. 'Strong, with just one sugar.' I must be the last person in the world who still has sugar in tea, he thought.

He was here to brief Commander Brown on the developing Flying Squad plan to ambush the Betson gang inside the Dome. He wanted to put the best plan possible forward, so he had waited until he was absolutely certain of his facts before he reported to Brown.

This was flat-out political dynamite.

If the gang was armed and the Flying Squad tried arresting them before they got to the De Beers vault, it could turn into a shooting match across the Dome, putting the public at risk. If things went wrong, there was a hair-raising worst-case scenario – multiple civilian casualties. That would make it a guaranteed resignation job. If the gang was armed, the operation fell apart and civilian blood started to flow, Shatford's bosses would be fired even faster than him.

Given all the risks and unknowns, it was a huge gamble. But the gang weren't going to simply give up and go away. They had to be caught inside, in the act. Anything less and they would walk away from the court.

Still, Shatford knew there was a good chance his bosses would shoot down the plan. They could decide that the situation was too risky. They might insist that the diamond exhibit should just be shut down, or that the Dome be surrounded by so many uniformed police officers that the robbers would be scared away. Shatford was hoping for Commander Brown's support, but with the potential for political fallout he was not banking on anything.

When he entered the office, Brown was sitting at a small meeting table drinking a cup of tea.

'Yes, Mr Shatford,' said Brown, adopting a teasingly formal attitude, 'what can I do for you?'

'Thank you,' said Shatford, squeezing around the table to sit at Brown's right. Realising the discussion was sensitive, the secretary closed the door quickly.

'We are back on,' Shatford began.

'What, the biggest jewel heist that never was?' Brown countered, ribbing his subordinate about the aborted operation on 1 September.

'Yeah,' said Shatford, 'with one small minor adjustment – it's going to take place *inside* the Dome.'

'What!' Brown exclaimed.

'It certainly looks like it. I have been firming it up as much as I can, but that's what it looks like.'

'How?'

'We don't exactly know yet,' said Shatford, 'but it will probably involve a raid on the diamond vault itself, and possibly a getaway on the Thames by speedboat.' Then he took Brown through the latest Intelligence on the gang.

'We've actually had them on the plot,' he reported.

'Doing what exactly?' asked Brown.

'They've been in and out the Jewel House,' Shatford responded, 'walking out to the river. Cockram was videoing everything, and eventually they ended up having a meet on the opposite side of the river.'

'But I thought the display area was secure?' queried Brown.

'So does De Beers, but it seems this gang thinks otherwise and they may be real pros.'

Shatford then took Brown through the Intelligence picture step by step, explaining how Terry Millman was linked to the Aylesford attack and to Tong Farm.

'The trouble is,' Shatford said, getting to the crux of the matter, 'we don't know how they will do it. If we move too soon on this firm we will lose them forever. The only thing I would say is that it is likely to be early in the morning. Both Nine Elms and Aylesford were early morning jobs. That means probably they'll hit the Dome right on opening time, or maybe just before, so we should have tight control of the area.'

'But of course the Intelligence picture might improve?' said Brown.

'Yes, it's likely to and it's getting better every day,' Shatford agreed. 'We know they have a speedboat at the farm, so the minute that moves we can scramble on the Dome. If we can't control it, then I can ask De Beers to close the Jewel House. At least it would put the gang off for that day without alerting them to the fact that we're onto them.

'All we know for sure,' he concluded, 'is that eventually they'll end up inside the diamond house. And in there, we can trap them and take them down.'

Brown proceeded to go through every detail of the plan. He checked through the 'Decision Log' that Shatford had been keeping which rationalised the need for every action taken:

> DECISION: Arrest gang inside the jewel vault.
> RATIONALE: The vault acts as a natural cocoon where the gang will be trapped inside. Least opportunity for the gang to use firearms. It will prevent them from running into the Dome and perhaps using firearms in an open area accessed by the public.

Brown saw that it would indeed be impractical and dangerous to try to ambush the gang outside the Dome. It could trigger a chase and a gun battle across open public spaces.

Shatford was relieved. He had worried that he was dropping an insurmountable problem in Brown's lap, but the senior officer responded with highly reasoned, methodical questions and calculations, all of them geared to the goal of protecting the public.

For now, the plan had the Commander's seal of approval.

That evening, Shatford pulled an all-nighter.

For no apparent reason, there was a rash of kidnappings around London that summer.

As one of the senior investigating officers at the Yard, Shatford had to do his stint and be available 24 hours a day.

This one really pissed him off. The kidnap plot just fizzled out. An Albanian car washer who was allegedly taken from his flat at gunpoint turned up safe and well.

Twelve hours after going missing he rang his sister begging her to get £500 or he would be killed. Rather than pay the money she called the police. Six hours later they tracked him down to a flat in North London where he was found stoned out of his skull on drugs. The whole thing was just a ruse to filch some money from his sister.

Shatford was not impressed.

By 10 a.m. he was exhausted and looking forward to getting home to bed.

His phone rang as he was leaving the Scotland Yard control room, where he'd run the kidnap operation.

'Boss, it's Sean.'

'Hi, Sean, how's things?' said Shatford, bracing himself as he detected an air of anxiety in Detective Constable Sean Allen's voice.

Allen had just talked to Malcolm Woods, the chief of security at the Millennium Dome.

'He told me that David James wants to see you.'

David James. The two words made Shatford freeze in his tracks in the corridor.

'Oh, no!' he exclaimed, leaning against the corridor wall for support.

'I know,' said Allen, adding sarcastically, 'I thought that would please you!'

'This could be a major problem,' said Shatford.

'What should we do?' asked Allen.

'Let me think on it and I'll get back to you.'

Shatford ended the conversation sensing the sword of Damocles above his head.

He had forgotten all about the kidnapping job.

'Shit!'

20. The Chairman

Millennium Dome Executive Office, 8 September 2000, 11 a.m.

He was a bastard.

David James was the brand new chairman of the Millennium Dome. He'd been on the job for two days. And, according to one expert, he was 'a self-opinionated, stuck-up, arrogant prig'.

The funny thing was that the expert who chose these words was actually David James.

He was a corporate rescue doctor. When British businesses were about to die, David James was the guy they called in to cut them open, find a pulse and stop the bleeding. He was ruthless, independent and Rottweiler-tough, and he thrived on chaos and crisis.

Three days prior to Shatford being summoned, in an act of pure desperation, the British Government hired David James to try to save the enormous pear-shaped disaster called the Millennium Dome. His official title was Executive Chairman of The New Millennium Experience Company (NMEC), the agency that managed the Dome.

James was a dapper 62-year-old art collector and fitness fanatic who got up every morning at 5 a.m. and ran ten miles.

He had his work cut out for him.

So far, the Dome had burned through at least £600 million of taxpayer's funds for no real purpose. It was being slaughtered in the press and in the halls of government. In a horrible miscalculation, Dome planners had budgeted for twelve million annual paid visitors, but it now looked like only 4.5 million people would actually show up.

One Labour MP called it 'a national disgrace'. 'This has gone well beyond a national joke,' charged shadow culture secretary Peter Ainsworth. 'Many people will be disgusted that money that could have been used for a whole variety of good causes is being used to prop up the Dome for reasons of political vanity.'

Tory leader William Hague called for the immediate closing of the exhibition, which he ridiculed as 'an empty, pointless tent in the middle of nowhere'.

Two days prior to that, under a headline demanding 'Close the Dome Today', the *Daily Express* newspaper asked, 'Do they think we are a nation of idiots? For the fifth time in eight months the Dome has been granted a bail-out.' Each time, the paper charged, 'the bumbling clowns responsible have insisted that no more money would be needed', but each time it was 'a lie'.

Although Dome executives reported that visitors gave it high satisfaction ratings, it was hard to see why, given the long queues and grim, sometimes nearly homicidal exhibits.

After experiencing the Dome for himself, John Walsh of the *Independent* called it 'the Great Horned Bomb of Greenwich,' and reported that it felt like 'a kind of modernist Hades, a subterranean crush of lost souls in a dungeon lit only by the jumping flickers of distant, wall-mounted screens.'

Two weeks into the Dome's planned one-year lifetime, the 'speaking toilet' exhibit on British humour caught fire and was closed down. Ten days later, as if in response, the British League of Pessimists used the Dome to announce 'National No Smiling Day'.

Soon after, the Brain exhibit in the Body Zone broke down and the Skin sprang a leak. In April, a child was injured by a falling metal sheet. As compensation, she was offered a ticket to come back to the Dome. The next week, eight more visitors were injured when an exhibit fell on them in the Journey Zone, and a schoolboy wound up in hospital after being hit by a giant pendulum.

Also in April, feng shui consultant Helen Oon condemned the structure as 'an upside down rice bowl with chopsticks sticking out of it'. The Dome roof sprang dozens of leaks, requiring £100,000 to repair.

Dome employees were said to be physically attacking the Dome's cartoon character mascots Coggsley and Sprinx, showering punches at Sprinx's green cheeks and taking pot shots at Coggsley's orange bobble hat and purple nose.

'There have been an increasing and disturbing number of incidents of alleged assaults', a staff circular warned sternly. 'Do not touch them, however playful your intentions are. These are real people inside – both male and female. Any allegation of assault could lead to instant dismissal, and be reported to the police.' The besieged actors playing Coggsley and Sprinx also complained of low pay and smelly costumes.

In May, *The Economist* described the Millennium Dome as 'staggering from disaster to disaster, short of visitors and bleeding cash'.

By June, so few visitors were showing up that Scotland Yard dissolved its 35-member Dome police patrol. A hoped-for summer pick-up in visitors never materialised, and by August the daily visitor count was 4,000 bodies below the break-even point.

Into this mess, on 5 September 2000, stepped David James. He was born one mile away from where the Dome now stood. At the age of ten he was incorrectly classified as mentally retarded, and spent the rest of his life trying to prove himself. He was offered a place at Oxford but couldn't afford it.

After a stint at Lloyds Bank, James went to work for the Ford Motor Company. When he was up for promotion, he eliminated his competitor by hiding a key file behind a cabinet. 'That was the end of him,' James recalled fondly. 'I had proved to Ford I was the right man for the job because they wanted people who would actually be that ruthless.'

After leaving Ford, he went on to specialise in corporate rescues and turnarounds, saving by his own count some 90 companies, including Eagle Trust, the LEP Group, the British Shoe Corporation, the Robinson Group and Dan Air.

In 1986, he paused to rescue twelve employees of a British consulting company who were taken hostage in Libya. He remembered it as the greatest two weeks of his life.

'I went out to try to sort it out, little knowing that what they were inadvertently building was supposed to be Abu Nidal's training camp,' he recalled to the *Financial Times*. 'The CIA decided to bomb it in the raid that Ronald Reagan unleashed on Libya as part of his anti-terrorist activity. We were swept up by the Revolutionary Guard and herded on to the beach.'

He escaped safely, and so did the hostages.

In July 2000, when James was first asked to consider saving the Millennium Dome mega-project he thought, 'Not bloody likely. The Dome is a destroyer of reputations and there is no way I'd get involved in that one.'

But as things got worse he eventually relented, for the sheer scale and inevitability of it. 'Like Everest, it's there,' he explained. 'You've got to climb it.'

On 5 September, he was literally given twenty minutes to save the Dome on his first day on the job.

The attraction was originally scheduled to close at the end of the year, on 31 December, but its finances were so cocked-up that the Millennium Commission met with bankruptcy advisors and decided to shut the whole thing down later that same day, 5 September.

The only way the Commission would release the money to keep the doors open was if David James took over as the Dome's chairman, in which case they would give him an extra £47 million to keep it going.

They gave him twenty minutes to make up his mind. James agreed, and the Millennium Dome stayed open. Just by showing up, David James saved the Dome from a premature death. Now he had to keep it open, and figure out ways of reducing the magnitude of the ongoing disaster.

According to James, he took over a grossly insolvent operation in a state of pure chaos, where contracts were fouled up, bills were unpaid, millions of pounds of fraud was ongoing, and no one even had a list of assets. The staff, James reported, were 'on the edge of nervous disorder'.

In other words, it was a perfect David James assignment.

In keeping with the perverted finances of the Dome, he was working for free.

No, actually he was *paying the Dome to work there*, shelling out tens of thousands from his own pocket to cover expenses, immediate staff, his driver and secretary, even phone calls.

It was a mission of mercy.

Jon Shatford had been following news of the David James appointment in the papers. He seemed like the perfect man to save the Dome. He also looked like the last man in the world who would approve a police plan to ambush a gang of robbers on his property.

It is a fundamental principle of British law that the Commissioner of Police in London, and Chief Constables in the Counties, have total independence over operational policing. But the Dome was public property, and the Flying Squad could not operate inside it without the approval of the government.

David James was the government accounting officer responsible for the Dome. The government accounting officer is the guy you shoot when everything goes wrong. And Scotland Yard had to have his approval.

This is why Shatford instantly felt woozy on 6 September when he heard that James wanted to see him.

There was hardly a chance in hell, Shatford figured, that James would take kindly to the police plan. He'd been brought in to sort out the Dome's problems, not preside over a spectacular diamond robbery.

When he left the Yard that afternoon, Shatford stopped at Bruno's for a tea and bacon roll. He took a seat in the window, and watched the commuters going in and out of St James's Park tube station.

People-watching would help distract him and focus his mind on something other than the Dome. He was not in the mood for company, so he purposely avoided eye contact with anyone he knew making their way to the Yard.

When his roll and tea arrived he tucked in, quietly cursing nearby smokers under his breath.

In the corner of his eye he saw the homeless woman who sold the *Big Issue* outside the station. Not only did she greet everyone with a smile, she never looked troubled or unhappy in any way. He was struck by how her face lit up when someone bought the magazine from her. He felt guilty because he never had.

Shatford's thoughts drifted back to David James, who he remembered as having a role in uncovering the Iraqi 'super-gun' affair. It was in the early 1990s, when there was an international weapons embargo against Iraq.

James was paying a visit to a subsidiary of Eagle Trust, a company he was involved with, when he noticed what looked like a muzzle of a giant gun. He tipped off MI6 and the whole scandal unfolded.

Shatford smirked at the thought of what a good detective James would make. Somehow this made Shatford feel better. James was a far cry from a conventional bureaucrat. He was not going to write James off too soon, but he knew he needed some help to win James over.

Despite the fatigue of the all-nighter, he decided to skip bed, go back to the Yard and see Commander Alan Brown.

Brown looked up from his desk with a cocked eyebrow.

'You look a bit rough, Jonnie boy. A late night I gather?'

'Good,' retorted Shatford as he took a seat, 'because I would hate to feel the way I do and look normal.'

'What can I do for you?'

'David James has asked to see me . . .'

'Oops,' interrupted Brown.

'It's one of two things – either he wants to know how he can help us – or he's going to tell us to piss off out of his Dome.'

'I'll go for the latter!' said Brown emphatically. 'Do you want me to come with you?'

'I think it might be helpful,' said Shatford. 'We need to spell out the consequences if he doesn't co-operate.'

'We can certainly do that,' declared Brown.

'He's meant to be a tough cookie,' Shatford speculated, 'but if we make our case well enough, you never know.'

'We shouldn't pull our punches,' the Commander recommended. 'How much are you prepared to tell him?'

'Everything, really: Nine Elms, Aylesford, the gang's reconnaissance of the Dome.'

'We will need to be direct,' Brown concluded. 'If he's the straight-talking man I hear he is, then he will respect that.'

It looked like Brown relished the prospect.

Shatford was grateful he had Brown on his side, as well as Detective Chief Superintendent John Coles.

Despite the sleep deprivation and the sheets of rain pelting the windows of New Scotland Yard, he felt invigorated.

When he left the office he got a call on his mobile.

This had better not be another fucked-up kidnapping, he thought.

Instead, it was John Swinfield, with an update on Operation Magician. Surveillance officers were dug into the mud around Tong Farm.

They were getting drenched.

'I'm David James,' he said, shooting his hand out in a friendly, animated welcome.

'Mr James, I'm Detective Superintendent Jon Shatford and this is Commander Alan Brown.'

They were in a Spartan conference room in Bronze Control, a grim clump of Portakabins on the edge of the Dome property. These were the Dome's sharply unglamorous management offices.

A picture of the Dome under construction hung on the wall.

The men from Scotland Yard were in no mood for negotiation. The gang they were after was probably going to keep going until they succeeded, and this could be the only chance police would have to control and stop them.

James introduced the policemen to a woman in her 30s who was going to sit in on the meeting. She was a lawyer.

'Where is PY?' asked James as they sat down, referring to the hyper-ebullient, 34-year-old, self-described 'little ugly Frenchman' and Dome Chief Executive, Pierre-Yves Gerbeau, nicknamed 'The Gerbil' by the press. Personally, he preferred 'PY'.

Gerbeau was nowhere to be seen, so James asked for him to be collected. Conscious of the time, he agreed to start without him.

'Now,' declared James as he locked eyes on his visitors, 'I have just been briefed about a robbery that is meant to be taking place here and I want to know all about it!'

'I will give you the facts as they have unfolded,' said Shatford, 'so you can understand exactly what is happening.'

He began outlining the Nine Elms job but had to stop when a lady came in with a tray of teas.

Shatford got going again, but he had to back up and start again with a re-cap when Gerbeau appeared, looking rushed and a bit flustered.

'PY, you need to hear this,' declared James.

The diminutive Gerbeau, a former professional ice hockey player, had endured a tough time in the press ever since his appointment as Chief Executive in February 2000.

The first reports hailed him as 'the man who saved Euro Disney from disaster', which was in fact a claim he never made. It emerged that he had really been more of a mid-level operations director, though a capable one. One Disney source sniped that Gerbeau 'was nothing more than the man who ensured that when an exhibit was broken, he got the staff to arrange that somebody came and fixed it'.

Gerbeau did have, however, boundless enthusiasm for the Dome, for the people who came to it, for Coggsley and Sprinx and everything else.

As Shatford described the Aylesford job to the group, he thought he noticed both James and the lawyer wincing slightly at the description of gunshots fired at the police. He continued taking them through each step of the investigation, wrapping up with how the gang were identified in the Dome on 1 September.

'It's now our very clear belief,' he said, 'that the Millennium Diamonds within the Dome are their next target.'

'It sounds incredible,' James said in absolute disbelief.

'We now have a real good opportunity,' ventured Shatford, 'to catch this gang in the act, with sufficient evidence to send them to prison.'

'But someone might get shot!' exclaimed the lawyer.

'We can reduce that risk to a minimum,' Shatford replied. 'We have a very good plan that will trap the robbers right inside the jewel vault.'

As he was speaking he noticed that Gerbeau was shaking his head in disbelief. This surprised Shatford because he thought that Gerbeau had already been briefed on the operation and had agreed to their plan.

'We have an advantage at the moment that we have never had before,' Shatford asserted. 'We know where the gang operate from, and we can control what they are doing. If we lose that advantage they will simply go to ground and commit another robbery in the future. And quite possibly kill people.'

'Does De Beers know about this?' James interjected.

'Yes they do,' the detective replied, 'and they have been very helpful.'

'Well, they can afford to be,' retorted James forcefully. The robbery is not going to happen on their property.'

Shatford could feel the situation sliding into full-scale bureaucratic combat. He tried to reassure James on the logistics of the plan.

'The Flying Squad have a lot of experience in these matters,' he pointed out. 'This is actually easier than many situations we have to deal with.

'A bank or post office, for instance, carries much more risk because of the open customer areas. We would never dream of ambushing a robbery gang inside such premises. In the Dome it is different. We can actually surround them and trap them inside the vault area.'

He spoke of the need to secure evidence, and the risks of moving in at the wrong time.

'Surely you can stop them before they arrive?' asked James. 'They do not have to get anywhere near here.'

'It's not as easy as that,' Shatford countered. 'While we know the days the gang seem to favour, we can't be sure we can stop the robbery even if we want to. By far the safest way is to let it go ahead so that we can control it.'

This approach wasn't working. David James was going into full combat mode.

'Bear in mind,' he later explained, 'that I'd just got £47 million pounds from the Millennium Commission to try to keep the place open, after all these problems and everyone saying it should be closed down. And I suddenly find myself about to stage the greatest crime since the Great Train Robbery. I thought, Jesus, is this something I want to get involved in? Oh no, this is one straw too many.

'My first concern,' James added, 'was that we were dealing with a government property, and there would be a massive scandal if anybody got hurt in the course of this. And did the police have any authority from within government to proceed with an exercise which might put staff or others at risk.' James discovered that nobody else in his government chain of command, which reported up to the Home Office, had yet agreed to the plan.

'There's just no way this is going to happen,' James told Shatford. 'We don't want to play. It cannot happen. Tell De Beers to take the diamond away. We're going to put it in the press that you're onto the gang, or we'll shut down the Dome.'

'No, that's just not feasible,' explained Commander Brown. 'We have a responsibility to catch this gang. I have personally looked at the risks and the Flying Squad plan and, believe me, this is the safest way.'

'What about the young mothers with children who might be visiting?' asked the lawyer, herself a mother. 'I can't believe you would even consider such a thing.'

Brown continued forcefully, 'Well, believe me at times we have to. The Flying Squad are very good at this and have lots of experience at it. If we lose this opportunity to catch them then you will have to reflect how you might feel if they kill someone in the future.'

Shatford was impressed at how strong Brown was, clearly not planning to compromise.

'But it doesn't have to happen inside,' insisted James.

'Yes it does,' insisted Shatford. 'The only thing we know for absolute certain is that at some stage this gang will end up at the Jewel House. Prior to that they could be anywhere, posing as tourists, employees, anyone. Inside the Jewel House we can control them.'

'But I am liable,' said David James. 'I have responsibility for the Millennium Dome. I would be responsible.'

'Well,' Brown disagreed, 'I don't think you will find that's right. The responsibility will rest firmly with the police, Mr Shatford and myself. I am telling you we can manage this.'

'It's far too risky,' argued James. 'Anyone could get shot. Our staff. Anyone.'

Equally adamant, Brown countered, 'We can actually cocoon them inside the diamond vault. They will walk straight into a trap.'

'But you cannot stop them shooting somebody,' declared the lawyer.

'No,' agreed Shatford, 'but what we will do is overpower them as quickly as possible to stop them from having the opportunity. We will choose the moment of optimum safety, and do all we can to keep members of the public away.'

'I hear what you say,' said James, 'and you make some powerful arguments. I still have the well-being of the staff and public at the Millennium Dome to consider.'

'Yes,' concurred Gerbeau. 'It's the staff and visitors we have to consider.'

Then Brown concluded as though he was summing up in court. 'We all have a public responsibility to catch this team of robbers,' he said. 'All we are doing is asking you to support a very good plan to do that. I have told you what the consequences might be if we do not.'

'I've listened to what you have said,' James said, bringing the meeting to an end, 'and I will think on it and let you know. I cannot give you an answer now because I will need to discuss the matter with Ministers.'

He was going to kick this up to the Cabinet level.

Shatford and Brown left the Dome that day on good terms with James, but fearing the worst.

The Government was bound to be sensitive and over-cautious about anything relating to the Dome.

If the operation went out of control and members of the public got wounded or killed, the scandal that followed could conceivably bring the Government down.

Several weeks later, the police got their answer.

James called up and said he had spoken to the Minister in charge of the Dome, Lord Falconer, as well as Sir Robin Young, the Permanent Secretary responsible at the Cabinet Office.

Lord Falconer advised that the matter be left in the hands of the police. Additionally, officials at the Cabinet Office had spoken to the Home Office, which oversaw the police, and came to the same decision.

Shatford was relieved, and impressed at Lord Falconer's guts.

A big hurdle was out of the way.

Now all the police had to do was to take down the gang without getting anyone killed.

21. The Trap

The Isle of Sheppey, 8 September 2000, 12.10 p.m.

'They're moving.'

Through his field glasses, a police surveillance officer spotted Lee Wenham's Ford Ranger driving out of Tong Farm, carrying four men.

He called the report in from his mobile phone. The police were on the technological defensive; they assumed the gang was monitoring police radio frequencies with sophisticated scanning equipment, so this ruled out using encrypted Cougar police radios.

The Ranger was towing a beige and cream-coloured Glastron Carlson speedboat on a trailer.

It was just after noon on 8 September.

The officers secretly tailed the Ranger for thirty minutes, until it reached Kings Ferry Bridge on the Isle of Sheppey on the coast.

The Ranger stopped at the gate to a slipway beneath the bridge, and the officers took up covert positions to observe the gang.

With long-range video equipment, the officers taped the scene as Ray Betson, William Cockram, Lee Wenham and Brian Mitchell gathered around the vehicle in conversation, looking out at the water.

The gang members quickly realised that the tide was too far out to launch the boat. Mitchell, The Boatman, placed the outstretched palm of his right hand over the top of vertically positioned fingers of his left hand forming a clearly identifiable 'T' sign.

They walked towards a tea stall and huddled in conversation while sipping hot drinks from Styrofoam cups. Fifteen minutes later they returned to the Ranger and drove off.

At 2.33 p.m., the group returned to Tong Farm. Apparently, someone in the gang had misjudged the tide.

Shatford received the news with mixed feelings. The chances were the strike date was getting close and that when the boat moved the strike would be on. That weekend he put a skeleton staff on at Tower Bridge just in case they had to scramble. The rest of the squad was on standby ready to respond to a phone call.

The chances of a weekend strike seemed low. The crowds at the Dome, such as they were, were bigger at weekends, and if this was the same gang that had committed the Nine Elms and Aylesford jobs, then they preferred working on weekday mornings.

Out at Tong Farm, crops officers noticed members of the gang working on the fittings and control systems of the JCB digger. There was speculation that it might be used in the robbery, but no one knew how. Incredibly, the gang did not know that they were under observation by the police. So far, Operation Magician seemed to be working.

At the Millennium Dome, police were slowly and secretly moving in and infiltrating the area in and around the exhibition, getting to know every nook, cranny and inlet for a mile around.

Shatford, Swinfield and other Flying Squad officers paid a number of visits to the Dome, pacing around, eyeing up every entrance, alcove and possible escape route. They had to stop thinking like policemen and get inside the minds of the criminals. In their own minds, they planned the robbery.

Working with SO19 firearms advisors, the officers were refining a series of contingency plans for ambushing the gang and trapping them inside the De Beers jewel exhibit.

It was like preparing for a major battle.

To prevent leaks, Jon Shatford and his deputies had to sneak police officers and weapons specialists, in teams ranging from 20 to over 100, in and out of the Dome area without anyone on the Dome staff or local police knowing about it.

The Dome building spanned an area measuring nearly 1100 ft in diameter, covered by what its promoters asserted was 'the largest roof in the world', covering an area twice the size of the old Wembley Stadium.

The main exhibits, including the Money Zone containing the De Beers diamonds, were spread in a circular pattern around a large empty space in the middle, which hosted an elaborate daily 'Millennium Show' featuring acrobats and fireworks.

The problem was that scores of people could be exposed to the gang in the open spaces – schoolchildren, tour groups, retired people and Dome staff. Depending on the day and time, there could be anything from a few dozen to over a thousand people at risk. In addition to the exhibits, there were several points where groups of people clustered, including two McDonald's restaurants seating 400 each.

There were multiple entrances to the Dome property, and there was no way of knowing how and from what direction the gang would approach. If they struck when the Dome was open, the police could not quickly shut it down without tipping the robbers off.

The key was for police to figure out a way to ensure that members of the public would not be in the path of the gang, and to spring the trap when the gang were inside the vault. To do that, police decided to deploy officers disguised as Dome guides, cleaners and workmen, who would move in and usher people away from the Money Zone before the gang reached that point.

Under cover of darkness, SO19's Inspector Mark Williams smuggled a team of workmen onto the Dome property to build a false wall into the Harrison Building, across the pedestrian walkway from the diamond exhibit. There was just enough room to conceal up to a dozen men behind it. When the Dome staff returned the next day, no one noticed that the room was 6 ft narrower.

Detective Constable Sean Allen was well ensconced in the Bronze Control Room, pretending to be looking out for drug dealers. He was actually using the CCTV to scan the Dome for Betson, Cockram, or anyone else who might turn up with them.

Shatford's attention now turned to the gang's apparent planned speedboat getaway across the Thames. If they somehow got into the boat and started to escape, he worried that police launches might not be fast enough for an ambush. There was the possibility of a gun battle on the Thames.

He called in Sergeant Clive Rew from SO19 and asked him to prepare a strategy for intercepting the robbers on the water. Sergeant Rew selected his team, and began special training on the river to prepare for the 'take out'.

At the same time, the gang were conducting naval manoeuvres of their own.

On 12 September, the crops officers at Tong Farm reported the gang were on the move again. At 11.33 a.m., a white transit van driven by William Cockram left the farm with several passengers, followed by Lee Wenham's Ford Ranger towing a speedboat.

The police tailed the gang to the coastal town of Whitstable, Kent. The Ranger parked near a slip road to the harbour. Betson instructed Mitchell to put on a set of disposable plastic gloves, and the rest of the gang followed suit. They were wearing baseball caps.

At 1.05 p.m., the men began unloading the boat into the water. It took some effort to get it into the sea, but they eventually managed it and all four men got on board.

Sporting a wetsuit, the tanned Mitchell took the wheel, started the engine and carried out a number of figure of eight manoeuvres and tight turns as police surveillance officers watched and taped from the distance.

The boat was spluttering and coughing and appeared to lose power. Ray Betson took the wheel, then Cockram. After twenty minutes they returned to the shore and loaded the boat back onto the trailer.

They arrived back at Tong Farm at 6.17 p.m.

One thing seemed clear – the speedboat needed repairs. 'This boat,' said Ray Betson, 'is a lump of shit'.

The Flying Squad officers were having their own problems. Protesters were blockading oil refineries around the country, demonstrating against the high levies of tax on fuel. Filling stations were starting to run dry. As a result, the Flying Squad had to restrict the numbers of vehicles they had on the road. Shatford was torn between wishing the gang would get it over with and move in on the diamonds sooner rather than later, and hoping they would at least wait until the protests were over.

That evening he travelled by underground to Tower Hill station, walked across the bridge and met Detective Inspector John Swinfield in a room on the second floor of the Flying Squad offices. They were the only ones in the building. They sat down and went through the latest Intelligence. Activity was picking up at Tong Farm. At the Dome, a police surveillance team noticed a bearded man in his late forties in combat trousers conducting reconnaissance from a spot on the north side of the Thames, near the entrance to East India Dock Basin.

He placed a large black equipment bag on the ground next to him, strapped binoculars around his neck, and set up a tripod-mounted telescope pointed at the Millennium Dome and Thames. He checked traffic, paced around, and then left.

'These may be signs that the time is getting close,' said Shatford.

'It could be,' Swinfield replied, 'but the boat did not perform very well today, which might put them off.'

'They should be able to tune that up,' noted Shatford, adding, 'they do seem to be going to the farm on a more regular basis.'

'They are, but we still don't know all the faces,' Swinfield replied. 'The Boatman seems to wield a fair amount of respect, but he's still an unknown. All we know is that he's come over from Spain.'

'As long as we know Betson and Cockram, we should be able to ID the others later,' said Shatford. 'We need to step up our response around the Dome now. We don't want to be caught out.'

The next day the Flying Squad and armed SO19 officers took up various positions within striking distance of the Dome. Nothing happened.

At 9.42 a.m., on Thursday 14 September, a man strolled into the Great Suffolk Street office of Hilti UK – a leading manufacturer of construction tools.

It was Terry Millman, the quartermaster of the Dome gang.

After a few minutes, he emerged carrying a red plastic tool case in his right hand. He drove off in his white transit van, oblivious to the police surveillance team following him.

Subsequent enquiries established that Millman had specifically requested a Hilti cartridge gun, model DXA-41. He also bought a box of nails and one box of cartridges. A Hilti gun is a heavy, hand-held, gunpowder-activated tool designed for firing nails and threaded studs into concrete or steel. The DXA-41 holds magazine strips of ten nails and ten cartridges. The latter contain gunpowder explosive which drives a piston onto the nails and then fastens into the base material. It is a powerful tool capable of penetrating up to 1 in of steel.

Millman paid £762.18 for it in the name of P J Cook with an address in Orpington, Kent. He signed the receipt in the name of A Weekes. This did not raise suspicion at the point of sale because employees often buy and collect property on behalf of their employers.

22. The Crisis

New Scotland Yard, 15 September 2000, 12.10 p.m.

The voice on the phone got his pulse racing.

It was Tim Thorn, the De Beers security chief.

'Jon, I've got someone at my office now who's got plans of our vault. He says he's been to the newspapers and told them how bad the security is.'

'What!'

Shatford could barely believe what he was hearing.

'Do you know anything about these plans?' asked Thorn.

'Nothing,' replied the detective. 'Are you sure they are of your vault?'

'Yes, certain. He said they are the wiring plans.'

Shatford asked, 'Can you take him to Snow Hill now?'

'Yes,' answered Thorn, 'I'm sure I can.'

Thirty minutes later the three men were in a locked interview room at Snow Hill Police Station in the City.

The man was in his early thirties, and he was carrying an artist's portfolio case.

He introduced himself as George Kehoe*. Early in the year, he explained, he had been employed as a stagehand for one of the many contractors working at the Dome. He said he had been barred from the Dome after he had discovered corruption taking place. He said he was aggrieved by the way he had been treated, and was now going to 'blow the lid off things'.

'Where did these plans come from?' asked Shatford, as he removed a plan from the case for closer inspection.

'I was asked to clear out everything in one of the executive offices and put it in a skip,' Kehoe explained. 'I found these plans in there and was told they were rubbish so I was going to throw them away,' said Kehoe. 'Later I decided to take them home.'

'Why didn't you hand them in to someone in authority?' asked Shatford.

'Because I was told to throw them away,' said Kehoe. 'No one was interested, but I knew how important they were so I took them home.'

'I will keep them for now and look into it,' said Shatford, grabbing the plans, anxious to buy time. 'Have you already been to any newspapers?'

'Yes, I went to the *Sunday Mirror*.'

Trying to conceal the panic detonating in the pit of his stomach, Shatford concluded by saying, 'I will contact the CID at Greenwich Police Station and let them know you have been in. They will need to speak to you later.' The last thing the police wanted was publicity about the diamonds just days before the robbery.

He took the plans back to the Yard and immediately contacted Angie Evans at the press office.

'I may have a crisis on my hands,' he told her.

He decided to be totally open with her about the impending robbery, knowing that he would need a press strategy no matter what happened. The Dome was already attracting more than its fair share of bad publicity, if not for poor attendance figures then for the various forms of mismanagement that kept coming to light. The Kehoe story could easily spiral out of control and seriously jeopardise the investigation.

He met Evans on the 13th floor of the Yard and escorted her to a quiet office.

'My God,' she exclaimed, astounded by his story of the impending robbery, 'that's incredible.' Her day-to-day job, in large part, consisted of managing the press and public impact of Scotland Yard's work. And the story of the robbery was bound to be huge.

'At the moment,' Shatford said, 'the biggest risk to us is if we get a leak, and that could happen at any time.'

'So you will actually let the robbery take place?'

'Believe me,' said Shatford, 'given the circumstances it's the safest way.'

Shatford took her through all the options, ending on the perfect scenario of trapping the robbers in the Jewel House. 'There's one more thing,' he said, as Evans sensed Shatford was about to deliver another blow. He explained the Kehoe crisis-in-progress to her.

'He has got hold of some plans of the wiring system for the De Beers Jewel House. Security-wise they are not a lot of cop, but it's the way it could be interpreted in the papers.' Evans could already see the headlines: 'PLANS FOUND TO JEWEL HOUSE CONTAINING PRICELESS GEMS', adding, 'I would say that could have the potential for quite a big story if it got out.'

'Well, that's the trouble,' Shatford confessed, 'it already has – he has been to the *Sunday Mirror*.'

'Oh no,' said Evans, 'that could be bad news for you.'

'Don't I know it,' Shatford conceded. 'If Betson and his cronies read that, they will automatically think security will be upped and call the job off. We'll lose our one and only chance of catching them.'

'I wouldn't think the *Mirror* would run anything without calling us for comment,' Evans predicted. 'If they do I will be able to judge how seriously they are taking it, and perhaps give them some guidance. If that is what you want?'

'Absolutely.'

Evans agreed to work on a strategy, but asked Shatford to consider what his position would be if it went wrong.

'If it goes wrong,' he replied. 'I'll be fired so fast I won't have to resign.'

An hour later, Evans called Shatford with bad news. The *Mirror* was in contact, saying they were going to run a story. And on 17 September, the article appeared under the headline, 'SECURITY THREAT TO £150M DIAMOND'. It was a smaller article than Shatford feared, but it could still create problems. There was a risk other newspapers would follow it up. In turn, the Dome management could be forced to respond with public declarations about increased security measures, and the gang would be scared off.

Out at the farms in Kent, however, the gang seemed to be in full swing despite the article and the appalling weather. The waterlogged crops officers were reporting a flurry of activity early in the week of 18 September.

The JCB was attracting a lot of attention from the gang, shuttling between Tong Farm and Starfields Farm. More vehicles were logged as they came and went, and Millman was spotted driving the speedboat off the premises by a white transit van filled with passengers.

By the evening of Wednesday 20 September, police realised that the JCB, speedboat and gang were nowhere to be seen. The job, it seemed, was on. The Flying Squad officers decided it would be too dangerous to follow the gang closely because of the sophisticated equipment they thought they had.

The Dome would open after 9.30 a.m. the next day, and presumably the gang had moved to a forward launching point for a possible attack. Shatford and Swinfield decided to deploy their troops around the Dome. Instructions were flashed out to nearly 100 Flying Squad and SO19 firearms officers to report to the police administration building at Lambeth at 2 a.m. the next morning, for a briefing.

The briefing would bring some risk, as it multiplied the number of people who knew about the impending attack.

Shatford went home at 8 p.m. and worried. He knew that SO19 and disguised police officers would be well prepared around the Jewel House, but a constant cause of concern was stray members of the public and Dome staff. They had to be kept out of the firing line.

The Thames was also well covered by Sergeant Clive Rew of SO19 and his firearms team. For days they had been practising for an ambush on the river – a thought that filled Shatford with dread.

At 9.30 p.m. that night, Swinfield called in to report that Intelligence signs were good for an attack. They still didn't know where the gang had gone, but it was not to any of their known locations.

At about the same time as the detectives were talking on the phone, a terrorist was hiding in a garden near Vauxhall Bridge, cradling a Russian-built, RPG-22 shoulder-fired grenade launcher.

Through a pop-up range-finder, he aimed the weapon at the highly secure MI6 building in central London, headquarters of the Secret Intelligence Service and the heart of the British Government's foreign Intelligence network.

The terrorist belonged to the so-called 'Real IRA', a hyper-violent splinter group that rejected the IRA's 1998 Good Friday peace agreement cease-fire with the British Government. The group were responsible for the bloodiest single atrocity of the thirty-year Northern Ireland 'troubles' – the 1998 bombing at Omagh that killed 29 people and injured 370.

The RPG-22 is a lightweight, highly portable anti-tank weapon that fires a 73 mm, fin-stabilised warhead capable of penetrating 390 mm of armour, or concrete 3½ ft thick, from 800 ft.

The terrorist squeezed the trigger and the rocket flew nearly 1000 ft through the night air, beyond its maximum effective range, and into an eighth-floor window, which deflected most of its impact.

The terrorist dropped the weapon and escaped. Nobody was injured, but the attack set off alarm bells throughout the security services.

At 10.30 p.m., Shatford switched on his television to see breaking news about the attack, which occurred less than half a mile from the Lambeth police building, where he was going to brief his troops in less than three hours. For Operation Magician, this could mean yet another crisis. The rocket attack would probably trigger heightened security on all public buildings, including the Dome. If it were publicised, it would almost certainly put the robbers off. Shatford was devastated – it might be back to square one again. It seemed that every time they had a breakthrough, something conspired against them. He couldn't believe his luck. Shatford arrived at Lambeth at 2 a.m. and met John Swinfield.

'Any more on the Intelligence front?' he asked.

'No, nothing,' answered Swinfield, 'we still don't know where the boat or JCB are, so we've got to assume they are ready for use.'

If that was all they knew, Shatford now had second thoughts about an inside-the-Dome deployment. It might be better to move instead to a rapid-response standby status with the police mobilised outside.

'I don't fancy deploying within the Dome unless we get more information than that,' Shatford concluded. 'Let's put everyone in hold-off positions, so we can be ready to move if we have to.'

'OK,' said Swinfield, 'Sean Allen is down at the Dome anyway with the Dome security director Malcolm Woods, so they will be ready to let us in.'

'Great,' Shatford said, 'now all we have to do is survive this terrorist attack. If they up the security on all high-profile buildings, we could be screwed.'

'You're telling me,' said Swinfield, sounding as disillusioned as Shatford.

The briefing went according to plan. The police officers were warned not to stop for burgers or coffee within a five-mile radius of the Dome in case members of the gang had the same idea. They were to go to their allotted locations and wait for a phone call. No radios would be used, and no driving through the plot was allowed.

It was drummed into everyone that this gang would be likely to have a third eye out looking for them. Shatford, Swinfield and Detective Sergeant Mark Drew were parked up behind a supermarket off Millennium Way with other Flying Squad cars. Detective Inspector Adrian Smales had again sneaked up the construction crane, and had a bird's eye view of what was happening.

The night was long and uneventful. The officers watched the dawn break and heard the Dome open up. Nothing happened. At 10 a.m., most of the team were stood down. They were instructed to return to Lambeth at 2 a.m. the next morning.

23. Reconnaissance

The Millennium Dome, 22 September 2000, 9.45 a.m.

'They're coming towards you.'

The surveillance officer was speaking softly into a tiny hands-free microphone.

'They're heading for the Jewel House.'

The CCTV cameras zoomed in on two men as they walked into the Dome.

It was Lee Wenham accompanied by an unknown man. They were being tailed discreetly by a team of Flying Squad officers dressed as Dome guides.

A small team of SO19 sharpshooters were standing-by, behind the false wall at the Harrison Building, ready to strike.

The two men entered the darkened diamond chamber and whispered to each other as they gazed at the gems, first studying the De Beers Millennium Star exhibit in the centre of the room, and then the surrounding wall displays housing the 11 vivid blue Millennium Jewels.

They walked out of the Dome, out to the pier at Millennium Point and looked across the river, both of them talking on mobile phones.

They took a slow walk back into the Dome, patrolling around the complex, then went back into the Jewel House for another look at the diamonds.

At 10.51 a.m., they got into a Ford Sierra and drove off.

That night, two detectives met at the Tower Bridge Flying Squad office.

'I don't see them holding off for much longer,' said John Swinfield. 'They must do it soon, unless they are put off by all the high visibility policing around there.'

'That's a real danger,' agreed Shatford. 'With the *Sunday Mirror* article and the attack on MI6, we've just about used up all our lives.'

In the wake of the Real IRA rocket attack on the MI6 building, the order went out to beef up uniformed police patrols around key high-profile buildings around London.

The Millennium Dome was one of them.

There was nothing the detectives could do about it, and it could trigger one of two bad situations.

Either the gang would be scared away from the police trap at the Dome, or they would tool up with heavier firepower to overcome the extra police presence.

'What the hell are they waiting for?' asked a frustrated Shatford.

'I think they're having trouble with the boat,' guessed Swinfield, noting that the speedboat and trailer were now positioned at Starfields Farm. 'They might be looking for another one. The weather out at the farms is impossible. Surveillance just can't get close enough.'

'Well, look,' Shatford said, 'our strategy is still sound. We should still be ready to deploy at the Dome. The movement of that boat will still be the key.'

The detectives reviewed all the Intelligence in detail, but one thing above all baffled them, what was the JCB for?

They wondered whether it might be used to gain access to the Dome site by subterfuge, perhaps to get the gang inside the main perimeter disguised as workmen, or even to knock out a power supply cable to the Dome to create panic and mayhem. They even wondered whether it might be a variation of the ramming vehicles used in the Nine Elms and Aylesford attacks. Perhaps a long arm would be attached on the rear of the JCB to stretch out into the Jewel House and try to smash the glass casing. But then what was the Hilti gun supposed to do?

Shatford concluded with a statement that was becoming a mantra for him.

'The only thing we know with any degree of certainty is that at some point they are going to end up at that Jewel House. That's what we must concentrate on.'

The detectives wondered where on earth the JCB had gone. They got their answer the next day.

Surveillance officers tailed Lee Wenham to an old coal yard in a rundown area on White Hart Road in Plumstead, South London, just three miles from the Dome. The yard housed a disused Railtrack engine shed. It was almost deserted, and well away from prying eyes.

Detective Inspector Gary Kibbey of the SO11 Intelligence branch quickly set up a long distance OP to monitor events. There, through the open door of an old repair shed, several gang members were spotted standing around the yellow JCB.

This must be a launch point for the Dome attack.

Ray Betson was having personnel problems.

Like many gangsters before him, he was having trouble recruiting talent and keeping the gang together for the weeks and weeks of planning and reconnaissance.

The members of a robbery gang, by definition, are an explosive mix of hoodlums in various states of mental stability. They can fall out without warning, and need to be fed and cared for, given payrolls and timetables.

The talent pool for a robbery gang is heavily polluted by boozers, pot-heads and all-round cut-throats – people often skating on the edge of spectacular personal failure.

Betson's complex plan to steal the diamonds was taking firm shape but, in late September 2000, he was at least two cogs short of a team after an unidentified pair was forced to leave the project for unknown personal reasons.

Betson decided to turn to an old friend for help: a 56-year-old convicted cocaine smuggler named Robert Adams.

In addition to being sentenced to a year in prison in France on a cocaine rap, Adams had spent six years in prison for trying to kill his wife. He was now living at what police called 'no fixed address', or on a borrowed couch somewhere, and was apparently in strong need of a gig.

Adams offered several assets to Betson. He had criminal experience, was well-built despite his advancing years, and he kept his mouth shut. The two men had been friends for nearly 25 years.

Police also believed that Adams was connected to the infamous Adams Family London gang, a vicious clan that the press called 'the most infamous crime family in Britain' and 'Britain's most feared gang of drug dealers and hit men'.

The Adams Family, in an intriguing footnote, was in turn reported to have links both to the Spanish 'Costa del Crime' and to London's gold and diamond centre in Hatton Garden.

Raymond Betson took his old friend Bob Adams out for a drink in Maidstone, briefed him on the Dome scheme and offered him £50,000 to join the plot.

Was he interested?

Adams jumped right on board.

On 27 September, gang member Terry Millman walked into the Whitstable Marine shop in Whitstable, Kent, put £3,700 in cash on the table and made off with a red-and-white Picton 180 speedboat capable of a top speed of 55 mph.

At 3.52 p.m., he attached the boat to the rear of his transit van and drove off. The name *Exstacy Royale* [*sic*] was clearly visible on the boat's side.

In a touch of bravado, Millman had signed the sales receipt with a fake name. His alias was 'T. Diamond'.

2 October, 11 a.m., Shatford and his senior detectives were finishing 'morning prayers' – a Monday ritual at Scotland Yard, when officers meet to review what happened over the weekend.

Today they discussed a rise in the number of kidnaps, the increase of armed robberies on bookmakers and, as always, the departmental budget. Everything had to be cost effective.

Shatford marched upstairs to his office on the fifth floor where Swinfield was waiting for him, coffee in hand.

'Do you think we've spooked them?' Shatford asked as he pulled the office door closed. He was concerned about the lack of Intelligence coming through on the Dome gang, and the seeming lack of activity at the farms in Kent.

'Maybe,' said Swinfield. 'We assume they're picking up technical equipment, or they could just be getting things together.'

Shatford sat down in his swivel chair and turned to face Swinfield. 'It's been a quiet few days and we're now into October; something must have happened.'

'Perhaps it's just the boat trouble that's slowed them up,' speculated Swinfield.

'I hope so,' said Shatford. 'I would hate to think that word had got out.'

There was a tap on the door and in walked Inspector Mark Williams, the firearms specialist.

'I have updated our options,' he said as he unfastened his briefcase, 'so I need to go through them again with you to make sure you are still happy.'

'Let's knock them about just to make sure we are not missing a trick,' Shatford suggested.

'First of all,' asked Williams, 'is there any significant Intelligence update?'

'No,' said Shatford. 'We still don't know how they are going to pull it off, except that a Hilti gun might be used. And we are still no wiser about the JCB. My own guess is that it will just be subterfuge to get them into the Dome complex. I'm pretty certain a boat will be used for the escape, though we mustn't discount the idea that they could all arrive in it as well. That would be a novel twist.'

'What about numbers?' asked Williams.

'Still none the wiser,' said Shatford. 'There's Beston, Cockram, the Boatman, Lee Wenham, Millman, but there could be anything up to a dozen or more in total, so we must plan for that.'

'So what are the certainties?'

'That at some stage this gang will turn up at the Jewel House.'

Now Williams posed a question that cut to the heart of the whole operation.

Shatford knew that as a weapons expert, Williams was playing devil's advocate; he was duty bound to explore the best options for a capture.

'Why can't you take them out for conspiracy at Tong Farm or the coal yard?'

'It's a fair question,' noted Shatford. 'But the fact is we could never prove conspiracy. We may have suspicions and indications that they are going to rob the jewels, but that's all they are. It's not evidence. If we nick this lot too early we can bank on "No comment" right through the interviews.

'That means we would need to catch them dirty, with guns wrapped round them and that's highly unlikely,' Shatford continued. 'Even if we did, we would have to prove whose guns they were, and the only realistic thing we would end up charging them with is possession of firearms without a licence.'

Williams asked, 'OK then, why can't you take them out en route to the Dome, when you know they are going to do the job?'

'Because even then all we will have is a group of men in a van – the chances of them having firearms with them en route are pretty remote.'

'Why?'

'Because,' Shatford explained, '(a) they know what the consequences would be if they got captured and (b), because when they visited the Dome on 1 September they were with a woman who was pushing a pram. There's a good chance they could secrete guns into the Dome.

'The guns could even be carried ashore from a boat,' Shatford continued. 'Anything could happen – the fact is we simply don't know. And to turn them over on speculation alone could lose us everything.'

Williams continued, 'What if you got traffic to do a stop on them en route?'

'Then they would smell a rat immediately and abort the whole thing.'

Williams was doing a good job challenging the rationale of Shatford's thinking. If it all went wrong, he would have to explain the same justifications in a court of law.

They continued discussing every possible scenario they could imagine. Each time they came back to the same conclusion.

Shatford wrapped up the argument: 'We have a once-in-a-lifetime chance here. For once we have the advantage. We know where the gang's safe house is, what their target is, and we can take them out on the plot.

'If we lose this chance to catch them, who knows where their next robbery will be? Who will their victims be? It could be a kid in a bank or jeweller's shop getting killed in the process. And what do we tell the parents when they find out that the police had the chance to take out this team, but bottled it?'

Both Williams and Swinfield nodded in agreement.

This was the clinching argument.

The Jewel House was the safest place to arrest the gang.

But only if they could keep the public out of the path of stray bullets.

24. The Lessons

Bruno's Café, St James's, London, 1 p.m.

He saw them out of the corner of his eye as he settled down in a window seat at Bruno's Café.

There were two very young-looking constables walking across Victoria Street, a man and a woman who looked like they were barely in their 20s. They were excitedly discussing something, maybe a bit of police gossip.

Shatford forgot about his lunch for a few moments as he watched the two, dressed in helmets, white shirts and black ties. The basic uniform hadn't changed much since Shatford first put one on some 25 years ago.

They looked fresh out of the Metropolitan Police Training School at Hendon, at the absolute bottom of the chain, just starting out on the job. Shatford remembered exactly how it felt.

'DULL IT ISN'T'.

That was the Metropolitan Police recruiting slogan when he joined. And dull it wasn't.

Nothing can match the feeling of your first day, patrolling on your own as a police officer. Dressed in the uniform you're so proud to have earned, you take to the streets like a pilot on a first solo flight.

Soon trepidation springs from every step, as you begin to sense that everyone is looking at you. It feels like you're wearing big 'L' plates posted on your back and front.

Your first moment of terror comes when a member of the public approaches you for the first time. Your mind is so jumbled with the legislation and regulations you learned in training school, that you wonder if you'll be able to solve your first crisis.

For Shatford, that first moment came in September 1975, in the form of a question: 'Can you tell me the way to Brixton prison?'

Internal panic ensued. Surely a police officer was bound to know where the prison was, on the ground that he policed.

Shatford gave it his best shot and, with the best of intentions, sent the member of the public totally the wrong way. When he realised his error, he spent the rest of his shift hoping he would not bump into his victim.

In the months that followed, Shatford directed traffic on busy junctions, stood on cordons around crime scenes, ushered children across the road, reported missing persons, dealt with burglaries, theft and domestic disputes, chased pickpockets through alleyways and filled out mountains of forms. His appetite for the job was insatiable. He loved London and he loved being a policeman.

The most amazing thing about being a policeman, Shatford quickly learned, was the feeling of being dropped into society's most heart-stopping, explosive and emotional situations, and instantly having to restore order out of chaos.

When you're called to a crime scene or an accident site, you're often besieged by people in extreme distress, people who are crying or screaming or attacking each other, sometimes bleeding, occasionally dying.

On the streets of London, Shatford learned that police officers always have to give the outward appearance of calm and confidence, regardless of the turmoil they feel within. He learned to be polite and respectful to everyone, even the suspects. If you start yelling or threatening to arrest someone, you've lost control. One of the golden rules is to not threaten to arrest anyone whom you're not prepared to arrest immediately.

He was once called to an old lady's flat when she managed to call the police after she fell out of bed. He broke in and found her lying on the floor whimpering. He helped her back into bed, and sat with her while an ambulance was called. She just wanted to hold his hand.

When the ambulance arrived she thanked Shatford for coming. Four nights later he received the same call again. She was lonely and just wanted some company. Police work can be a balance between law enforcement and social work.

When he started his first foot patrols in Brixton, South London, in 1975, Shatford absorbed everything he could. He listened to more experienced colleagues talking about their cases, watched them in action and copied everything he thought was good.

He learned on the streets and in police stations, watching criminals and officers in action.

Shatford learned one particular lesson from an officer named Colin Parffit: 'First, cool the temperature.'

Parffit was a supervisor's nightmare. If there was an angle to anything, he'd figure it out. But when it came to dealing with volatile situations, he could charm the birds out of the trees.

One day Shatford found himself standing next to Parffit at a front door, facing a husband and wife who were screaming at each other.

Each had called the police, convinced they were in the right. That's the way it is with domestic disputes. The two parties were competing to put across their point of view, which was leading to blows as each tried to shout the other down.

PC Parffit nodded to Shatford, and signalled him to follow him indoors to the living room. Parfitt switched on the television, and he and Shatford plopped down on the sofa.

When the couple followed them in, Parffit looked up and said, 'Well, who's going to make the tea?' The couple was so surprised that they both went into the kitchen and prepared it.

When they returned, Parfitt acknowledged them, took his cup, and carried on watching TV.

The husband and wife were so befuddled that they looked at each other in total astonishment, forgot all about the argument and focused instead on the two policemen sitting on their sofa, who seemed to have no interest in them whatsoever.

Upon finishing his tea, Parffit thanked the couple and led Shatford out the door. The police never received another call to their house.

The lesson was, cool things down and don't argue with members of the public, particularly in domestic disputes. Passions run so high that people only hear what they want to hear, and if things go wrong they will unite against the police officer.

He learned another lesson on his own, when he was called to a report of 'suspects on premises' in Brixton Hill.

Shatford was the first responding officer to enter the unoccupied house. After a thorough search no one was found. He then levered himself up into the attic and spotted a dark mass in front of him.

'The easy way or the hard way?' hollered Shatford with as much authority as he could muster.

'The easy way,' was the reply, much to Shatford's astonishment.

With that, a six foot three tall, middle-aged man appeared. Shatford arrested him for 'being on enclosed premises for an unlawful purpose', an offence under the Vagrancy Act that no longer exists. The unlawful purpose, Shatford concluded, was to steal some of the fittings.

At the trial that followed some months later, Shatford was asked a strange question by the defence barrister.

'Did you look behind all the doors, officer?'

'Not all, no,' said Shatford, expecting him to allege an accomplice had got away.

Then the barrister looked at Shatford and asked with grand theatricality, 'What about *excrement,* officer?'

Shatford froze in the witness box.

'Did you see *excrement* behind any of the doors?'

'I can't recall,' said Shatford, oblivious to where the questioning was heading.

'Did you look?'

'Not specifically, no.'

'Thank you, officer,' smiled the barrister.

A police officer knows he's fouled up when a defence barrister thanks him in court.

The defence went on to allege that the defendant was only in the house to relieve the call of nature, without criminal purpose, and he was acquitted.

The incident illustrated that you have to think like a criminal, predict what their defence might be, and be prepared to rebuff it. When a detective prepares a case for trial, he knows that the prisoner will have a year or more to prepare a defence, and every detail of evidence will be pored over by a defence barrister. Careful attention to detail and excellent report writing are among the most formidable weapons a detective has.

Shatford learned a valuable lesson that day: always check for shit behind doors.

It was chance, rather than any particular desire to join the CID, that led Shatford to become a detective. He had some good arrests to his credit, so after three years at Brixton he was asked to put in for the local crime squad as an aide.

Four weeks after passing the selection board, he was at Clapham reporting for work on the L District Crime Squad. He would now cover the South London area of Brixton, Clapham, Kennington, Streatham and Gypsy Hill in plain clothes.

Working in plain clothes required a whole new lot of skills. The protection of the uniform is removed and you have to rely far more on your personality, street sense and nascent acting skills.

Joining the Crime Squad as an aide meant Shatford was a 'scrote', back at the bottom of the food chain. Scrote was an abbreviation of scrotum, and reminded trainee detectives of their station in life. He was paired with an experienced aide called John Hicks who had tried for years to get into the CID. He was an excellent thief-taker, but had some difficulty passing selection boards.

The two of them worked closely with John Reid, the DC in charge of their little group, and Tony Sowden who joined at the same time as Shatford. Sowden was a biker with long hair and a scraggy beard, and resembled a Hell's Angel Rasputin, the perfect disguise for a plain clothes officer. The four young detectives were driven by the same goal: they loved nicking criminals.

Sowden had such high morals he would never take a drink off anyone unless he was allowed to return the compliment. He despised corruption which, by his definition, extended to an officer accepting a free cup of tea.

On one of their first nights working together they went to search a house in Kellett Road, Brixton, for stolen property.

It's always a scrote's job to cover the back of a house being entered, so Sowden volunteered. After Reid, Hicks and Shatford entered and began questioning the suspects, a deafening shriek was heard outside the back window. It came from a bearded figure crumpled in agony outside the window.

'I fell off the wall,' screeched Sowden. 'I think I've broken my foot.'

Shatford, Hicks and Reid dissolved in fits of laughter as Sowden surfaced above his pain to take down the suspect's statement. He refused to go to hospital, and came back to Brixton police station with the three prisoners who could be forgiven for thinking they had been arrested by the Keystone Kops. He was off work for three weeks with a badly sprained ankle.

The incident illustrated some cold realities of police work – you had to work through the pain, and there was little sympathy for a scrote.

From John Hicks, Shatford learned an effective technique for questioning suspects: bore them to death.

Hicks was a master at this.

He would sit down with a prisoner and talk to him for hours on end about anything – his weekend, football, you name it.

Hicks believed that once a prisoner started talking to you, it was only a matter of time before he gave in and told you what you wanted to know.

Once, Hicks talked to a prisoner for over an hour and he still had not replied. Then he noticed that the prisoner was continually playing with a ring on his finger. Hicks regarded him curiously.

'That's a nice ring,' he said.

'My mother gave it to me,' said the prisoner, looking up for the first time.

And bingo, he was in.

They spoke about their mothers for an hour.

She proved to be the most important and influential person in the suspect's life. Hicks revealed similar feelings about his own mother, and soon after the prisoner confessed to everything.

Later, there would be strict rules on questioning imposed by the Police and Criminal Evidence Act, and it wasn't quite so easy, but the principle was the same. You have to find a level on which to connect.

Shatford had some good teachers on the L district crime squad, and enjoyed his life as a scrote. It struck him how sincere his colleagues were when it came to helping people in trouble. Their station in life, politics or ethnic origin didn't matter. If someone was in trouble, it was the detective's job to help them.

When Shatford passed a selection board, he went on to work in the Brixton CID office and then Stoke Newington as a DC. He undertook a very intensive CID course at the Detective Training School at Hendon, which gave him insights into the criminal law. British law is based on case studies, some going back hundreds of years, and this training enabled him to interact with barristers on equal terms.

Stoke Newington is north of the Thames and, for Shatford, it was like joining a different police force. The divide between North and South London is marked, both in sociological and policing terms. The Thames serves as a great divide. People tend to stay in one half or the other, and those in South London only tend to head north to visit the West End. Criminals are no exception. For Shatford this was a whole new ball game.

His Detective Inspector at Stoke Newington was John Farley, likened by his colleagues to a ferret because once he got his teeth into something he would not let go. He scoured all the crime sheets to ensure that no stone was left unturned, and would not tolerate anyone who cut corners. Working for Farley was like an advanced degree in itself.

Over the years, from these detectives and many others, Shatford learned lessons and sharpened his instincts.

Today, as he watched the two pink-cheeked young constables disappear around the corner, Shatford wondered what lay in store for them, what lessons they'd learn and how they'd make out.

Some of the officers being assigned to Operation Magician seemed almost as young. Shatford was asking them to enter a possible combat zone. And if they got wounded or killed, the fault would lie with the criminals, but their blood would be on his hands.

25. Battle Stations

Tower Bridge Flying Squad Office,
4 October 2000, 3 p.m.

'This must be it,' he muttered, stuck between fear and exhilaration.

Shatford was reviewing the Intel reports on the Dome gang with John Swinfield.

'All the signs are good, fingers crossed,' concurred Swinfield. 'The Intelligence looks spot on, especially as all the firm are coming together.'

On the previous day, 3 October, members of the gang towed the speedboat *Exstacy Royale* into Starfields Farm using a Ford Sierra.

This morning, the same Sierra drove into the coal yard at Plumstead, and the JCB was seen being washed and driven short distances, apparently being tested.

This coincided with information that the gang members had booked rooms in low-class lodging houses in South-east London. Millman had booked into a lodging house in Kent.

This information convinced Shatford that the job was imminent.

'What about the boat?'

'Conditions down at Starfields are bad,' said Swinfield. 'We've got it on a long eyeball, but can't guarantee we'll see the boat if it leaves. There's been a lot of coming and going, but it's impossible to see who or what.'

'That's not good news,' grumbled Shatford.

'I know, but the lads are doing their best. They are still waist deep in mud.'

'If we can't be sure, then we must assume the job's on,' said Shatford. 'Better that way than to miss it. Let's deploy inside the Dome tomorrow night.'

'I've spoken to Malcolm Woods,' reported Swinfield. 'He will be down there from 1 o'clock in the morning to let us in.'

'Have you got any doubts?' he asked.

'No,' said Shatford, 'I think we'll take them out OK, but those SO19 boys and girls are going to have their work cut out.'

The good news, it seemed, was that fewer people than ever were going to the Dome. This week, the Dome reported dismal attendance numbers for September, the lowest monthly number of visitors since it opened in January.

But what the policemen didn't know was that this was about to change. A big rise in attendance was coming in October, fuelled by the half-term, and perhaps by morbid interest in the Dome's imminent closure on 31 December.

That month, an average of 20,000 visitors would come to the Dome *every single day.*

When Shatford arrived at the Lambeth police building on the night of Thursday 5 October, there was a real sense of optimism in the air.

The second floor conference room filled up with over 100 officers, and they intently absorbed a briefing from Shatford, Swinfield and Williams.

'Tonight, for the first time,' said Shatford, 'we are going to fully deploy inside the Dome. If the job comes off then it will not matter who sees us, but if for any reason it doesn't, we must get out as quietly as we got in. I ask all of you to bear that in mind. Do not draw attention to yourselves.'

That remark yielded an outbreak of smirks in the audience, from officers wondering how such a large number could possibly go unnoticed.

Swinfield followed with a tactical briefing, detailing where individual officers would be posted, what their responsibilities would be, and the fact that there would be a radio blackout.

Next, Williams went through every detail of how the armed SO19 officers were to respond. He asked the plain clothes officers to stand up so that everyone could get a good look at their faces.

If there was to be an exchange of fire, it was good to know which faces were on your side.

Two hours later, Sean Allen drove Shatford and Swinfield to the Dome. They stopped at a service station and each bought a pack of stale cheese sandwiches, crisps and a soft drink.

At the Dome they were met by security director Malcolm Woods, who escorted them to a conference room in Bronze Control, the prefab building about fifty yards from the Dome. This would be Shatford and Swinfield's operations base. Allen left them to take a seat in the CCTV room to monitor the cameras.

Shatford looked at the clock on the wall and checked it against his watch: 3.15 a.m., 6 October. In a couple of hours he expected movement, in Kent and at the coal yard.

'All we can do now is wait, Guv,' noted Swinfield.

'Power of positive thought, Swinni,' replied Shatford. 'Betson and the gang are probably getting ready right now.'

A nearby team of SO19 officers was well prepared with tasty-looking sandwiches and flasks of tea and coffee. Shatford and Swinfield looked on enviously, considering their own less appetising garage specials stuck together in cellophane packs.

Swinfield cracked some jokes, and soon the war stories started. Whenever policemen get together, you're bound to hear stories about their cases, what went wrong and how disaster was averted, always ending with a laugh. When the story sounds overcooked, the teller will be shouted down with accusations of 'swinging the lamp'.

After an hour the SO19 officers lay down on the floor to get some sleep.

Firearms specialists are held in awe by other police officers for their ability to sleep anywhere, anytime, in full battle dress, and wake up refreshed and ready for action.

Swinfield's mobile phone lay on the table.

The next call, they assumed, would be the signal that the gang were moving into place.

At 6.30 a.m., the phone rang.

Suddenly everyone was awake and staring at Swinfield, trying to figure out the conversation.

'Yeah, OK then. . . keep an eye out.'

He shook his head – a false alarm.

'It was Mark saying it's all quiet at the coal yard.'

Shatford ventured, 'I would have thought we'd have movement by now if it was going to happen.'

'They're cutting it a bit fine,' agreed Swinfield.

By 8 a.m., Shatford was ready to give up.

The Dome staff was arriving, and soon the first visitors would be strolling around.

At 8.20 a.m. Swinfield's mobile rang again.

'Yeah, right,' he said, nodding to his colleagues. 'How many? Right, keep us posted.'

He ended the call with a smile on his face. 'That was Mark,' he announced. 'There's movement at the Yard. A white transit with two up has just entered and gone towards the engine shed where the JCB is.'

'They're cutting it really fine,' worried Shatford.

The Dome opened to the public in sections, starting at 9 a.m.

The obvious best-case scenario would be to trap the gang in an empty Dome.

'They could still be here by 9 a.m.,' said Swinfield.

His mobile rang again.

'Is it? I'll tell the boss, he's with me.'

Hanging up abruptly, he announced, 'The JCB is on the move here with its amber light flashing.'

'Excellent!' said Shatford. 'That's the best news yet.'

'In a half an hour we could have it in the can.'

The phone rang, this time with Detective Sergeant Jools Lloyd on the line.

'The boat is in the river further east,' he reported. 'We haven't got it under control yet because we don't want to risk showing out.'

'The boat's in the water and the JCB's en route, so it's game on,' said Shatford. 'This really is it.'

The Dome was starting to fill with people.

Police officers and cameras were sweeping the area from multiple observation points around the Dome, the Thames, and the coal yard, but there were gaps in their coverage and limits to their field of vision.

It was morning rush hour, and thousands of vehicles were swarming around Greenwich on hundreds of roads. Gang confederates could come from anywhere.

Plain-clothes surveillance officers were beginning to move into the vicinity of the De Beers Jewel House, ready to block any visitors from the area.

Malcolm Woods was preparing to pull his Dome staff members out of the area.

Everyone held their breath.

9 a.m. passed. The route the JCB would probably take to get to the Dome was lined with surveillance officers hiding in side roads.

The JCB was sighted by three of them, but had not yet passed to the fourth.

9.30 a.m. came and went with no sign of the gang, the JCB or the boat.

At 10.05 a.m. Swinfield's mobile rang. His disappointment was obvious when he announced, 'The JCB has just returned to the coal yard.'

'Oh shit!' cried Shatford, 'What could have happened?'

Was it an elaborate exercise by the gang to test for a police presence?

Were the gang scanning the police frequencies and measuring radio traffic?

Shatford gave the order to withdraw from the Dome thirty minutes later. Detective Sergeant Mark Drew was beginning to wonder if they were working on the biggest robbery that would never actually happen.

The covered lorries that smuggled the firearms officers into the Dome appeared at a rear loading-bay and, as discreetly as possible, the firearms officers climbed aboard, their guns concealed in holdalls. Remarkably, they attracted little attention, partly because of the number of clowns and performers that were warming up close by. Most onlookers must have assumed they were just part of the entertainment.

'Guv, can I have a word.'

It was SO19's Sergeant Clive Rew, the man leading the planned boat interception on the Thames. He pulled a piece of paper from his pocket and said to Shatford, 'Look at this. It's the table of tide times on the Thames.'

'Oh yeah,' said Shatford, 'what does it tell us?'

'Each time we think this gang is going to strike, it coincides with a high tide. The river rises and falls as much as twenty-one feet. Unless the tide is high, they won't be able to scramble ashore. There's no way to climb back up.'

Shatford and Swinfield studied the paper and looked at each other, then Rew. It was a moment of realisation.

'Of course,' marvelled Shatford. 'They need a high tide to pull the job off!'

'It looks like it,' Rew said, 'and the Marine Support boys think they would have a job to launch their boat unless it was a high tide because of all the mud on the inlets.'

'That's it, we've got it,' smiled Shatford.

'Well done, Clive, this could save us a hell of a lot of time.'

The next high tide was 19 October.

'Jon,' said Commander Alan Brown, 'there's a lot of nervousness about this Dome job.'

It was Monday 9 October, and the tone of Brown's voice warned Shatford that bad news was coming next.

Sure enough, the Commander added: 'I've asked for an independent review of your plan.'

'Who from?' asked Shatford.

'John Bunn. He should be down with us shortly.'

Bunn was the Detective Chief Superintendent in charge of Scotland Yard's anti-terrorist branch, SO13. He was a seasoned detective with a tough intellect and plenty of experience in highly complex armed operations such as the one they were planning.

From an institutional perspective, this review made perfect sense. But

Shatford was now afraid of a new worst-case scenario – that Operation Magician might get shut down for being too risky.

'Well, that's good,' Shatford remarked, not sure if he meant it. 'I'm more than happy to have the plan scrutinised, although Mark Williams, Swinni and I have been through it time and time again.'

'We are playing for high stakes here, Jonnie boy,' Brown pointed out.

'I know,' said Shatford, 'but I challenge anyone to find another way.'

There was no hiding his disappointment as he returned to his office and collected his decision logs, plans, maps and various notes. When he returned to Brown's office, John Bunn and Mark Williams were already there, along with Shatford's immediate superior in the Flying Squad, Detective Chief Superintendent John Coles.

Commander Brown ordered the four officers to lock themselves away and review everything.

They went to Coles' office on the fourth floor of Scotland Yard and started unravelling the Operation Magician plans.

Bunn asked every conceivable 'What if?' question about weapons, risks and public safety – questions informed by years of experience working on terrorist investigations.

For hours, the officers scrutinised every bit of Intelligence, and analysed every possible option and scenario. They discussed what the consequences might be if they did not act.

The dilemma was obvious. If being 'Intelligence-led' meant frustrating crimes that police have Intelligence on, then how could they justify not going ahead with Operation Magician? Followed to its natural conclusion, a gang of Betson's pedigree would continue until the police lacked the Intelligence to frustrate them.

In the end, John Coles asked the bottom-line question: 'Are we as sure as we can be, given the circumstances, that we need to carry out this operation in the way we have discussed?'

'Yes,' answered Shatford. 'There are risks, but the greater risk is to let this gang escape from our clutches.'

Coles nodded and turned to Williams, who agreed: 'We will have many advantages by trapping them at the Jewel House, and I think that is the safest way.'

Detective Chief Superintendent Bunn concluded: 'I really think you have anticipated every scenario.' The plan looked sound.

Operation Magician was alive, having survived a very tough review.

But a troubling reality kept drifting in the back of Shatford's mind: in the end, police have authority only to succeed.

Never to fail.

26. Nightmare Scenarios

The North, 14 October 2000, 10 a.m.

He gunned the accelerator and broke free of London.

It was a Saturday morning and Shatford was on top of his BMW K1200 motorbike, among a pack of ten Hondas, Triumphs, and more BMWs, all travelling north on the A1.

Shatford was the only policeman in the group of friends, and he was trying not to think of Operation Magician for a few hours. The Dome was becoming his whole life, and the tension had become unbearable. But now, this morning, he was concentrating instead on his driving; on taking corners and on the wind blasting his helmet.

But the Dome seemed to travel with him in the back of his mind; it had become a Pandora's box of nightmare scenarios.

Every day, Shatford and the Flying Squad were living in fear.

Fear that the gang would strike – or wouldn't strike.

That the gang would kill a member of the public or police.

That the gang had an inside agent at the Dome or even in the police.

That the police couldn't sustain such a high level of alert for much longer.

That they couldn't arrest the gang quickly and safely.

That the gang would come with heavier-than-expected firepower.

That the operation would leak to the press.

That if the gang called it off they would be lost to the police, wait a few months, strike somewhere else and slaughter a bunch of people in a botched operation.

And Shatford was afraid of guessing the wrong day for an attack – what would happen if the gang struck on one of the days when the police were not covering the Dome. He could never explain that away.

To plan for this contingency, the Flying Squad prepared a crude but creative plan. On these 'off' days, a skeleton crew of police was standing by near the Dome. If the gang were spotted approaching the Dome, the officers would stage a fake traffic accident with two unmarked Flying Squad vehicles on the main approach road. Hopefully the police presence would deter the gang without alerting them to the fact that the game was up.

Shatford speculated on what was motivating Ray Betson and his gang.

It wasn't just the financial pay-off, Shatford assumed. It was pure bravado – the adrenalin boost, the excitement, the thrill of beating the police and making a name for themselves.

If they got away with this, they would be ten times more famous than the Great Train Robbers. They would not only be rich but immensely famous and anonymous.

As the fear of civilian casualties escalated, Shatford and his officers had been quadruple-checking every possible detail of a series of nightmare scenarios where bystanders could be killed.

Children could get hit in the crossfire.

The gang could sneak into the Dome through different entrances with high-powered weapons.

They could take hostages.

They could smuggle in guns and explosives hidden in prams.

They could try to stage explosions or disturbances to distract attention.

The gang members could disguise themselves as Dome employees, even as clowns!

The gang could infiltrate the Dome the day before, hide somewhere in the vast property overnight and strike the next morning.

They could land a helicopter near the Dome to make their getaway, using the speedboat as a diversion.

Or they could arrive on foot very subtly, sneaking through separate entrances and linking up for the attack.

The first bike stop that Saturday was a service station to the north of Birmingham.

Shatford reached for his mobile, eager to hear if there had been any developments.

'Any news, Swinni?' he asked anxiously.

'Nothing,' came the reply.

A woman's voice hollered in the distance. 'Put that phone down!'

Realisation dawned quickly. Mobiles should not be used anywhere near filling stations as they transmit electrical signals that could ignite highly volatile petroleum. His mind had been elsewhere.

Shatford cringed as he cut the call short and cursed himself for being so stupid. He mimed an apology to the furious woman and made his way to the cafe, and joined the other bikers who were talking excitedly about the trip.

It was an annual ritual where grown men escaped the shackles of life to indulge in a second childhood. They were from different walks of life, but were bound together through their love of motorbikes. Shatford studied them with a strange detachment. They had no idea what he was going through, and he felt like he was looking down from a parallel universe.

The bikers manoeuvred their way up the A1(M), shaking off the motorway just past Scotch Corner. As they eased onto A68, the scenery opened out in front of them to reveal the hills of the Northumberland National Park. One by one, the throttles opened. Shatford glanced in his mirror at the lights of the bikes behind. They stretched out in a snake-like trail that weaved with the turns.

He tucked in tight to the rear wheel in front. A touch on the brakes at this stage would be fatal. Warning signs in the road pointed to blind summits for four miles. The road descended to a steep downward hill, then up to the horizon where visibility was lost.

Too fast at the brow and the bikes would fly into space.

Once over the horizon, the bikes raced downhill before rising to the next blind summit.

The sensation of speeding over the top was thrilling, and he felt a shudder pass through his body. It took total concentration to hang onto the handlebars, and position himself for the road ahead.

He was not thinking of Operation Magician.

It was late afternoon when they arrived at the pub in the Scottish border town of Jedburgh that was their overnight stop. Splattered flies on their visors bore testimony to some rapid riding.

While the others made for the bar, Shatford made for the phone. Swinni had nothing to report.

Shatford gave a sigh of relief as another day had passed without event.

He was hungry after the day's ride, and got to the bar just in time to order a meal. He chose the Scottish pie with vegetables and potatoes. For the first time in what appeared to be an eternity he felt he could relax. He was too far away now to do anything, even if he wanted to.

That night the beer flowed and stories from the trip the year before were exaggerated to such an extent that roars of laughter followed each one.

The next day, they travelled further north to the Highlands. They skirted Glasgow and avoided Edinburgh stopping only at petrol stations. The journey north was swift.

Mountain ranges opened out as they headed for Glencoe. When they stopped midway to admire the beauty, Shatford discovered he had no signal on his phone.

They were so remote and cut off that he couldn't make a call.

He egged his biker friends to move off but no one understood his panic. The more he protested, the more amusing they found it.

He finally realised that there was absolutely nothing he could do about it. That at least brought him some solace. If anything happened, it was over to Swinni.

The journey north continued with long straight roads punctuated by hairpin bends. It was a biker's dream. In late afternoon they bypassed Fort William and headed for their stopover at Loch Ness.

Shatford got a signal. He checked in with Swinni. Still no news.

He surveyed the beautiful landscape around him and couldn't help but think that the Dome had become his own monster. It was consuming everything he did.

The evening's antics began with ten middle-aged bikers jumping into Loch Ness for a swim. The water was freezing but invigorating. He was grateful for another distraction.

The next day, the journey south began. Shatford decided to head straight home and get back to work. He was afraid the gang were about to strike.

His friends had booked into a pub just outside Edinburgh, and when they arrived he had a meal and put his head down for an hour before leaving. They all lined up outside to wish him well.

As night was falling he passed over the Northumberland hills – beautiful in the daylight but strangely chilling at night. He missed the comfort of seeing his friends' headlights in his mirror and felt very alone. His thoughts settled on the Dome, and he went through every possible scenario.

The isolation of the night and the wind against his body exaggerated all his fears.

In the distance he could see the lights of Newcastle.

It was starting to rain.

On Wednesday 18 October, signals seemed to point to an attack on the Dome at high tide the next day.

A Ford Sierra driven by Lee Wenham entered the coal yard carrying two other men whom the observation officers did not recognise.

They got the JCB started and drove it out into the yard. They seemed to be working on the front bucket, but the officers couldn't see exactly what they were doing. When they finished, they drove the digger back into the engine shed, and left at 11.41 p.m.

Shatford thought they might be preparing the JCB for the next day.

He arranged another full deployment around the Dome.

Not a damn thing happened.

There had been other false alarms in the last week, when the gang were spotted moving the speedboat and manoeuvring the JCB around the yard.

On three separate occasions the gang appeared at Tong Farm. The boat was seen to leave, then a white van. The job was surely on. The Flying Squad were in a state of high readiness. SO19 officers had their fingers on their triggers. Anything could happen.

Each time, the police continued their complex deceptions to sneak in and out of the Dome. The SO19 sharpshooters were smuggled into the Dome in closed panel trucks, and hidden in full battle gear and gas masks behind the secret wall.

But each time the gang pulled back. No one could figure out why.

Suddenly, there was very limited Intelligence coming in. Tong Farm, Starfields and the coal yard were nearly silent, with limited activity and few visitors.

What did it mean? Shatford feared the worst and suspected the gang may have called the job off.

'It's out, the papers have got it!'

It was Saturday morning, 4 November, and Scotland Yard press officer Angie Evans was calling with urgent news. Shatford was at home listening to classical music, trying to grab a few relaxing hours. When his mobile rang, he was dangling a piece of fresh turkey in front of his cat.

'What do you mean?' asked Shatford, feeling all the life draining from his body as he gripped himself for whatever was coming next.

The next high tide was expected in two days, on Monday 6 November. All things being equal, this could be the last anxious weekend he would spend for a while.

Sounding like she had the weight of the world on her shoulders, Evans explained gravely, 'The editor of the *Sunday People* knows the whole story, right down to the fact that the gang will use a JCB.'

'Oh, God!' said Shatford.

Somehow, news of the secret Operation Magician had leaked.

It didn't matter how, and he really wasn't that surprised. So many people knew about the job now that it was bound to happen. The police were lucky to have made it this far.

Months of work, it seemed, could be on the verge of going down the drain.

The whole operation was about to be blown away.

'Is he going to run the story?' he asked.

'No, that would be very irresponsible,' predicted Evans. 'But we will have to tell him something. My bosses are talking to him.'

'What do you suggest?

After knocking around a number of ideas, Evans hit upon an ingenious solution: the police could confirm the outline but try to persuade the paper not to run it before the robbery happened, out of concern for public safety. In exchange, Scotland Yard would allow the paper early access to the Dome when it was over. Their reporter could then claim an exclusive.

What worried Shatford most was that the paper might send photographers to the Dome on Monday morning to try to get some action shots. This could have a devastating effect. At the very least, the gang could spot them and abort the job, thinking they were police officers.

At worst, the gang could open fire on them and the Dome could be a scene of carnage.

Evans brokered the arrangements through her bosses, and agreed that she would go to a police station near the Dome on Monday morning with the reporter and photographer. She would then facilitate their access to the Dome after the job went down.

To their credit, the newspaper's editor made it clear from the beginning that they would not run anything that would compromise the operation.

Another bullet fired. Another bullet dodged.

Meanwhile, the Betson gang was having its own crisis. The Boatman was bailing out.

For reasons unknown, Brian Mitchell, the imported boat specialist from the Costa del Sol, had to drop out. He was at least the third gang member to do so over the last eight weeks.

But, as of 4 November, despite various operational setbacks and aborted attempts, the job was still on. The equipment seemed to be working. Most of the gang were lined up.

Boss Ray Betson and 'lieutenant' Bill Cockram were still on board, in charge of getting into the Dome and into the vault.

Bob Adams, nicknamed 'Bob the Builder' by the gang, was the new arrival, designated with providing muscle for Cockram.

Aldo Ciarrocchi and Terry Millman were standing by, ready to handle look-out duty, scan police radio frequencies and do counter-surveillance, with Millman driving the getaway vehicle.

Lee Wenham and at least two unknown gang accomplices were standing by in support roles.

The gang had access to over fourteen vehicles at various locations, at least four of them stolen. The fleet included two JCBs, three transit vans, a speedboat, a BMW and a Mercedes.

The gang had put together a meticulous five-minute plan to break into the Dome and escape with the diamonds, the details of which were still a mystery to Shatford and the Flying Squad.

Everything else was ready, but now that Mitchell dropped out, they didn't have a boatman.

Bill Cockram had a brainstorm.

Kevin Meredith was a chartered boat skipper down in Brighton. He worked at the marina, piloting a boat called the *Random Harvest*. He was 34 years old, and had no criminal record. People at the marina thought he was very nice chap, a pleasant fellow. But he was struggling to make ends meet, and finding it difficult to pay his mortgage.

In early 2000, according to Meredith, one of his customers was William Cockram, who took the boat out a few times for fishing trips.

On one of those trips, Meredith complained to Cockram about the steep costs of doing business and paying for moorings. To his surprise, Cockram took out £1,400 in cash and handed it to Meredith.

'No pressure,' said Cockram as Meredith accepted the money.

The debt was called in on Saturday 4 November 2000, and would ruin a good chunk of Meredith's life.

That day, Meredith got a phone call from Cockram.

'This is Bill,' said Cockram. 'Do you fancy a drink? I might have something for you.'

Reminding Meredith about his debt, he said: 'You're in for a drink and we'll forget about the money you owe me.' He arranged to come down and meet Meredith in Brighton, explaining, 'I've got something to put to you.'

They met later that day, over coffee in a noisy pub at the marina.

Cockram asked for the money.

'I haven't got it, said Meredith. 'I'm skint.'

Cockram sulked, sighed and said, 'Can you do me a favour? Can you drive a speedboat?'

'What do you mean?' asked Meredith.

The reply: 'Can you drive a speedboat for fifteen minutes?'

'I'm not too sure,' said the skipper. Speedboats weren't his speciality.

'I need to know now,' Cockram announced.

'It's not what I'm used to,' he said.

'I need you to do it,' Cockram insisted.

'I don't know,' replied Meredith. 'What are you doing?' he asked.

'You don't need to know,' Cockram declared. 'It's something to do with the Dome . . . That's all I can tell you.'

He was getting emphatic. 'Drive the speedboat,' said Cockram. 'Do it. Pay your debt off.'

This was a direct order, but Meredith was slow picking it up. 'I'm not sure,' he demurred.

'Look,' said Cockram, 'remember your wife and kids.'

The look in Cockram's eyes, the tone of his voice and the words he chose all conspired to create one effect on Meredith. He was shocked. He took it as a threat.

'I am not a strong person,' he later explained. 'If somebody says something like that, I'll do whatever I'm told.'

He agreed instantly. The gang had a new boatman.

And Meredith had every reason to be scared shitless.

27. The Briefing

New Scotland Yard, 5 November 2000, 10 p.m.

The fifth floor of Scotland Yard is a lonely place on a Sunday night.

Shatford was at his desk reading through Intelligence reports and waiting for the latest news from Swinfield.

At the same time he was going through what he would say at the next briefing, in four hours.

He knew that all the previous false starts had naturally bred some sceptics among the 200 plus police involved in the operation, and that spelt danger. If his officers became complacent, then standards could slip.

It would only need one of them to show out on surveillance and the game would be up.

It might also mean a shoot-out.

High tide was coming on the Thames, but at least tomorrow was Monday, which should mean fewer people visiting the Dome.

When the call came from Swinfield, he almost expected it to be a stand down.

Swinfield was his usual calm self.

'It's on,' he said. 'The speedboat left Tong Farm at 3.56 this afternoon being towed by a white transit. Earlier in the day it was heard being revved up in the farm.'

'Sounds promising,' said Shatford. 'Do we know where it went?'

'No, we couldn't follow it and, of yet, it has not returned.'

'It must be up near the Thames ready to be launched,' speculated Shatford.

'There's more,' said Swinfield. 'Looks like they've dispersed and are staying apart overnight.'

This was the tip-off Shatford was waiting for. When a gang split up like this, it was often a counter-surveillance step that actually meant they were preparing for dirty work.

The reasoning was simple. If the gang were seen gathering together just prior to the crime, it could reach the wrong eyes and ears. The gang could expect a lot of heat after the robbery, and the Flying Squad were bound to be into every snout for miles around after a crime this big.

It looked like the Betson gang was good to go.

The two detectives wrapped up the call on an optimistic note, arranging to meet at Lambeth in South London at 1.30 a.m. to prepare for the briefing at 2 a.m.

Shatford was picked up by a squad car, driven round Parliament Square, past Big Ben and across Westminster Bridge to Lambeth. It was a hive of activity.

Squad cars were pulling into the covered parking area. Small groups stood around discussing matters as important as where the nearest open burger bar was. Others were transferring exhibit boxes and clothes from one car to another.

'Spike,' someone called to a very capable, long-suffering Flying Squad driver who was renowned for his cautious driving. 'When this job goes down, I hope you manage to get out of second gear or it will be all over before you get there!'

This provoked roars of laughter.

The SO19 firearms officers were already in place on the second floor, wrapping up a pre-briefing from Inspector Mark Williams.

A steady flow of officers filled the plain white room. It looked like a classroom, with rows of chairs arranged to face a small stage. The first officers to enter claimed the seats furthest from the front. It always happened. Most officers preferred not be in direct line of sight of the guv'nors.

The customary police humour kicked in, with Spike being the butt of continued teasing. He took it in good faith, and gave as good as he got.

The firearms officers filled the front right side of the room, many of them in battle gear, tooled up in body armour and ammunition belts, with standard-issue Glock 17 self-loading pistols in their holsters. They all looked ready for action.

Their longer-range weapons, the Heckler and Koch MP5 carbines, were stashed outside in the ARVs along with night sights, 'flash bang' stun grenades and ballistic shields.

Despite their surface jocularity, the SO19 officers faced an abyss of unknowns. They hold the power of life and death in their hands, over criminals and innocent bystanders. They have no idea what weapons a gang might bring, and they have to prepare for the worst. These days, police are often outgunned by gangsters who have access to high-velocity semi-automatic and fully automatic weapons like black-market Beretta machine guns, Tokarev automatic pistols, Uzi sub-machine pistols and Mac 10 machine pistols capable of firing over 1,000 rounds a minute.

There were about 300 firearms officers in SO19, and they were battling a sharp increase in gun-related crimes. Given the inherent risks of the job, mistakes could sometimes happen. In 1999 a 46-year-old man named Harry Stanley was tragically killed when a chair leg he was carrying was mistaken for a firearm, both by the civilian who made the 999 call and the officers who responded.

But the overwhelming majority of SO19 firearms operations ended successfully – hostages were freed, kidnap victims rescued, drug dealers and killers taken off the streets and brought to justice, and untold numbers of members of the public were protected.

Whenever a firearms specialist discharges a weapon, he or she is then immediately subjected to an extremely stringent internal investigation, which sometimes takes years and can, in extreme cases, result in disciplinary action. The officer can be treated almost like a criminal – isolated, stripped of his clothing and hands swabbed for forensic evidence. He can be suspended or placed on restricted duty for four years as the investigation grinds on, and he'll have no idea if he'll actually be prosecuted.

The impact on these SO19 officers and their families could be devastating. They could be vilified in the press, have their pay reduced, go into debt and risk bailiffs taking away their property.

Whenever they go into action, SO19 officers face a paradox. They have to legally justify every shot but, at the same time, act quickly enough to squeeze the trigger to stop a suspect from opening fire on the police or public.

By now the room was almost overflowing, as Flying Squad detectives from across London squeezed in between SO11 Intelligence specialists and Marine Support officers. The marine police were used to patrolling the Thames in launches, not participating in a Hollywood-style, diamond counter-heist.

At 2 a.m., the banter died down and was replaced by an air of expectation. Everyone wanted to know the latest news.

Was the job on or off?

Shatford, Swinfield and Williams were huddled on the small stage discussing the latest Intelligence. Some officers sitting within earshot were leaning forward and trying to eavesdrop.

'It's on,' whispered one, satisfied he had heard enough to convince him of the fact.

A flurry of nods and glances bounced around the room. By the time they reached the back, even the cynics were convinced the job was going down.

Shatford walked to the front of the small stage.

He looked at the 250 officers, all of them anxious and silent.

'Ladies and gents,' he began. 'Firstly, thanks for coming out at this time of the morning. I know you haven't seen much of your families lately. In a minute Detective Inspector Swinfield will brief you on operational deployments, followed by Inspector Mark Williams who will deal with the firearms issues. I will then round things up before we deploy.

'But let me start by saying this. Every indication we have is that the job is on. I want to remind you that we have to assume these people are dangerous and may be armed. We have to assume they may use weapons against you. We cannot afford to let our guard down for a single second. If we do, it could prove fatal. They have a lot at stake. You will be all that stands between them being very rich or serving long prison sentences.'

He continued, 'Now it is really important that everyone listens to the tactical briefings by Mr Swinfield and Mr Williams. I do not want anyone leaving this building without being absolutely certain what his or her role is. Do not be afraid to ask questions. If something occurs to you it may well occur to others who just don't want to speak out.'

He scanned the room to be sure his words were striking, and added, 'I am not going to forgive anyone who fouls up over this.'

He stood back and Detective Inspector Swinfield came to the fore.

Swinfield began by posting each Flying Squad officer to teams prefixed Alpha, Bravo, Charlie, Delta, Foxtrot, Golf and Hotel.

Each team was also assigned a number, so their location could be identified in every communication.

Five Alpha teams were to be posted out of sight but within striking distance of the Dome. One Bravo's posting was inside the London Underground station at North Greenwich, close to the entrance of the Dome to block any escape attempt by that route.

Four Charlie teams were posted to the north side of the river to intercept the robbers if they escaped, and to try and identify the getaway vehicle.

Swinfield ran down a list of team leaders, explaining which officers would be in what vehicles, who would deal with prisoners, and who would be in charge of exhibits.

He explained which police stations had been nominated to receive the prisoners, and which officers would search their addresses afterwards.

'What is absolutely critical,' said Swinfield, pausing to stress the point, 'is that there be NO radio communication whatsoever. The gang are extremely surveillance-conscious. We expect them to be monitoring police frequencies.

'They have already been to the Dome, and probably measured radio traffic in the area. If they take new readings while we're using our radios, they'll know we are right on top of them.

'There must be total radio silence until the job goes down.'

He explained that the only limited communication allowed was from team leader to team leader on mobile telephones.

Now, SO19's Inspector Mark Williams stepped forward, a portrait of confidence and precision.

'To avoid confusion,' he announced, 'I have broken the armed operation down into four smaller ones. First: armed deployment outside the Dome on the Millennium Peninsula; second: armed deployment inside the grounds of the Dome; third: armed deployment on the Thames; and fourth: the armed deployment on the north side of the river.'

He specified the objective for each operation – protecting the public, arresting the robbers, and covering incidents around the Dome and on the Thames.

Shatford was impressed by how meticulous the planning was.

Inspector Williams then turned to the limits of each team's operation, which were essential for everyone to understand so that they didn't get caught in a crossfire.

He went through them one by one.

Armed officers on the outside of the Dome were not to enter unless ordered to do so.

Those on the inside were not to exit the grounds of the Dome unless ordered to.

Those on the river would not come ashore unless specifically called upon, unless they were in immediate pursuit of a suspect.

Armed officers on the north side of the river were not to enter the Thames or its embankment.

By now, each officer knew what his or her individual role was, and how it fitted into the overall puzzle.

Shatford stepped forward to perform a final task. Scanning the eyes of the armed officers, he was duty-bound to give them a warning.

Everyone already knew the warning but, given the circumstances, it had to be repeated.

'It is my obligation to warn you that the use of a firearm is an individual decision which you may have to justify in court.'

Shatford almost felt sick as he said this, because it almost felt like he was abdicating his responsibility. He had just told these officers that they were going up against a potentially dangerous gang. Now he was saying if they got it wrong they would have to answer for it.

The Criminal Law Act of 1967 makes it clear that only such force as is reasonable in the circumstances can be used. The European Convention on Human Rights added a further stipulation that it must be 'absolutely necessary'.

Lethal force must always be the very last option, and the officer only has a split-second to decide whether to fire or not. If he gets it wrong, he could end up in the dock at the Old Bailey on a manslaughter charge.

And if he moved too slowly, he could end up dead.

The meeting broke up into groups of chattering officers who made their way downstairs to the car park.

In everyone's mind was the fact that, in just a few weeks, the Dome would close. There were very few high tides left.

A contingent of SO19 firearms officers piled into the back of a large, covered box lorry specially hired for the purpose. When the last officer entered, the steel shutter at the rear was rolled down and they were locked inside. As it pulled out onto the streets of London it became just another anonymous vehicle moving through the capital.

So many police vehicles were involved that they had to stagger their journey to avoid suspicion. Each was designated a separate route to get to the Dome.

Surveillance officers from SO11 headed for the old coal yard and various locations – disused factories, tower blocks and ditches – along the route to the Dome. Their job was critical – to track the robbers through each checkpoint and report their progress to the next group.

Conditions were lousy.

Rain, fog and winds were heavy, as England was gripped by record rainstorms and the most severe flooding in thirteen years.

Shatford and Swinfield were in a vehicle driven by Detective Constable Sean Allen.

They turned right out of Lambeth, past the Imperial War Museum and into the one-way system to the Elephant and Castle. They were travelling into the heart of South London, through the very streets that spawned Raymond Betson and William Cockram and generations of villains and thieves. When the SO19 lorry arrived at the Dome, it was met by Dome security chief Malcolm Woods who waved it through the security gates. It was not unusual for lorries to pass through the entrance; all Woods had to do was tell the guards that there was night work going on.

The lorry stopped outside the Harrison building and, one by one, the covert cargo entered.

Sergeant Mark Adams led them towards the cavity of the false wall. Piling in, they took up crouched positions.

When the last man entered, Adams squeezed in behind and, with the help of Woods, sealed the false wall behind them.

Once they were safely inside, they stretched out their legs, ready for a long stay. For those who needed it, there was a can to relieve themselves.

Ten minutes later, Shatford was in the Bronze Control Room, with Swinfield and the SO19 control contingent: Inspector Mark Williams, Chief Inspector Andy Latto, Police Constable Kevin Bird and Sergeant Steve Manning.

'Here we are again,' said Williams.

'For the last time I hope,' replied Shatford.

'We all want to see you pacing tonight,' said Williams.

This was an in-joke; when Shatford jumped up and started pacing around thoughtfully it could only mean one thing – the job was on.

'Me too,' chuckled Shatford, 'I never quite made it the last time, did I?'

'You will,' predicted Swinfield. 'It is going to come off this time.'

'That's what I want,' said Shatford, 'positive thought!'

Officers Williams, Bird and Manning lay down on the hard floor and in minutes they were asleep.

'I can't believe how these SO19 people can sleep anywhere,' said Shatford enviously.

Latto explained: 'It's not easy. It comes from years of interrupted sleep patterns. In the end you can sleep anywhere.'

Hours passed.

At 6.10 a.m., the silence was pierced by Swinfield's mobile ringing.

'Right, really?' he said, nodding emphatically. 'OK, I'll pass it on.'

'The speedboat has just been spotted being towed by a white transit van to the Isle of Dogs,' Swinfield announced.

Everyone in the room looked at one another, and smiles crossed their faces.

'I wonder where the hell they will put the boat in?' wondered Shatford.

28. The Countdown

The Isle of Dogs, 6 November 2000, 6.30 a.m.

'Don't fuck up.'

The voice came from inside the white van as the new boatman, Kevin Meredith, got out to check the speedboat.

He was scared. In fact, he was in a state of panic, probably shitting bricks, realising there was no way out of his predicament. According to his later testimony, Meredith still didn't know what the job was, except he was supposed to drive a speedboat across the river.

The previous day, when Bill Cockram had introduced him to the imposing figure of Ray Betson, Meredith realised the job had to be something criminal.

The three of them did a quick reconnaissance of the Dome area. Pointing out two mooring points near the Dome, Betson warned Meredith not to go to the QE2 pier because there was too much security there.

'That's no good,' said Betson, indicating another spot called the Millennium Pier. 'It has to be the other pier. Has to be.'

They then went to a point on the north side of the Thames, directly opposite the Dome, called Lower Lea Crossing. Pointing out a spot near a traffic roundabout and a mud track, Betson told Meredith, 'That's the point to wait.'

The boat plan seemed simple enough.

Terry Millman and Meredith would put the boat in the water at a point on the Isle of Dogs, south-west of the Dome, and Meredith would drive the boat up and around the Thames to wait at Lower Lea Crossing.

There he would wait for a radio signal to cross to the Millennium Pier, pick up the gang and cross back again to rendezvous with Millman, who by then would have driven up to Lower Lea Crossing to drive everyone away.

That morning, as the job was about to start, Kevin Meredith apparently had no idea he was about to help commit the biggest robbery of all time.

'What is it you're getting?' he asked one of the gang.

'It is to do with the Dome. That's all I am telling you,' was the terse reply.

Probably a drugs drop-off, Meredith thought.

'What happens when I drop the boat off?' he asked Bill Cockram.

Cockram wouldn't answer the question, instead saying cryptically, 'Sweet as a nut, sweet as a nut.

'Everyone's kosher,' he added, 'known them for years.'

When they got to the other side of the river, Meredith wondered if he was going to get a concrete block tied around his legs or be knocked out and soaked in petrol.

He felt powerless to run away.

He didn't want his wife and kids to get hurt.

When Ray Betson strapped on his Tetranike body armour that morning, he had every reason to believe that by 10 a.m. he would have got away with £250 million in diamonds.

The comfortable, lightweight body armour would protect him from small-arms fire, stab wounds or flying shrapnel.

He'd figured out an audacious, ingenious way into the diamond vault, and a split-second plan to escape. Everything was lined up. His vehicles and equipment were ready, as were his gang members. Weeks and weeks of planning and reconnaissance were coming together. And there was no sign of the Old Bill.

The full amount of cash that Betson was supposed to have received is still unclear, but it can safely be assumed to be a huge amount. He'd probably have enough for a lifetime of Armani and Louis Vuitton; of Rolexes, top-of-the-range sports cars, amazing luxury holidays, and oceans of caviar and champagne.

He could, perhaps, retire to Spain. Buy himself a nice villa down the mountain from the Saudi royal family; maybe open up a pub by the sea – his own personal spot.

He might keep a scrapbook of the next day's press clippings tucked away in his study, with frenzied headlines like 'ROBBERY OF THE MILLENNIUM – BRAZEN ATTACK YIELDS £250 MILLION IN GEMS, or 'POLICE BAFFLED AS MASTER CRIMINALS GET AWAY SCOT-FREE' or, 'BIGGEST HEIST OF ALL TIME EXECUTED IN PERFECT JAMES BOND STYLE'.

Over the years, the headlines would subside, but every five years or so there would be anniversary pieces in the tabloids: 'DOME ROBBERY STILL UNSOLVED' and WHERE AND WHO ARE THE DOME GANG? A SPECIAL REPORT'.

Some poor Scotland Yard detective would be interviewed, glumly admitting there were no leads, but the police were still working the case. Then the movie would come out, and Betson would be fascinated by how the screenwriters tackled the challenge of a totally unsolved crime. They'd have to fudge it, of course, make a lot of it up, and create a fictional cast of characters. But who would play the gang leader when they didn't even know who it was? Pierce Brosnan? Robert De Niro? Tom Cruise was about the right age – like Betson he was turning the corner of forty.

But all that would have to wait. Right now Betson had to pull the crime off first. The whole thing was fully planned out in his head, with every action timed. The entire operation would take twenty minutes, from the break-in and escape to the cash pick-up and final getaway. Before the alarms could summon a full police response to the Dome, the gang would be across the Thames. They would jump into Millman's white van and simply disappear into thick traffic – one among thousands of other white vans buzzing around London at any given moment.

They would then double back to the south side of the Thames, probably through the Rotherhithe Tunnel, to a spot on a quiet street outside the Mayflower pub in Rotherhithe.

Waiting there for the pay-off would be the Money Men, the middlemen to the buyer of the diamonds. They would have a holdall stuffed with cash ready for the exchange.

But both Betson and Cockram were worried about what might happen at the handover spot, when they traded the De Beers Millennium Star and the eleven other jewels.

Betson later explained, 'That'd be a different gravy. We would have had a high-value product that they were purporting to do this cash exchange for, but we would have just stolen them and we wouldn't have wanted them stolen off us.'

For protection, Betson was bringing along Cockram and Ciarrocchi to the handover, and they would all be keeping their body armour on.

They were afraid anything could happen.

They had no reason to trust the buyers.

They thought they could get double-crossed.

Or ripped off.

Or shot to pieces.

The police were on full alert and ready to pounce, zeroing in on different members of the gang through cameras and field glasses.

At 6.34 a.m., the white transit van was filmed, with Millman at the wheel and Meredith in the passenger seat, going onto West Ferry Road on the Isle of Dogs, towing a speedboat. Fourteen minutes later, a Ford Escort entered the coal yard in Plumstead and drove directly to the engine shed where the JCB was hidden. The JCB's engine was switched on; its amber light flashed.

Inside the Dome's Bronze Control Room, detectives Shatford, Swinfield and Williams were keyed up. It looked like everything was going according to plan.

At 6.59 a.m., the Ford Escort drove away towards Woolwich and the coal yard was quiet again.

'What the hell went on there then?' asked Shatford.

Swinfield speculated, 'Could be someone just making sure the JCB will start.'

'But what will they use it for?' wondered Shatford. The use of the digger was still a constant source of speculation within the team.

'I still favour the theory that they will masquerade as workmen,' said Shatford. 'It's an ideal cover to drive right up to the gates. I doubt security would blink twice at them.'

'Hopefully, we'll know soon enough,' said Williams.

The minutes ticked by and the optimism started draining from the room.

At 7.56 a.m., a second white transit van entered the coal yard and went straight to the engine shed. A short while later the amber lights on the JCB were seen flashing, and the engine being revved was heard.

This news re-energised the Control Room and, for the first time, Shatford got out of his chair and started pacing.

Swinfield noted, 'They'll have to leave soon if they want to get to the Dome before opening time.'

'Maybe they'll do it when it's open,' said Shatford, inwardly digesting the risks that would bring.

The speedboat was at the river, the JCB was being revved, and gang vehicles were manoeuvring around the area.

It had to be happening.

'Oh, shit!' exclaimed Shatford.

Just before 9 a.m., in a case of atrocious bad timing, a German tourist slammed his car into the back of a bus in Millennium Way, just outside the front entrance of the Dome.

Police were called.

Instantly, this raised traffic levels in the area and the communication levels on the police frequency. Shatford and the Flying Squad were still using minimal radio contact to avoid alerting the gang, whom they assumed were measuring police transmissions. The accident also threatened to draw police cars to the scene. All this could easily spook the gang into aborting the attack.

And right now, local traffic police were on the way.

'That just can't happen!' said a highly alarmed Shatford. 'It will blow the entire job. Stop them getting there.'

'Too late,' reported Swinfield. 'Traffic is on scene reporting it.'

'Shit, shit!' said Shatford, his head buried in his hands.

'See if you can get someone to get them out the way as quick as they can.'

Simultaneously, a crisis was erupting with the gang.

At Newcastle Drawdock on the Isle of Dogs, Terry Millman and Kevin Meredith were struggling with the speedboat and trailer.

They reversed the van down a slip so that the trailer settled into the water's edge with the speedboat attached. They fiddled with the ropes, and tried to float the boat off the trailer into the water.

But Meredith noticed a disturbing sight. The tide was dropping very quickly.

'Terry,' he said, 'I don't think we'll be able to get it in.

'There's not enough water here . . . I can't get the boat in.'

The water was pulling away from them quickly.

'The tide's wrong,' concluded Meredith. 'Call it off.'

Terry got on his mobile and said, 'We will have to stop.'

They pulled the boat and trailer up the slip, and stuck chocks under the wheels.

At 9.22 a.m., the other white transit van was observed leaving the coal yard. The JCB did not move.

'Either they saw us dealing with that accident,' said Shatford, 'or they're doing it without the JCB. Make sure everyone's on alert.'

At 9.29 a.m. Millman's van was seen leaving the Isle of Dogs, towing the speedboat.

'Shit,' snapped Shatford, 'this is not going to happen.'

An hour later, Shatford gave the order to stand down.

The SO19 officers were smuggled out of the Dome but, since the place was now open for business, several people saw them. They hoped they would be mistaken for performing artists as the sight of armed officers would be too surreal to be true.

The police triple-checked their charts of the tides. There would be one more high tide tomorrow, 7 November. They would stage a full secret deployment in and around the Dome.

Shatford headed back to New Scotland Yard. He would have to explain to his bosses yet again why the job did not happen.

He felt like he was fast running out of lives.

'It should have been high water,' said Bill Cockram.

Somebody in the gang had fucked up on the tide front.

Later that day in a safe house in Bermondsey, Kevin Meredith explained that day's boat problem to Cockram.

Actually, Meredith was relieved, as he thought he could now get the hell out of there. He did not want the boat to be launched. He had been told that if they couldn't do the job that day, it would be put off for a couple of weeks.

Meredith thought he was going home.

But at 6 p.m. Bill Cockram had devastating news.

'Doing it tomorrow,' he said.

Meredith called his wife, who thought he was in London on a building job. He was due back home that night for a fireworks party with his kids.

'We couldn't get the roof finished,' he lied to her, 'because of the weather.' He said he had to stay another night.

Now Meredith was afraid she thought he was with a woman. The job had to be done, he explained; they had to get the roof on. His wife sounded pissed off.

'Get home now,' she said.

29. The Dawn

The Millennium Dome, 7 November 2000, 2 a.m.

We are making fools of ourselves, he thought. This is a complete waste of time.

In the middle of the night, David James, the Chairman of the Dome, sat in the CCTV room of the Dome's Bronze Control room, armed with a cup of coffee. Over the past eight weeks, he and his deputy had gone through this exercise no less than sixteen times, trooping to work in the wee hours for a long vigil as scores of armed police infiltrated his Dome and waited to spring their trap.

And sixteen times nothing happened.

By now, James was fed up. He had a day job, which was trying to stop the Dome from haemorrhaging millions of pounds of taxpayers' funds. He had a board meeting today at 9.30 a.m.

This diamond robbery was never going to happen. If anybody was so stupid as to try something like that, he thought, then they were the most incompetent bunch of crooks that have ever walked the earth. He settled in and started drinking a lot of coffee.

At 3 a.m., 200 police officers gathered at Lambeth for yet another operational briefing. It was almost a carbon copy of the briefing 24 hours previously. Jon Shatford was wondering if he was stuck inside a twisted version of Bill Murray's movie *Groundhog Day*, condemned to relive this day for eternity. Time was running out, he worried.

This was an exquisitely difficult and complex police operation. There was no way they could maintain this level of high alert for much longer. Once more he briefed the officers on firearms procedures, in accordance with the Criminal Law Act and the Human Rights Act.

Detective Inspector John Swinfield delivered an Intelligence update and a recap on Operation Magician, the Flying Squad's responsibilities, forensic retrieval processing and crime-scene management. Inspector Mark Williams delivered the tactical firearms presentation. The briefing was over by 4 a.m. and the officers began deploying to dozens of ambush points and observation posts around the Dome and the Thames.

The police plans had been shaped and refined over the weeks, and catered for every possible contingency. As with any plan, anything could go wrong and a lot could change, except one thing – everything the police did was geared to protecting the public and getting these men off the streets. In case the gang landed or escaped by helicopter, a police chopper was placed on standby five miles from the Dome. It was not equipped for air-to-air assault, but it was fuelled up and ready to intercept and follow the gang for a radius of over 100 miles.

A team of armed officers prepared to infiltrate the North Greenwich tube station near the Dome entrance, to block a getaway. Other armed officers fanned out to their ambush points – behind the false wall in the Harrison Building, the inflatable boats up the Thames and the ditches around the Dome complex. Others, dressed as Dome cleaners, stashed their firearms in rubbish bins and prepared to patrol the floor with mops and brooms.

One police officer stood on top of a Canary Wharf skyscraper and studied the Dome through field glasses. The night air was clear and the building glittered in the distance, illuminated by floodlights and crowned by twelve red aircraft warning lights on the 330-foot-high pylons, which were painted in what one writer called 'van Gogh cornfield yellow'.

At the Dome, security chief Malcolm Woods was escorting police units into the complex, a process that took an hour and a half. He had been working on this nerve-wracking operation for eight weeks, and in the event of an attack he would be the ground commander of the Dome security staff, only a handful of whom were aware of Operation Magician.

When an attack came, Woods would race to the De Beers Millennium Jewels exhibit, order his staff to keep people inside nearby exhibits and out of the line of fire, and shepherd visitors in the open areas away to safety. The police had told him the most likely times for a raid were between 8.30 and 10 a.m.

This created a whole series of nightmare scenarios.

The Millennium Jewels vault opened to Dome staff at 8.30 a.m., and there was usually a blue-and-yellow-jacketed staff member posted at the entrance. On high-risk days, he was pulled away for fear he would be killed or injured. The Dome then opened to the public in four sections from 9–10 a.m. every day. The diamond exhibit was in the first section, Area 1. It opened at 9 a.m. Despite the popular image of an empty Dome on the edge of oblivion, there were now thousands of people coming in every day, including busloads of tour groups, VIPs, contractors, performers, visitors with special needs and schoolchildren.

At any given time between 9 and 10 a.m. there could be 300–400 people in or around the area of the diamonds. The De Beers Jewel House was a popular exhibit and, on busy days, unexpected pockets of pedestrian congestion could erupt around it.

The last section of the Dome to open was Area 4 at 10 a.m., and it included the McDonald's 'Own Town Story' display, where scores of children gathered each day with teachers and Dome staff to participate in displays about their home towns. Thankfully, it was some distance from the diamonds, so if an attack came, the children would be held in there safely.

At 6.30 a.m., Flying Squad detectives Sean Allen and Lester Oakley infiltrated the Bronze Control CCTV room, removed the overnight security tapes and replaced them with blank Metropolitan Police video cassettes. Then they began monitoring the CCTV system.

Dome Chairman David James was still drinking coffee. And he was getting more and more pissed off.

The Betson gang were tooling up for action with a wealth of paraphernalia and tricks. The JCB was standing ready at the coal yard, specially modified to take four men – Ray Betson, William Cockram, Robert Adams and Aldo Ciarrocchi – instead of the usual one.

These four were the break-in team. All of them wore flexible, lightweight body armour and safety gloves to block fingerprints. They were equipped with gas masks as protection against their own smoke grenades, and to screen their faces from security cameras. As a bonus, the masks would probably terrify anyone who got in their way.

The JCB's windows were partially screened by black reflective material so that no one could see what was happening inside.

To impersonate a construction worker, Betson was wearing a reflective waistcoat. He was wearing a latex 'old man' face mask and a black balaclava on top of his head, which he planned to roll down when they escaped from the Dome. Two of the gang's vehicles, the JCB and the getaway speedboat, were rigged to explode and wipe out forensic evidence with two full petrol cans.

After dropping off Meredith and the speedboat, getaway driver Terry Millman was preparing to park on the north side of the Thames disguised as a road worker, complete with a red hardhat, reflective waistcoat and road barriers that would give him the cover to linger in the area.

The JCB would approach the Dome from the east, driven by Betson and followed by a white support van containing two police radio scanners – one tuned to air traffic, the other to ground.

The radio man, Aldo Ciarrocchi, was multi-tasking, with at least five different jobs to take care of. For weeks he had been memorising computer maps and street names in the area, in order to calculate police response times from radio transmissions. He would monitor the radio through headphones, poised to abort the operation at any moment.

During one of the gang's earlier advances on the Dome, on 6 October, they had all had a collective panic attack when a police car started following them. Ciarrocchi frantically scanned the police radio signals, but could not detect anything unusual. It turned out to be a coincidence. The police car, which was not part of Operation Magician, peeled away. The advance was aborted by Betson and the then-boatman Mitchell when the escape boat developed engine trouble.

Today, Aldo Ciarrocchi was in charge of a small arsenal of smoke grenades stashed in the JCB. The twelve devices contained a blend of potassium chlorate, lactose and dye. When ignited, they would set off large billows of red and lilac blue smoke.

The grenades contained toxic materials, and were supposed to be used outdoors under highly controlled conditions. But the gang were planning to detonate the grenades indoors, inside the Dome. And inside the confined De Beers vault this ran the risk not only of creating panic and chaos, but of triggering eye and skin irritation and even respiratory failure in bystanders.

Besides working the radios and setting off the grenades, Ciarrocchi had to guard the De Beers vault while Adams and Cockram went into action to seize the jewels, and set off a stink bomb in the JCB to throw police dogs off the gang's scent as they made their getaway. Ciarrocchi may have also been in charge of detonating the petrol containers in the JCB and speedboat, as he was carrying weatherproof matches.

He had a lot of responsibility. As a backup anti-forensic measure, Ciarrocchi was carrying a solution of ammonia in a small spray bottle which he would use to coat the cockpits of the JCB and speedboat in order to remove any DNA, sweat, blood or fingerprint traces the gang left behind.

Bill Cockram, Betson's number two, had a hip torch to help find his way in the darkened diamond vault and was wearing a sleeveless vest with zip-up pockets under his hooded jacket. All twelve diamonds could fit into the single pocket, the De Beers Millennium Star plus the eleven electric-blue diamonds. £250 million in one pocket.

Bill Cockram and 'Bob the Builder' Adams were armed with their own ammonia spray bottles, as well as a pair of bolt croppers and two 14 lb sledgehammers.

Cockram had wrapped both his arms in bandages. This was to protect his skin as he reached through the broken glass of the diamond cases, and to prevent leaving blood samples behind in case he cut himself.

He was also armed with the high-powered Hilti nail gun.

At 7.26 a.m., Millman and Meredith put the plan into action. By 8.15 a.m., they had managed to float the boat off the trailer and launch it. But now, just off shore of Newcastle Draw Dock, Meredith couldn't get the starter to engage. It kept conking out. So he pulled it to one side and ran the engine awhile to get it warmed up.

At 8.11 a.m., at the coal yard in Plumstead, the JCB was started up. Sixteen minutes later, Terry Millman gave a thumbs up and Kevin Meredith headed the speedboat north and then east, past Canary Wharf and towards the Dome, heading for Bow Creek. Ever the professional boat pilot, Meredith was sporting a life jacket.

Scotland Yard surveillance cameras were recording the boat as it knifed through the Thames.

At 8.43 a.m., the JCB drove out of the engine shed and the yard, followed by the white transit van.

In the Millennium Dome Control Room, Flying Squad officers abruptly took over the CCTV controls and expelled Dome security staff.

As he scanned the TV screens, Jon Shatford was praying that this time it would really happen.

30. The Raid

The Millennium Dome, 7 November 2000, 8.43 a.m.

'Stay with the JCB,' said Shatford. 'Let the van go.'

Shatford, Swinfield and Adams were studying the wall full of CCTV screens in the Bronze Control Room, which were now also being fed by police observation cameras.

The JCB had just turned north into Anchor and Hope Lane, after briefly passing through a blind spot in police surveillance.

This was a final approach road to the Dome, and the gang had never made it this far before. Their white van was pulling away from the JCB, blending into heavy rush-hour commuter traffic.

Shatford had to make a split-second decision. The van could be a diversion, intended to draw police away. Or it could just be an escort vehicle. Either way, he feared that if police followed and stopped the van, the gang would be alerted and the raid called off.

The van, Shatford concluded, was probably the least significant part of the attack, and the JCB had to be the crucial vehicle. He decided to concentrate all his resources on following the JCB. He could probably deal with the van later, when the gang was in custody.

The police focused on the JCB, and the white van vanished.

It was 9 a.m. and, right at that moment, a motorcycle slammed into the back of a bus on the Blackwall Tunnel southern approach road, close to the Dome. It was a gut-wrenching, *Groundhog Day* replay of the previous day when a car ran into a bus in almost the exact same spot.

'Oh, Christ, how is this happening?' moaned Shatford.

The JCB was less than two miles away.

In a frantic attempt to head off any traffic police, Shatford scrambled a Flying Squad gun ship to the scene.

The motorcyclist was shaken, but not injured seriously. He must have wondered why a pair of burly plain-clothes detectives in an unmarked car was bundling him off to hospital. Shatford punched in a secure text message to his boss: 'They're coming in.'

Inside the super-secure operations control room of New Scotland Yard, Detective Chief Superintendent John Coles read Shatford's message and gazed at his own bank of video screens. The room was packed with police, and the noise and excitement was at fever pitch.

This could be the best day of his entire working life. It was exceedingly rare to get this close to such a heavy mob for so long. The gang were planning the biggest robbery of all time. And they were manoeuvring right into the Flying Squad's trap. Catching them red-handed would be the ultimate prize.

'Sometimes police evidence in court is not believed,' Coles later explained. 'Catch them in the act, and that's the end of it.'

The video screens were picking up traffic all around London, including plenty of JCBs. 'And I have to tell you I wasn't watching the right one,' Coles later recalled. 'Not to begin with.'

At 9 a.m., the Dome opened to the public, and security director Malcolm Woods started quietly steering people away from the diamond exhibit. Police officers disguised as Dome guides were doing the same thing.

Normally, there could be several hundred people approaching the area in the next hour. To add a special layer of horror, two large groups of schoolchildren were approaching the Dome's entrance gates right now. One group, a party of 100 from the All Hallows School in Farnham, Surrey, was heading for the Mind Zone to hear a lecture. The other, a group of 64 kids aged from twelve to fifteen from the Ferndown Middle School, in Dorset, was going to the 'Our Town Story' open theatre area to put on a show about their town.

Woods dispatched a manager to divert these children to the enclosed McDonald's restaurant in the main square, some distance away from the diamonds, and ordered another manager to hold the Farnham group inside the safety of the Mind Zone.

The children began singing hymns.

At 9.07 a.m., the JCB turned left off Bugsby Way, moved underneath the A102 Blackwall Tunnel approach, and parked out of sight, in a police blind spot.

Betson was communicating through his portable radio with his getaway team, boatman Kevin Meredith in the speedboat and Terry Millman waiting in the van across the Thames.

Inside the JCB, Aldo Ciarrocchi was hunched down out of sight, covered up by a sheet and listening intently to a hand-held police radio scanner as he braced himself against the bumpy ride. He couldn't detect anything unusual.

One of the many things Ciarrocchi had to worry about was drowning. He was not a good swimmer, and he was loaded down with body armour, boots and radios. He didn't know Meredith well and, if he tipped the boat over during the getaway, there was a good chance, Ciarrocchi thought, that he'd go to the bottom of the Thames.

Right next to him, Cockram was afraid they might get pulled over by traffic police. To him, this approach stage of the operation was the most nerve-wracking, and this is where he felt most vulnerable. It felt like it was taking hours.

Meredith was moored up on the north side of the river, at the entrance to Bow Creek, with the boat's engine running. He was absolutely petrified. There was a chance, he feared, that this could be his last day on earth.

Through the radio crackle and interference in his earpiece, he heard the command, 'Five minutes, five minutes.'

Increasingly, Dome Chairman David James's mind was dominated by a single, powerful thought.

I need the loo.

He'd been up in the Bronze Control Room all night drinking coffee. 'Coffee,' he later explained, 'was pouring out of my ears as well as nearly everywhere else.' And his executive board meeting was in twenty minutes.

Then he heard that the JCB had vanished, again stopping short of the Dome. He was fed up. So at 9.15 a.m. he stood up and made an announcement.

'I've had enough of this. I've got a bloody board meeting to hold, and I'm going to the bloody loo. I think this whole nonsense is ridiculous. There's never going to be a robbery. The police are pulling our legs. I'm sick and tired of this, and I'm going to stop this nonsense,' he concluded.

He was going to shut down Operation Magician.

'We are doing it no more.'

At this, he spun on his heels and stormed out of the Control Room. The door slammed behind him.

On the video screen, the JCB re-appeared, resuming its advance.

David James was charging down the stairs breaking his neck to get the loo, when he heard a voice shouting after him, 'Come back, it's happening!'

'Fuck off,' said the chairman. 'I'm not falling for that one.'

In the Control Room, Jon Shatford focused on one decision – when to order the ambush. He had to protect the public *and* catch the gang red-handed. The two objectives might be moving into full-scale collision.

A police observer called in, 'Eyeball One, JCB moving forward.'

'Stand back,' said Shatford.

At 9.27 a.m., the JCB turned left into Ordnance Crescent and stopped in Drawdock Road, just short of the Dome's perimeter fence.

At the Dome CCTV controls, Detective Constable Sean Allen swung a camera round to cover this junction, but the view of the JCB was mostly blocked by the fence.

The Flying Squad watched as the digger moved forward, heading for a small gap in the fence.

It stopped, reversed and then shot forward, increasing in speed until it pushed straight through the 10 ft metal fence and flattened a concrete bollard.

Shatford still wasn't sure what the hell their plan was, even though they had just recklessly smashed their way through a fence. Next to him, Mark Williams relayed an order by mobile phone to the ground commander inside the Dome, Inspector Vincent Esposito.

Esposito quietly moved his advance team of firearms officers to a forward position nearer the diamonds.

Ray Betson shouted the radio alert to Meredith and Millman: 'ATTACK ATTACK ATTACK!'

Kevin Meredith was freaking out. He unhooked his moorings, pointed his boat directly across the river to the Queen Elizabeth II pier, and opened the throttle.

The pick-up spot was supposed to be the Millennium Pier.

He was heading straight for the wrong pier.

Meanwhile, the JCB picked up speed as it circled the roundabout near the Dome entrance and drove onto an access ramp.

It headed towards Gate 4 of the Dome, its scoop raised. This was the point of no return. The heavy steel double doors of Gate 4 were right ahead. The gate was locked.

Betson hit the accelerator.

A pair of Dome guides was startled to see a JCB heading straight towards them. 'What the hell?' thought one. 'It came so near us we had to jump out the way,' he recalled.

As the vehicle sped towards the gate, the guide thought, 'Hold on a second, mate. The door isn't open yet. You can't just drive straight through it.'

But that's exactly what it did.

To the amazement of the police, the JCB charged right into the gate and rammed the doors open.

The doors gave way easily, as if they had been fastened with tape.

Shatford watched the screen in disbelief. They were literally smashing their way into the Dome.

The JCB's like a tank, he thought. Nothing's going to stop it. It was too big and too fast. They couldn't even shoot the tyres out.

This was the one contingency Shatford hadn't anticipated. But still he decided to hold off the police counter-attack until they went for the jewels.

'Stand back,' he announced into his mobile.

The JCB vanished out of camera range under the rim of the Dome canopy. Ray Betson then turned the vehicle, and launched it towards the shell of the Dome.

At 9.33 a.m., the JCB crashed at high speed through its third and final barrier, the closed Perspex shutter forming the skin of the Dome.

The plan to escape with the diamonds was based on shock, force and, above all, speed.

'It was all based on time,' Cockram later explained. 'It would have taken a very short time from hitting the main gate to getting back across the Thames.' He estimated, 'Five minutes maximum.'

The plan was so good that Cockram thought the worst part was now over. 'Once we went through the actual Dome doors,' he explained, 'I thought that was it and we were then in the clear.'

Betson elaborated: 'It took us thirty seconds to get from the bollard area and to outside the [diamond] exhibit. It would have taken 45 seconds to get in the cabinets to get the stones, allowing ourselves a minute. So we're talking a minute and a half now.

'By the time we spun [the JCB] around,' Betson continued, 'it would have took a further 45 seconds to get from outside the vault, then out through Gate 10, then down to the beach.'

Betson continued, 'So now we're talking about two-and-a-half minutes, and then it's a sixty-second crossing. So even if they [Dome security and police] had responded to it according to textbook guidelines, they would have had no chance.'

As the JCB crashed through the Dome wall, anyone standing on the other side didn't stand a chance, either.

31. The Break-in

The Millennium Dome Money Zone, 9.36 a.m.

When the JCB crashed through the wall, it created a small shower of debris that flew 70–100ft into the Dome concourse.

'Oh, shit,' thought a Dome maintenance contractor who was suspended on top of a hoist, working on partitions. He thought a piece of heavy equipment had crashed into the side of the building.

Ozcan Ocha, the thirty-year-old manager of the Baker's Oven café, heard what he called 'a terrible crashing noise as if there was an accident'.

A Dome chef, Jason Forest, was getting ready for work when he heard a loud bang. 'It sounded like something was collapsing,' he told a reporter. 'All I could see was a JCB passing me at high speed. At first I thought it was someone crazy trying to destroy the Dome.'

'I heard this enormous crashing noise,' said another witness. 'My first thought was that something had fallen on top of the Dome, it was so loud.'

The immediate area was being guarded by two SO11 surveillance officers in plain clothes, Detective Constables Carol Brockelsby and Michael Hayward, but now they were directly in the JCB's flight path.

Members of the public were at a safe distance, but many were frozen in place, watching the spectacle of the JCB as it charged straight at the officers.

'I remember the look of fear on their faces,' explained one tourist. 'They seemed to be being chased by the JCB and were trying to get out of its path.'

One woman compared the digger to 'a tank in a war film'.

Others thought someone had gone berserk and was on a rampage.

Several people thought a terrorist attack was under way, especially when they caught glimpses of the gas-masked gangsters, one of them now hanging off the side of the digger.

'They looked like terrorists coming in to destroy the Dome,' said one witness.

One Dome worker, watching the running figures of Brockelsby and Hayward, recalled, 'I saw them both run to the left in front of the visitors service centre, and the digger turned in the same direction and seemed to chase them. The shovel of the digger was raised and it was only a couple of feet behind them.'

The two police officers were trying to get out of its path, she added, 'but it appeared that it was stuck to them like a magnet as it continued to follow them wherever they went.'

A startled Japanese couple stumbled backwards as the JCB shot past them.

One visitor wondered if this was part of the live entertainment.

The arrival of the JCB did add a fresh burst of surrealist detail to an already bizarre landscape.

In the central stage area, technicians were calibrating strobe light effects for the 'Our Town Story', as a musician energetically tested the drums. School children were singing hymns in the safety of the holding room in the Mind Zone, guarded discreetly by police and Dome security.

When the JCB rammed through the wall, a pair of stilt walkers in Victorian costumes who had been conferring with a group of pensioners from Reading, scrambled away from the scene as fast as their stilts could manage.

Betson made a sharp right turn and steered the JCB to the open entrance of the De Beers Jewel House in the Money Zone, which was lightly guarded by an elasticised barrier.

He braked hard near the entrance, and Adams, Ciarrocchi and Cockram were poised to jump out of the cabin, ready for action with body armour, gloves, pulled-up hoods, gas masks and tools.

'Get out,' announced Betson, 'we're here.'

Ciarrocchi was first out, and he pulled the barrier aside before trotting to the front of the JCB to detonate the smoke grenades.

A strange feeling gripped Ciarrocchi, of time slowing down. 'It was like when your car's about to crash and you start braking. The skid feels like it takes forever,' he later said.

He pulled a grenade out of his pocket, popped off the cap and threw it on the ground.

A blue smoke cloud billowed up from the concourse.

'Chuck some more out,' ordered Betson, who was turning the JCB around to face the Gate 10 exit, pointing it towards the Thames.

Out on the river, Meredith was nearing the southern shore at the QEII Pier.

Adams and Cockram were already dashing into the De Beers exhibit with their tools. Cockram paused to stick a wedge in the door so that they wouldn't get locked inside.

'Eyeball three,' announced the excited voice of a spotter on the police mobile phone line, 'they are forcing entry into the Money Zone – they are inside!'

'Wait for them all in, I have control,' ordered Shatford in as calm a voice as he could muster. 'Hold your positions.'

Meanwhile, a few miles to the north-east in the City of London, in the security control room of De Beers, an officer's eye was caught by a flurry of activity on the CCTV screen that broadcast a constant live image from the diamond vault at the Dome.

Only a tiny handful of De Beers people were yet aware of the robbery threat, and he wasn't one of them.

The officer snapped to attention and exclaimed, 'Oh my God, did you see that? Do you see what's happening?'

He and his colleagues studied the images intently, which seemed to be of a pair of terrorists scampering into the vault and pouncing on the De Beers Millennium Star display case.

Instantly, the officers sounded the alarms at 17 Charterhouse Street.

Back at the Dome, the dark jewel chamber was empty when Adams and Cockram entered, and the pinpoint spotlights fell upon a glittering, incandescent object on top of a small column in the display case.

Cockram was moving with a speed and confidence that was fuelled by months of planning and a single, stunning technical insight. It was an insight built upon the laws of physics, as expressed in the brute force of the construction industry and the Hilti nail gun he held in his hand.

Cockram had figured out an ingenious, low-tech way to penetrate the specially treated armoured glass of the De Beers Millennium Star display and the surrounding Millennium Jewel cases.

'I knew of a way to get into those cabinets,' he later explained.

The designers of the display cases had assured De Beers that they would withstand any known drilling instrument for at least thirty minutes, and up to thirty tons of pressure. As a test, De Beers' security people had even attacked a prototype of the glass with a variety of power drills, hammers and saws. Not only couldn't they break or shatter the material, they couldn't even crack it.

But Cockram had realised something the experts hadn't. If he fired industrial-strength nails hard enough at point-blank range into several spots in the glass, even glass as heavily reinforced as this, it would heat up, causing a temporary structural weakening. The heating effect would mean that, for a few moments, the glass could crack under a sharp impact. The trick, according to Cockram, was 'to to hit it very quickly, while it was still warm'.

Cockram placed a set of bolt croppers on the floor, a back-up tool he planned to use in case the jewels were fastened to their holders inside the displays.

He reached up and placed the Hilti gun against the glass and fired one, two and three shots in a vertical row, spaced a few inches apart.

He stepped aside and 'Bob the Builder' Adams swung his sledgehammer full force at the glass.

The first swing weakened it.

Adams instantly fired another shot, aiming at the same spot.

At 9.37 a.m., the second swing punched a small fist-sized hole in the glass and sent glass fragments spraying into the case.

Adams was amazed at how fast the glass gave way.

The glass had been treated by its designers with a substance that was supposed to bind the glass together in case of impact, and prevent large cracks from opening up and shattering the whole panel. It did this job well, limiting the crack to the impact area, but the damage was done. A hole. There was a hole.

It took the gang just 27 seconds to blow open the case instead of the minimum thirty minutes promised by the display's designers.

It would be the greatest 'smash and grab' of all time.

Now that the case was breached, Cockram and Adams swung around and started going to work on the other case that protected the eleven rare blue diamonds, firing and smashing.

Outside, Ciarrocchi was patrolling the exhibit entrance, dropping blue and yellow smoke grenades.

All three getaway drivers – Betson, Meredith and Millman – were ready and in position.

There was no sign of the Old Bill.

Cockram decided to reach through the glass and grab the De Beers Millennium Star.

In the Dome's Bronze Control Room, CCTV video recorders were capturing the whole crime as it happened, relaying the feed from a security camera in the ceiling of the vault onto fresh Metropolitan Police evidence tapes, already labelled and coded.

Cockram and Adams were creating vivid action photos of themselves doing what they loved doing best, immortalising their criminal careers in a blaze of grainy black-and-white 'caught-on-tape' images.

They were cocooned inside the vault.

This was the airtight, bullet-proof evidence that was needed by Shatford, the Flying Squad and the Crown Prosecution Service – the kind that would stand up in court.

He gave the order he'd been waiting to give for more than eight weeks.

'Go – Go – GO!'

The trap was sprung.

32. The Ambush

The Millennium Dome, 9.38 a.m.

'Strike, strike, strike,' Shatford shouted into his mobile phone.

'All units, STRIKE,' ordered Swinfield, and the command ricocheted around the Dome.

'It really was like something out of a film,' said one of the customers in the Baker's Oven café. 'It was very surreal – one of the officers had actually been sweeping the floor next to me and suddenly he was pulling out a gun.'

The café manager, Ozcan Ocha, remembered, 'There was a loud crash and a series of bangs, and suddenly half the people I thought were visitors or cleaners were pulling out guns. I had been talking to some of them a few minutes earlier and I had no idea they were police officers.'

The plain clothes officers deployed around the Dome put on high-visibility police caps to avoid confusing each other for gang members in the heat of the action.

Sergeant Mark Adams was team leader of the SO19 unit assigned with penetrating the vault. The team had two jobs – to isolate and capture the suspects in the vault, and to cut off any attempted escape into the public domain.

He got the strike order as he was holding his men in the cramped room behind the false wall in the Harrison Building.

They were a full stick of twenty heavily equipped firearms officers. On many occasions over the last six weeks they had been stuck in this windowless concrete corridor for hours at a time. It measured 6 ft wide and 30 ft long, and they were packed in head-to-toe like sardines, having to perform their bodily functions in an open thunder box.

At last, they got the order to move.

They burst into the open and charged across the concourse.

'Keep back! Keep back! Get down!' they shouted to people in the distance as they advanced and converged with other officers.

The uniformed officers were dressed in full SFO operational kit:

black overalls, body armour, ballistic helmets, respirators, plasticuffs (modern handcuffs), goggles, Glock 9 mm self-loading pistols and MP5 carbines.

Their ammunition was SO19's standard 95-grain, 9 mm blunt-tipped bullet. In contrast to military-issue 'full metal jacket' round-nosed bullets, their blunt-tipped bullets were specially selected to dump their energy into the target and reduce the danger of 'over-penetration', or flying out of the target and hitting bystanders.

Near the head of the column was an officer carrying a Hatton gun, a short-barrelled pump-action shotgun that fired a 'Hatton round' made of compacted lead dust in wax, designed for blowing down bolted doors and other barriers.

Other officers carried stun grenades, or 'stunnies', and long ballistic shields.

The last man in line was the team medic, carrying a medical pack.

In seconds, they closed in on Ray Betson, still at the wheel of the JCB, and Aldo Ciarrocchi, who was preparing to fire off another smoke grenade.

'It was a hell of a lot of noise,' remembered Flying Squad Detective Sergeant Mark Drew, who was watching an overhead CCTV view on a monitor in the Dome security control room. 'There was a lot of shouting and screaming. There was smoke everywhere.'

A Dome maintenance worker was horror-struck as he watched Ciarrocchi lobbing the smoke grenades. Considering Ciarrocchi's gas mask and what appeared to be a white scientist's suit, the workman feared he was releasing toxic gas.

Ciarrocchi tossed a grenade towards an oncoming policeman. It detonated with blue smoke, and the officer kicked it away like a football player fielding a practice shot.

'ARMED POLICE, ARMED POLICE, GET DOWN!' the police ordered, guns aimed at Ciarrocchi. This was one of SO19's rules of engagement – to shout clear warnings to a suspect.

Ciarrocchi wasn't precisely clear on what was happening, since his hood was up, he had radio signals crackling in his earpiece and his vision was impaired by the smoke and his goggles.

He wasn't sure if the police were screaming 'get down' or 'get out the fucking way', but he'd heard enough to dive directly onto the hard floor.

He later explained his feelings at this exact moment.

'I shit myself.'

'Armed police, armed police,' the SO19 officer called up to Ray Betson in the elevated cabin of the digger. 'Show me your hands!'

The officer's MP5 was pointed at Betson's torso, but the villain seemed a portrait of indifference. He had just taken off his latex 'old man' mask and was preparing to strap on his gas mask.

He was perhaps frozen in shock, confusion or defiance.

His hands were hidden in his jacket pockets.

The engine was running.

Despite repeated commands to show his hands, Betson wasn't responding.

Officers were circling around the vehicle in a wide arc, trying to block an escape.

One officer aimed his Hatton Gun at the cabin, ready to blast the door off.

The police had no idea whether or not Betson was carrying guns, grenades, detonators or explosives, and they couldn't take chances.

Fully prepared for Betson to pull out a gun, one of the SO19 officers was preparing to fire at Betson, his finger on the trigger.

Betson's hands started coming out of his jacket. They were empty.

'Out, out of the vehicle!' ordered the police.

The door opened and Betson came tumbling out almost head first, police forcing him face-down flat on the floor.

For whatever reason, Betson still wouldn't show his hands.

An officer put his foot on Betson's back and shoulder, to restrain him, pulled his hands behind him and assisted a colleague in wrapping plasticuffs around Betson's wrists.

Both Betson and Ciarrocchi were now prisoners, face down on the floor.

The advance team of SO19 officers was flooding into the narrow corridor that led to the diamond vault. They could detect movements in the display area, but had no clear line of sight.

Inside the vault, Bill Cockram was just about to grab the De Beers Millennium Star but had not yet pushed his gloved hand through the hole.

SO19 team leader Sergeant Mark Adams shouted repeatedly into the exhibit: 'Armed police – come out.'

There was no response, so he gave the order to deploy stun grenades.

'Stunnies, stunnies,' came the request, and a bunch of them were passed up the line.

'Armed police – come out and show yourselves.'

Two officers advanced to the entrance from behind a tall, hand-held ballistic shield. One of the gang members popped into view, wearing a gas mask and torch strapped to his forehead.

An SO19 officer pointed his carbine at him and challenged him with a shout of 'Armed police, stay where you are.'

But the suspect immediately ducked back around the corner, out of sight.

Two stun grenades were tossed in, setting off multiple flash-bangs that were designed to temporarily immobilise and disorient their target.

At nearly the same instant that the grenades were in midair, Cockram and Adams made a joint emergency decision to drop their tools, kneel down, and dive face-first on the floor as fast as they could.

Any doubts they might have had were quickly removed by the deafening bangs of the stunnies, and the swarm of police who charged through the darkness and smoke, and overwhelmed them.

Over and over, the officers ordered, 'Armed police – show me your hands.' But, like Betson, they weren't complying.

One of the suspects struggled with an officer as he tried to handcuff him.

'Show me your hands,' ordered the policeman. 'Put your hands out – release your hands!'

Finally, kneeling on the suspect's backs, the officers pulled their hands free and cuffed them.

Then the officers noticed a sharp chemical smell coming through their gas masks.

The suspects were choking.

The door to the conference room banged open.

David James had just started his Dome board meeting in an adjacent building when a woman burst in and commanded, 'Come here immediately – I need you.'

There weren't many people David James would tolerate addressing him like this, but Linda Thomas was one of them. She had been his secretary for the last twenty years.

'The robbery's happening. They need you urgently,' she told him after they'd stepped out of the room.

Looking around for his deputy, Pierre-Yves Gerbeau, he asked, 'Where's PY?'

James raced to one of the Dome's little electric transport buggies and went off in search of PY, whom he soon found having his own operations meeting close by.

James stormed into the meeting and said 'PY, get your ass out of here – it's happened!'

'We picked him up,' remembered James, 'put him on the back of the golf wagon with me, and went to the Dome.'

When police launched the ambush, Terry Millman was at his assigned getaway spot on a footway at Lower Lea Crossing, above Bow Creek, wearing his red builder's hardhat and fluorescent jacket.

The road barriers were neatly set up by the side of the road near his parked van. To complete the deception, Millman had even placed an amber flashing light on top of his roof.

He was looking south across the river at the Millennium Dome and monitoring his gang radio and police scanner. He was waiting for the thrilling sight of the JCB triumphantly cruising out of Gate 10 and over to the pier with a quarter-billion pounds of diamonds zipped up in Bill Cockram's pocket.

But at 9.40 a.m., inside a passing gun ship, an officer spotted the van's registration plate and exclaimed, 'N770 – that's it!'

The gun ship swung across the road and three police officers got out and approached Millman, their guns drawn, shouting, 'Armed police, armed police, do not move.'

'We are police officers from the Flying Squad,' announced one officer as Millman put his hands in the air. 'You are under arrest on suspicion of armed robbery at the Millennium Dome.'

After Millman was cuffed and cautioned, an officer asked, 'Do you have any weapons on you?'

'No.'

'Who are you?' the officer asked.

'My name is Terry Millman. I've got nothing more to say.'

'What's this?' asked an officer as he pulled a clear plastic bag out of Millman's pocket.

'It's a bit of hash,' said Millman.

'You are also under arrest for unlawful possession of cannabis,' said the officer, who again cautioned the suspect.

Millman was then wrapped up in a blue forensic suit to maintain the integrity of any later forensic examination of him or his clothing. This was a sterile wraparound sheet that police use to lock in key forensic evidence on suspects, including hairs, fibres, glass, paint, body fluids and firearms and explosives residues.

The cape also protects against cross-contamination, for example, when a suspect sits in a police car and picks up firearms residue from the seat or from a police officer's clothing. The cape was the next best thing to dropping suspects into plastic bags and bringing them to the police station.

Millman shut up, this time for good.

'Right, OK, the job's on!'

It was 9.39 a.m. And it took less than sixty seconds for Sergeant Clive

Rew and his squad of fifteen SO19 officers to break out of their secret holding area, dash down to the boats and launch towards the Dome in the western distance.

This was one of the biggest operations in SO19's history. But beyond the scale and complexity of the job, it didn't really seem that unusual to the men behind the goggles and armour. It was one of some 1,000 pre-planned firearms operations that SO19 conducted every year, covering everything from hostage rescues and domestic sieges to robbery stakeouts and executing warrants. There were far more pre-planned firearms operations in London than in the rest of England, Wales and Scotland put together.

The highest-risk warrants were for known robbers, armed suspects, drug dealers and killers, and they required extra robust levels of force and surprise.

Most SO19 jobs were so well planned and well rehearsed that they rarely resulted in shoot-outs. Surprise was often the key, and total surprise was what they hoped for today.

But as the boats bounced through the water, every man on board was aware of the possibility that things could go wrong and a shoot-out could erupt.

Sergeant Rew was the longest-serving member of SO19, having joined the unit in 1980 when it had only 25 officers. Now there were 300. He had a multitude of things to worry about.

Although his strike team were travelling in three fast, rigid, inflatable police boats with powerful diesel engines, there was a chance, he feared, that the Betson gang's light fibreglass Picton speedboat could outrun them on the river. It might be capable of forty or fifty knots.

The response time was another problem – they had to be far enough away so that they didn't compromise the operation, but not so far away that they were too late getting to the Dome peninsula. The gang could have a lookout watching the river, poised to abort the operation if police were spotted.

But the biggest problem was the water.

The chance of surviving a fall into the Thames can be 'lower than falling in front of a Tube train', reported Sonia Purnell of the *Independent*. The tide can fluctuate by 40 ft and run at 10 mph. 'Near bridges the speeds can be even higher,' Purnell wrote, 'producing deadly whirlpools and back eddies that can sweep away victims at breakneck speed or crush them against or under obstructions such as jetties, boats or piers.'

The Thames was a very tough place to stage a firearms operation. It's hard enough to hit things accurately when you've got both feet on the ground, but when you're flying along in the water shooting from a moving platform, your skill level has to be truly extraordinary.

Even in skilled hands, the maximum reasonable range you can expect to get hits on a man-sized target from an MP5 carbine is 100 metres (328 ft), and that's if you're standing with both feet on the ground.

But if you're moving along at a fast speed across the Thames, the range over which you can manage an accurate shot is reduced to about forty or fifty metres (130–160 ft). The only thing you can hope to do from a fast-moving boat is get a shot in the centre of the target, in the chest area.

As part of their regular training, SO19 officers drilled on the Thames throughout the year with the Met's Marine Support Unit.

To rehearse for hostage rescues and anti-terrorist operations on the river, they practised jumping onto fast-moving vessels, rappelling down river barriers and jumping 50 ft off the back of ships suited up in FRIS (fire-retardant immersion suits), weapons and survival gear.

This morning, Sergeant Rew and his officers had waited hidden away in the gymnasium of the Marine Support Unit base near Thames Wapping. Some of them slept and others read books as the hours ticked by. As they waited for the order to deploy, they had to stay 'booted and suited', kitted up in all their gear.

'I know it sounds a bit blasé,' remembered Sergeant Rew, 'but we're used to playing the waiting game, sitting around in cars or vans sometimes for hours and hours waiting for things to shape up. Then it happens – fast and furious action for two or three minutes, and then it's all over.'

When the strike order came at 9.38 am, they moved out at full throttle.

'Eyeball One,' said the voice on the police radio, 'waterborne moving in on the jetty.'

For the past eight weeks the police had observed strict radio silence. It was no longer necessary.

There were six officers per boat, a Marine Support specialist and a medic, prepared to treat and evacuate casualties in case of an exchange of shots on the water.

Sergeant Rew was in boat Delta Two with Inspector John Terry and four SO19 specialists.

They were heading straight for the Picton.

Sweeping north of them was Delta Three, providing a pursuit and cut-off capability.

The third boat, Delta One, was assigned with boarding the pier, searching for suspects and shutting down the pier.

When Delta Two closed to within 200 ft, the officers could see the back of a hooded figure crouching in the well of the boat.

Kevin Meredith was idling his engine at the wrong mooring-up point, on the Queen Elizabeth II Pier, and it was about to dawn on him that he was being closed in on by a pair of hovering police helicopters and three fast-moving inflatable police boats.

'I had my weapon raised a good 150–200 metres (500–600 ft) out,' recalled Sergeant Rew. 'We were closing rapidly on the boat, and he was coming into a shootable distance. As soon as I could see the boat, I saw he had his back to us. As we got closer and closer, I had to have the sights of my weapon on him before we started to shout 'armed police', since that might have triggered him into pulling a weapon up and firing.'

When they closed to within a few dozen yards, Sergeant Rew shouted, 'Armed police, armed police – stand still – don't move.'

Meredith froze as the police launch pulled up next to him and he stared into the barrels of a small arsenal of weapons.

'Hands up in the air,' ordered Rew.

Meredith complied. He looked totally shocked, like a man who suddenly realised he'd been caught in the act.

'Now kneel down and interlock your fingers on top of your head.'

Meredith did as he was told.

The officers slung their weapons to the side, pulled Meredith horizontally over into the well of their boat and plasticuffed him as he lay flat.

Police helicopters were directly overhead, videotaping the spectacle.

At 9.42 a.m., an officer leaned over the suspect, told him he was under arrest for conspiracy to commit armed robbery, and cautioned him.

Meredith seemed to be in a state of shock and despair.

'What am I going to say to my wife and kids?' he asked.

33. The Prisoners

The De Beers Millennium Jewels Vault, 9.45 a.m.

In the diamond vault, Sergeant Mark Adams smelled what seemed like ammonia and saw that both Cockram and Adams were having real trouble breathing.

He pulled up their gas masks and his officers helped the cuffed suspects sit up on their sides, which seemed to help.

The sergeant called back for the team medic to examine the suspects.

'Are you breathing OK?' he asked Adams.

'Yeah, OK,' replied would-be super-jewel thief Robert Adams, who had minor injuries to his scalp and forehead.

His gas mask was on top of his head and he was sitting in a powerful stink of ammonia.

Bill Cockram was bleeding from both nostrils, had a small contusion to his left temple and a bruise on his cheek bone.

Outside on the pedestrian concourse, Ray Betson was nursing minor contusions to the left cheek and temple and a swollen, bleeding nose.

A medic treated their wounds. It wasn't clear if the injuries had been sustained during the gang's traumatic entrance to the Dome, or when they dived onto the floor, or during the arrests.

At 9.45 a.m., a Flying Squad detective introduced himself to Cockram and announced, 'I am arresting you for committing this armed robbery.'

He was cautioned, but made no reply.

The officer asked, 'Have you got anything on you?'

'What, tools?'

'Yeah.'

'I've got ammonia in my front pocket,' said Cockram.

In the pockets of Adams and Cockram, the officers found Sinex bottles containing ammonia, both of which had burst when they hit the floor. Betson and Ciarrocchi had them too. This explained the fumes and the choking.

As Robert Adams was arrested and cautioned, he had a question.

'Have I been bubbled up?'

'You know I can't answer that question,' said the arresting officer.

'I am arresting you for attempted robbery of the Millennium Jewels,' an officer informed Raymond Betson, who had nothing to say for the moment.

Betson was cuffed and spread out on the floor, wearing an expression on his face that looked like his world had come to an end.

The gang members appeared to be totally stunned.

'You should have seen their faces when we turned up,' remembered one policeman. 'They looked like someone had cancelled Christmas.'

Later, one officer reported that Betson had regained his composure long enough to throw him a wink and a smile, saying, 'It was worth a try.'

The police lined up Betson, Ciarrocchi, Adams and Cockram on the floor near the entrance to the Jewel House. The cabinets in the De Beers diamond exhibit were smashed, but twelve exquisitely beautiful sparkling objects were still secure on their pedestals, shining in the spotlights.

Thanks to months of amazing police work by over 300 officers of the Metropolitan Police and the Kent County Constabulary, Operation Magician seemed to have come off . . . magically.

Jon Shatford was urgently calling all his team leaders, asking over and over, 'Is everyone all right? Are there any casualties?'

There were none.

A delighted voice appeared on the police radio.

'Six arrests and no shots fired!'

Every major crime scene has an exhibits officer, and on this job it was Detective Constable Gill Blakebell of the Flying Squad's Tower Bridge office.

The exhibits officer is in charge of securing the crime scene and keeping track of all the evidence. It is a crucial job since some crime scenes, like this one, can have hundreds of pieces of evidence that will become exhibits at the trial.

There is no margin for error. If one exhibit gets mixed up, a defence lawyer can pounce on it and challenge the credibility of the whole case. If police cannot conclusively prove that an exhibit being reviewed in court is the same one taken from the scene or the suspects, then the case could collapse.

And if the defence smells a breach of exhibits regulations, they will leap on it and try to get the trial thrown out.

The tools of the exhibits officer are a pen, an exhibits book, gloves, and dozens of cardboard boxes and hundreds of plastic bags, all coded and cross-referenced.

The police 'box system' of exhibits processing is so complex and crucial that it's part of the standard training drill at Hendon, and is required instruction for every police recruit.

The Dome job was a massive crime scene – there were no less than 700 different exhibits spread across a wide area, including parts of the Dome, the shores of the Thames, the coal yard, the JCB, the white van and the getaway boat.

On top of that there were six 'human crime scenes' – the gang members. Each suspect was a crime scene, and had to be treated as such.

As soon as the arrests were made, Detective Constable Blakebell moved in and quietly began the mammoth job of recording all the exhibits in her notes. She posted officers to stand watch at various key spots to make sure evidence was undisturbed, pending the arrival of SOCOs.

A team of police photographers armed with digital video equipment recorded Betson and his gang members as they were searched, right there at the scene.

The SOCOs soon moved in and began examining everything, lifting fingerprints and footprints, collecting DNA and blood samples to be submitted to the police laboratory.

The captured gang members were quickly swaddled in standard-issue blue forensic capes, sealing in forensic evidence.

Perhaps it was the excitement of the moment or the ammonia fumes, but for some reason Robert Adams briefly became a chatterbox and wise-cracker in captivity, despite having been cautioned by police.

'I was twelve inches from pay day,' he blurted to his captors. 'I cannot believe how easily the glass went. I only hit it twice. I almost had it in my hand! It would have been a blinding Christmas,' he lamented. 'Then that fucking mob of a hundred policemen came in and jumped on us.'

A detective cautioned Adams against making incriminating statements, but he kept babbling on.

'I just can't understand all the fuss,' he laughed. 'It was an accident – we just crashed into the Dome! They should employ me as a guide!'

'We mustn't discuss this any further,' said a detective, 'it's in your best interest.'

'What's the chances of a fag?' asked Adams.

David James and PY Gerbeau hopped off their buggy and entered the Dome.

According to James, they had a Miss World photo-call and dress rehearsal scheduled for that morning in preparation for the televised competition, which was taking place at the Dome in a few weeks.

'That day we had three whole coach loads of 96 young women being brought in from London for the rehearsal,' recalled James. 'We didn't stop it, we let it go on. It happened in the central arena, and the robbery took place in its perimeter wall.

'By now, the robbers were on the ground trussed up with binding tape,' James later recalled. At the time, he thought they looked like turkeys tied up for Christmas.

'There was a lot of blood around. They're all tied up on the ground and obviously in some distress, and meanwhile all the would-be Miss Worlds were parading off the coaches. They were all parading past us, a stream of little girls in their little costumes that they'd been told to wear for the day, advancing past a stream of police mounting armed guard over these guys on the ground. Then 96 little Miss Worlds trooped into the arena.

'It was very weird,' he recalled, describing a scene of children singing hymns in the distance, police working the crime scene, 'and the Miss Worlds all jigging up and down on their stage in the centre.

'The saddest thing of all, at the end of the day for me,' James remembered, 'was the sight of all these young girls on the centre stage, looking forward to competing as Miss World whilst on the floor trussed-up like turkeys were the criminals who were obviously going to prison for many, many years, and who had nothing left to come. No more girlfriends. And they were seeing all these girls traipse past them as they were waiting to get carted off to the slammer. I thought it was one of the saddest wastes of human endeavour that I've ever seen.'

His deputy PY Gerbeau was a bit more upbeat.

'It's another crazy day at the Dome,' he told the BBC.

One of the first reporters on the scene was Lucy Panton of the *Sunday People*. In her story, she described a scene of vivid strangeness: 'Surreally, a lost Dome acrobat wandered past in a leotard, then five men in coloured costumes appeared. I felt I was in Tellytubby land.'

Stilt-walkers, jugglers and clowns were looking on and, from somewhere in the distance, she heard a brass band playing, 'in a desperate attempt to persuade visitors nothing was wrong'.

As the Dome Raiders were led away by police at 10.45 a.m., the journalist described them as 'dazed', with each wearing 'a steely stare'.

But she would never forget the 'cocky smile and wink' offered to her through a bloodied eye by William Cockram as he passed her. Nor would she forget his last words in the Millennium Dome: 'We knew we might get caught, but at least we can say we had the balls to give it a go.'

By 11 a.m. scores of London-based reporters from all over the world were flocking to the Dome to cover the spectacular story.

Out at Tong Farm, in Kent, armed police had just arrested gang accomplice Lee Wenham as he sat in the passenger seat of a BMW.

Detective Superintendent Jon Shatford walked down a long ramp towards the gaggle of excited journalists waiting in the sunlight, accompanied only by Scotland Yard press officer Angie Evans. Shatford had prepared several worst-case statements in his mind, to try and explain things in case everything fell apart.

He was ready to resign on the spot, to apologise, to say he hadn't told his bosses everything about the operation. He had braced himself for the nightmare possibility of headlines screaming about a botched police operation gone horribly wrong, with scores of dead or wounded. He was ready to place his head on the chopping block, sacrifice himself and turn in his warrant card.

But everything had gone perfectly.

For once in his life, Shatford wasn't exactly sure what to say.

The capture of the Millennium Dome gang on 7 November 2000 was a decisive victory for Scotland Yard and the Flying Squad. The event triggered a brief cascade of worldwide media coverage, with headlines in the British press proclaiming: 'THE GREAT DOME ROBBERY', 'THE DOME IS NOT ENOUGH', and 'IT WAS JUST LIKE A BOND MOVIE'.

The six suspected Dome Raiders were taken to different police stations for questioning on the day of the raid, and charged the following day.

In press interviews, Shatford said he understood public concerns over the risks of Operation Magician. 'There were risks,' he admitted. 'We mitigated them but we could never eliminate them. The bigger risk,' he added, 'would have been to let them go free.' He explained, 'I know they would have committed equally dangerous robberies.'

When he was asked why police didn't intercept the gang before reaching the diamond vault, he answered, 'The biggest danger would have been to let them escape or frustrate them before they could commit the offence. We have to produce the best evidence. If we fail to do that we are letting the public down because we are saying it is too difficult for us, and we are letting them go and commit crimes elsewhere. The planning we went through and the result vindicates the strategy used.'

Despite some press speculation that a police informer aided the gang's capture, that was not the case.

Detective Sergeant Mark Drew later said that 'without Operation Magician, I have absolutely no doubt they would have been across the river to Bow Creek, into the van and they would have escaped.' He added, 'I think they were the best robbery team in the United Kingdom, but I think they met their match.'

Without the Scotland Yard and Kent County Constabulary investigations, there was an excellent chance that the gang would have vanished with £250 million in diamonds.

34. The Trial

The Old Bailey, Central Criminal Court, London

On 8 November 2001, the five accused members of the Millennium Dome gang went on trial for robbery at the Old Bailey. Terry Millman, the accused getaway driver, had died that summer of cancer in a Clapham hospice while awaiting trial.

The presiding justice was Michael Coombe who, at nearly seventy, was one of the Old Bailey's most senior judges. The snuff-taking, Oxford-educated Coombe was called to the Bar in 1957 and, over the years, had developed a reputation for toughness.

Since they were caught red-handed, Ray Betson, William Cockram and Aldo Ciarrocchi did not deny that they'd attempted to snatch the diamonds, but argued for the lesser crime of conspiring to commit theft, not robbery.

The difference is that theft is the dishonest appropriation of property, and does not involve harming or the threat of injuring a person. Theft carries a maximum sentence of seven years; convicted robbers can be sentenced for much longer terms.

The replacement boatman, Kevin Meredith, denied having conspired to steal or rob, and argued that he had been coerced into joining the plot. The prosecution proceeded with the more serious charge of conspiracy to rob against all five.

Martin Heslop QC led the formidable prosecution team, which included Edward Brown of Treasury Counsel and Julian Evans of Counsel.

Heslop had considerable experience with major criminal cases, as both a prosecution and defence counsel. Distinguished by a large pair of spectacles, he punctuated the air with his fingers as he laid out carefully crafted questions.

Heslop's voice was eloquent and refined, and when it reverberated off the courtroom walls it could easily send shivers down the spine of whomever he was cross-examining. Even hardened police officers were known to quiver when they had to face him in the witness box.

Heslop said of the gang, 'They were playing for very high stakes. This was no ordinary robbery. The value of the diamonds is conservatively estimated, and I will pause here, at £200 million.

'Had they succeeded, it would have ranked as the biggest robbery in the world in terms of value. It could properly be described as the robbery of the millennium.

'The operation was planned professionally, down to the last detail,' added Heslop.

In January 2002, Betson, Cockram, Ciarrocchi and Meredith each entered the witness box to tell their side of the story, excerpts of which follow.

Adams did not testify.

Betson, Cockram, and Ciarrocchi argued that they had been set up to do the crime by a Betson family friend who was a London policeman, working in league with a mysterious character named Tony who, supposedly, was a former Dome security guard. Tony in turn, they claimed, had inside agents on the Dome staff who conspired to assist the crime.

The police officer accused by Betson entered the witness box, and he categorically denied under oath any involvement with the crime, any prior knowledge of it or any knowledge of Tony.

'You told Mr Betson,' said Andrew Mitchell QC, Betson's defence counsel, 'that you had struck up a friendship with somebody you had appreciated subsequently was an acquaintance from school, that his name was Tony, that Tony was a bright man with a cunning plan to steal the Millennium Diamonds.'

'No such conversation took place,' said the police officer.

'That there were people prepared to back him,' Mitchell asserted, 'that there were money and facilities to carry out the theft available, and it was a piece of cake.'

'No such conversation took place,' maintained the policeman.

Mitchell continued, 'That Tony would, through his friends, provide and pay for everything that was necessary to carry out this job, and that the security at the Dome was crap.' He added, 'There were discussions about the possibility of getting keys to the cabinets, and was he, Ray, interested in meeting Tony?'

'No such conversation took place,' declared the officer.

'Did you know anything about the planning of this?' asked the counsel.

'No I did not,' insisted the PC.

'I suggest you knew something about a plot involving the JCB as you disclosed to Betson,' charged Mitchell. 'You told him no member of public or staff would be involved and it was a foolproof plan. You wanted to know whether he was interested.

'After you discussed this,' he added, 'in particular the importance of you keeping in the background because the authorities would be looking for an inside man, did you leave the conversation with Mr Betson saying he wanted time to think about it?'

The policeman denied it, insisting, 'No such suggestion was put to him.'

A thoroughly bizarre twist occurred soon after the policeman's testimony, when an usher found a cryptic handwritten note in the courtroom that read, 'Who will care for the widow's son?'

Fearing that the note might be a threat on the life of the police officer who testified, Justice Coombe immediately halted the trial and ordered a full inquiry. The message turned out to be a derivation of the Masonic distress call, 'Oh, Lord, my God, is there no help for the widow's son?'

In Masonic ritual, the passage is known as 'The Grand Hailing Sign of Distress', and it obliges any Mason hearing the call to come to the aid of his fellow. Betson later admitted he wrote the note when all his privileges were stopped, and he got away with it by saying it was just a joke. The trial was resumed.

In their testimony, gang members variously alluded to at least two other confederates who joined them at different stages of the plot, but they remained unidentified. Police had arrested two suspected accomplices after the failed robbery, but they were later released for lack of evidence.

Betson, Cockram, and Ciarrocchi appeared to try to charm the jury of seven women and five men by appearing as likeable rogues or cheeky cockney chappies.

In the witness box, the accused gang members argued that they intentionally did not carry guns, and that they took pains not to use violence or threaten people with force or injury. Indeed, police did not find any firearms on any gang members when they were captured.

This was a tough argument to make, however, given that they detonated smoke grenades, were armed with ammonia sprays, and were dressed in clothing that reminded at least one witness of terrorists.

On top of all this, they were travelling in a speeding, barrier-crashing piece of construction equipment.

Of the JCB, Heslop pointed out, 'It is a very large and powerful bulldozer-type vehicle – an enormous galvanised steel shovel at the front. When driven fast and with criminal intent, it's extremely frightening.'

A large number of witnesses to the attack, the prosecutors maintained, 'were absolutely terrified by what they saw', including

Dome staff, hosts and visitors – several of whom testified to this in court.

Meanwhile, Aldo Ciarrocchi clowned around by winking at reporters and pretending to tickle a guard. When asked how he felt, he testified, 'Now I'm in the dock at the Bailey, obviously completely stupid and embarrassed, really. It's just stupid, absolutely stupid.' He added, 'It seemed almost plausible at the time.'

Despite the fact that the stratospheric value of the gems had been reported in the press prior to the robbery attempt, Ciarrocchi argued that he had no idea of the magnitude of the robbery he was committing.

'No, not at all, no, no,' he testified. 'I'm not into jewellery myself and I mean, I guessed if there's an exhibition, then obviously it must be pretty special. But the first time I found out the figure was when a solicitor come to see me in Carter Street police station, and I almost fell off me stool.

'I have seen all Mr Heslop's hype,' said Ciarrocchi, 'and I've seen all the stuff in the papers and it seems like an absolute crazy James Bond nutty thing to do. At the time, I was under the impression, basically, it was like walking into a warehouse, taking something out of it and going away. It was, I would just about call it, a 'smash and grab'.

In the witness box, Ciarrocchi drew a self-portrait of an earnest young man from an underprivileged background who was keen to start a nice family life with the £50,000 he'd allegedly receive for the job.

When asked why he joined the plot, he responded, 'I can say for the money, obviously. It is obvious for no other reason. I was looking to start a family with my girl, and I mean I was brought up with no money. My mum and dad didn't have any money and I've got enough responsibility to know that if you can avoid that, it's not the best way to, you know, bring up a child. So I thought if I was financially secure, that would be the time to start a family.'

One of the reasons he signed up, Ciarrocchi claimed, was because 'Ray mentioned that his brother-in-law [the policeman] was involved, and the fact that [there was] no way anyone would get hurt, including us.' The whole operation, he thought, would be 'a piece of piss'.

Things were 'so nutty' at the Dome, that the scheme seemed plausible. 'It seemed to me like an easy thing to do,' he remembered. 'You ain't got to hurt anyone, you'd be in there for a minute or something and be gone, and that would be the end of it.'

Junior Prosecution Counsel Edward Brown challenged Ciarrocchi on the key point of the use of force, and how the gang frightened people inside the Dome.

'Have you ever been next door to a JCB that is coming towards you at speed?' asked Brown.

'Next door to?' asked the defendant, 'What, do you mean on a pushbike or something?'

Brown: 'In front of it, or just to the side of it as it is passing you or coming towards you at speed?

Ciarrocchi: 'Yeah, yeah, on a building site, yes.'

Brown: 'It is not much fun, is it?

Ciarrocchi: 'It's not much fun working on a building site.'

Brown: 'No, come on, Mr Ciarrocchi.'

Ciarrocchi: 'What are you trying to imply?'

'If a JCB was coming towards you,' asked Brown, 'you would be terrified, would you not?'

The diminutive Ciarrocchi twisted himself into a contradictory contortion: 'If a motorbike was coming towards me, I'd be terrified if it was coming towards me at speed, as you're saying. A car, a bus, anything, a lunatic on a mountain bike, anything. I wouldn't be terrified, but it'd make you think.'

'It would not terrify you?' asked Brown, 'It would make you think?'

Ciarrocchi: 'If there's someone on a pushbike coming towards me and there's a motorbike coming towards me.'

'We are talking about a JCB,' declared the counsel.

'A JCB,' Ciarrocchi granted. 'You'd think: There's a JCB coming towards me, yes.'

'Is that a serious answer?' asked Brown.

'Yes,' insisted the accused. 'You would think there's a JCB coming towards me. You might be terrified if it touched you or come right up on you, or you actually thought you was down a manhole and you couldn't get away, you'd probably be more concerned.'

Brown: 'It would probably kill you.'

Ciarrocchi: 'Well, if you're down a manhole and couldn't get away. So would a motorbike.'

Brown: 'Forget the manhole joke.'

Ciarrocchi: 'It wasn't a joke.'

When asked why he wore body armour, Ciarrocchi said he thought it was 'over the top' but in the end, why not? 'It's a billion to one chance that something may go wrong. So why not have a bit of insurance?'

'You were determined, were you not, Mr Ciarrocchi?' asked Brown.

'I was, of course I was determined,' said the accused, who invoked his affections for American fashion model and live-in girlfriend Elisabeth Kirsch. 'I wouldn't have got involved in anything that could have took away my girl if I wasn't determined. I knew I was taking a chance. I'm not stupid.'

To illustrate his non-violent personality, Ciarrocchi argued to Brown, 'I know you're trying to suggest we're all like on *The Bill*, but I'm not on the TV and not the sort of person who would run around with firearms and have shoot-outs with people.'

Ciarrocchi provoked chuckles in the courtroom following an exchange with Judge Coombe, when he described his accomplice William Cockram as 'a funny guy'.

'He's a bit of a clown, really, if I can say that without being insulting.'

Judge Coombe asked, 'a bit of a what?'

'A clown,' replied the defendant.

'You want to see him when he's had a drink, my Lord.'

'I hope I shall not see him in that position,' dead-panned the judge.

One of Ciarrocchi's most colourful outbursts came when he described his moment of capture by agreeing with the account of a witness. It wasn't an eloquent oration, but it got the point across.

'You got to remember it's fourteen months ago and I was shitting myself,' announced Ciarrocchi. 'And I ain't got a great recollection, but my memory has been jogged by the videos, and the videos go along exactly with what he said as far as me shitting myself, and I ain't proud of shitting myself – but I did.'

In the witness box, William Cockram was alternately defiant, argumentative and jocular, leading prosecutor Martin Heslop at one point to comment on his 'laughing and joking'.

'I am a bit excitable, Your Honour,' Cockram told Judge Coombe, 'I do get like that.'

'All right,' said the judge, 'calm down.'

'I'm not a complete imbecile,' Cockram pointed out.

Cockram openly admitted his long friendship with career criminals Betson and Millman, and admitted to a string of criminal offences of his own dating back to 1970.

But he argued that he drew a firm line against armed robbery. 'I have never done an armed robbery,' Cockram testified. 'The difference is with armed robbery you get twenty years, and theft you only get eight years. There's no way I would have entertained an armed robbery.

'I wouldn't threaten anybody,' Cockram insisted. 'I'm not that kind of person.'

Sticking to the gang's account that they'd been manipulated into doing an inside job, Cockram said, 'If there had been no inside help, I wouldn't have even entertained it. The fact there was inside help, I knew that there was going to be nobody there.'

The sight of the lightly defended diamonds, Cockram remembered in the witness box, was irresistible: 'I'd seen the cabinets and I couldn't believe the security on the cabinets. So I had to go for it. It was a chance in a lifetime, really. Nobody was going to get hurt. There was no one there to hurt.'

'The Dome was always empty,' Cockram declared, despite the fact that many thousands of people were appearing there each day as its life drew to a close. 'That's why it went skint, Your Honour.

'The actual job would have gone sweet as a nut,' he recalled wistfully. 'I just couldn't believe how simple it was. I couldn't sleep at night. I just used to think about it and I thought, this can't be true. It's a gift, you know.'

Cockram claimed that he had fairly modest financial ambitions for the crime: 'Well, they could have been worth a trillion dollars to me. I could never have sold them diamonds. I was on wages. The £100,000, that is all I was interested in, paying me mortgage off and buying a new car.'

He explained how he came up with the insight of using the Hilti gun: 'I'm in the building trade, Your Honour, so I know about glass and stuff like that. Plus I've been in burglary and I know about windows.'

Cockram maintained that boatman Kevin Meredith had misunderstood what he'd said at the Brighton marina on 4 November 2000. What Meredith remembered as a threat to 'remember your wife and kids' wasn't a threat at all, said Cockram, but an offer of cash that would enable Meredith to take his family 'on a nice holiday'.

When Cockram was asked why the gang used body armour, he testified that it was for their protection at the cash exchange with the buyers, whom they'd 'never trusted'. He asked rhetorically, 'Well, they shoot people for anything nowadays, don't they?'

The whole crime, Cockram speculated, was being organised and directed by the mysterious Tony character, with the possible help of a police informer. The gang had been 'grassed up' he declared. Tony 'may have been a policeman, for all I know,' he said.

Cockram even ventured a physical description of Tony, a creature who police doubted even existed. 'He was about, I suppose, six foot,' said Cockram, 'maybe six foot one, quite muscular, a bit like Vinnie Jones, that type of build, sort of short-ish hair . . . like a modern haircut, you know, where they have, sort of, gel?' Tony had a tan, he said, and seemed a 'nice enough guy'.

The rest of Cockram's testimony was sprinkled with avuncular asides and quips that sometimes had even the police smirking.

He explained his zipper-pocket plan for carrying the diamonds: 'I didn't want to lose them if I was jumping in the boat and one fell out; you know, it would be upsetting for me and the boys.'

As soon as he heard the cries of 'armed police' prior to his arrest, he remembered, 'I dived on the floor a bit lively, I can tell you.'

'Stink bombs?' Cockram asked indignantly at one point in his testimony. 'I'd be slung out of the underworld. I don't know nothing about stink bombs.'

Commenting on Kevin Meredith's statement to police that Cockram had coerced him into the plot, Cockram scoffed to prosecuting barrister Martin Heslop, 'Cock and bull, sir, isn't it?'

To testimony from eyewitnesses that the JCB seemed out of control, Cockram exclaimed, 'It's all balderdash ... What are you trying to say – to be frightened of a JCB digger? For God's sake, I work on a building site. I've seen them all the time.'

Heslop persisted: 'Imagine this, please. The JCB pulls up at a vault and out jump three men, all wearing gas masks. Just imagine that, please?'

In the witness box, Cockram responded with a weak attempt at humour: 'You're not suggesting I'm kinky now as well, are you?'

To evidence that in the first hour of the Dome's opening there would have been at least 500 to 600 members of the public on the premises, Cockram said 'Balderdash, absolute balderdash.'

'This is just a farce, Mr Cockram, is it not?' asked Heslop. 'You go into what seems to have been the biggest attempt to rob in the world?'

'Still,' noted Cockram.

'Being organised,' the barrister added, 'by a man whose last name you do not even know?'

Cockram: 'It's obvious now he's grassed us up, isn't it? That's why he never told us his second name.'

Heslop: 'Does Tony exist?'

'Well,' asked the accused, 'who was driving the white van, then?'

Heslop: 'I do not know, you tell me?'

'I told you,' said the defendant. 'It's Tony.'

Heslop asked, 'Does he feature anywhere in a way that he can be identified on any of the video material we have on the case?'

'Quite conveniently he doesn't,' replied Cockram. 'That's why we're here, isn't it?' he said, trying to raise the spectre of a police informant. 'It is strange how he disappeared with 140 policemen around, and just drives off into the wild blue yonder. No wonder they called this Operation Magician.'

In fact, police did not know the driver's identity.

Cockram seemed untroubled by stirrings of modesty or contrition.

As the video played in the courtroom of Betson charging into the Dome, Cockram noted admiringly, 'He drove very well, actually, didn't he?'

'We didn't do bad,' he said at one point, remembering his speedy penetration of the De Beers diamond cases despite wearing body armour. 'Twenty-seven seconds.

'We would have got away with it,' he declared, 'but for the fact there were 140 police waiting for us.

'Was I proud of what I did?' Cockram asked the court. 'I would have been proud of myself if we had got the diamonds.'

By far the smoothest performance in the witness box, thought Shatford, was given by Betson. His demeanour was calm, reasonable and conversational and, unlike Ciarrocchi and Cockram, he stayed cool and unrattled throughout almost all his testimony.

In fact, Shatford marvelled that Betson seemed to be the most self-assured criminal he'd ever seen. He thought he saw Betson even throw a wink at a female juror at one point, but he couldn't be sure.

In the box, Ray Betson denied being a robber, either armed or unarmed, and testified that he had never been accused of violence.

He freely admitted that he was a 'very successful' career criminal who had rarely worked an honest day in his life and had engaged in various smuggling operations, among other crimes.

Betson asserted that he was supposed to be paid £500,000 for the Dome raid.

To demonstrate Betson's career-long penchant for deceit, prosecutor Martin Heslop asked him, 'Do you accept that you are an elaborate deceiver by occupation?'

'I accept that I'm a criminal, yes,' said Betson.

'You are a professional criminal?'

'Yes.'

'And a very successful professional criminal, by your own confession?'

'Yes.'

'Your particular expertise involves, amongst other things, deceiving people, does it not?'

'With the traveller's cheques, yes.'

'Deceiving people?'

'Yes,' agreed Betson. 'I make no bones about it. You are 100 per cent right, yes.'

'Your particular involvement in crime is all about dishonesty and conning people into what you are representing?'

'Yes.'

'You are a past master at it, Mr Betson, are you not? That is why you have been so successful.'

Betson countered, 'It doesn't necessarily follow that everything I say is trying to deceive someone.'

The gang decided 'We wasn't getting involved in violence,' he explained. 'We're not callous people and also the bird would have been so outrageous as well, and of course there was no need for it in any case.

'Given all the information and all the help we was supposed to have had,' Betson claimed, 'I didn't really think there was anything that could go wrong.'

Betson's reasonableness even extended to his granting the prosecution some points.

During cross-examination on 10 January, Heslop asked him, 'Do you accept the evidence given in this case about the JCB that, as it drove through the Dome, it was very frightening, with the bucket up; it appeared as if it was out of control, as if somebody had gone off their rocker? Do you accept the evidence from the witnesses that that's how it appeared to them?'

'I've got a mixed view, to be honest, on the witnesses that came forward and the testimony that they gave,' Betson replied. 'There was a couple of middle-aged ladies who I felt were sincere and genuine, and they seemed that they was shaken up and they was frightened.

'All I can say is that wasn't in our plan,' he claimed. 'I didn't envisage that was going to happen. I didn't drive directly towards them. I couldn't see them at the time and I'm sorry that that was the case. But obviously that wasn't what we agreed to do. That wasn't what we thought would happen. We thought the area was going to be empty.'

There was another witness, who Betson said 'looked like Jennifer Lopez' and who had said she was 'terrified' during the attack. 'Then,' recalled Betson, 'she said that she was at a bus stop three months later and she saw another JCB and was terrified all over again. I mean, she deserves some sort of Academy Award, really.'

Justice Coombe asked, 'You think she was making it all up?'

'Yes,' said Betson. 'I think she was hamming it up to the ceiling. Why would I want to hurt anybody?

'You know, I'm not a callous person. That wasn't my motivation. My main motivation was trying to get the stones as quickly and as smoothly as possible.'

Betson had an explanation ready for the question of why the escape speedboat was equipped with a 25-litre container filled with petrol. He said the boat's tank had been topped up during the gang's trial runs, and the container had just been left in the boat.

With a colourful illustration, Betson rejected the idea that the gang would have blown up the boat.

'If this had been a real deal and we had got over to Bow Creek,' Betson testified, 'we was home and dry, if you excuse the pun. Now, to set fire to that amount of petrol, and bearing in mind the boat has an outboard engine and there's just rubber pipes going down to underneath the floor of the boat, and that's where the tank was housed and that was completely topped up, I think that was 90 per cent full of petrol. I mean, you are talking now ridiculous amounts of petrol.

'We have in theory accomplished the job,' he added, we've got the stones and no one's been hurt and everything's hunky dory. All of a sudden, you want to set fire to this boat? It'd be like a bad night in Vietnam.'

Judge Coombe interjected, 'Sorry?'

'It'd be like a bad night in Vietnam when the war was on.'

The justice said, 'I see.'

'You'd have a plume of flames going up,' Betson concluded, 'and the boat would explode and it would be like something out of a war movie, and the amount of attention that would attract, it would be just stupid for us to do that.'

On the question of why the gang used a JCB, Betson explained, 'There wasn't supposed to be anyone there, and what we was told was they (the Dome) had their own JCB, or used JCBs in there. So the post needed to be knocked down. So we needed something like that, and it became the perfect machine to use again because you could get close up the approach road. A lot of building work was going on, and no one would take any notice of it, and in itself it was not out of place in the Dome.'

When prosecutor Heslop asked if the gang had planned for the possibility of the JCB being delayed on its journey, Betson seemed to lose his patience, asking, 'Did you think I was going to stop for a sandwich or something? How would I be delayed? Come on. You put the question. How would I be delayed? I wasn't going to stop, was I? I wasn't going to pull up and have a chat with the fellows over there.'

At one point in his testimony, after Betson said he couldn't identify an unnamed black accomplice, Betson got so tangled up in his own story that Judge Coombe accused him of perjury.

Martin Heslop moved in for the kill, asking the defendant, 'Did you realise that you were lying through your teeth?'

'Of course I did, yeah,' said Betson.

Judge Coombe stepped in to clarify: 'You did just now lie to the jury?

'Yes,' he admitted. 'In order to protect him, yes.'

Coombe said, 'Just pause there, Mr Betson. "Of course I realise I was lying to the jury in order to protect the black man?"'

When Betson agreed, Coombe announced, 'Now the jury have heard you admit perjury.' Coombe declined, however, to formally charge Betson over the incident.

In his testimony on 9 January, Betson tried to explain why he crashed the JCB into the Dome.

He alleged that on the day of the robbery attempt, there were 'inside men' positioned inside the Dome, dressed as Dome staff, who were co-ordinating his arrival. He later alleged that he was in radio communication with them that day.

It was a story that was unsupported by any evidence or eyewitness testimony.

'Indeed there was someone standing there, as arranged, on the right-hand side,' Betson claimed. 'They had a radio. I done a left and I see that the shutter was closed.'

This dismayed him, Betson said.

'I was making an on-the-spot decision, but I wasn't making a reckless decision because the machine was going so slow and because there was no one at all in that area and I could see to the left of the shutter. I could see to the right of the shutter. I could see through the shutter . . . the arrangement was that one of the yellow coats should be standing just to the left of the shutter, where he was in position, and just back a bit.'

This person, Betson alleged, was waving him into the Dome and shouting 'Clear – come straight through.'

Defence Counsel Mitchell asked, 'What led you to go through the shutter, rather than pull out because it was shut?'

'Because,' Betson explained, 'I thought it was safe to go through it as there was no one there to be injured, and because I further thought there was no one in there because the guy who was supposed to be working with us was there, and he was encouraging me to do so.'

'You are in,' said Mitchell. 'Did you chase people down the pathway leading to the jewellery exhibition?'

Betson agreed that it might have looked that way, but said he thought instead that he was being escorted into the building by two Dome workers in the yellow and black kit that Dome hosts wore.

'One of them again made a gesture to me, like a waving forward gesture, and then they started running in front of the machine. I suppose they was about twenty foot in front of the machine, slightly over to the left, not in my direct path, and my understanding was that they were running me in.'

Judge Coombe asked, 'Your what, sorry?' Referring presumably to the two police officers who in fact had been guarding this area, and were now running for their lives, Betson said with a straight face, 'They was actually running me in, your Lordship. They was with me. This was part and parcel of the inside help.'

Defence counsel Mitchell, apparently reflecting Betson's line of being grassed up and manipulated by unseen forces, noted, 'In one sense, that is exactly what happened.'

'Well, yes,' agreed Betson.

'They was running me in. Yeah, I didn't get the joke myself.'

In his testimony, Betson speculated that the Flying Squad orchestrated the crime as a PR operation.

'I suppose for the robbery squad this is like one of the biggest things they've ever been involved in,' he said. 'It's something that will give them a lot of kudos. Perhaps they were shortly to be disbanded. I don't know, because they don't do a lot nowadays.'

This line of thinking provoked an odd series of flippant replies by Betson to questions put by his defence counsel.

Mitchell: 'Did you tell the police that you were going to the Dome on 1 September?'

'Yeah,' said Betson. 'I phoned them up and I told them.'

Mitchell: 'Did you tell the police that you were going to try and steal the Millennium diamonds on 6 October?

Betson: 'Of course I did, yes.'

Mitchell: 'Did you tell them you were going to try and steal them on 6 November?'

Betson: 'I am being facetious.'

Mitchell: 'Did you make sure they were already in place and armed and ready to strike?'

Betson: 'There's nothing that I'd like to do more than be standing here now.'

Betson insisted in the witness box that he'd been roped into the Dome raid through his family friend and de-facto brother-in-law, the police officer, working in league with 'Tony'.

'He told me the complete skeleton plan in a few sentences,' said Betson. 'I had every confidence in him. I thought there was no way he would fit me up. If it had come to me from anyone else I probably wouldn't have entertained it, but he was more or less my family.'

When prosecution counsel Martin Heslop asked Betson about the identity of the elusive Tony, the defendant responded, 'It may not be his real name.'

Heslop asked, 'It may not be? You meet with this man and you discuss an operation to steal the diamonds over a substantial number of months, yes?'

'Yes,' said Betson.

'You never discover his name?' Heslop asked, 'his last name?'

'That's not odd at all,' reported Betson. 'As you already pointed out, and I did myself. I am crooked, and that is not odd at all in the crooked world. You don't ask people for surnames.'

The last defendant to testify was Meredith, the gang's getaway skipper.

In his testimony, Meredith maintained that he had been coerced into the plot by Cockram's threat to harm his wife and children. He said he'd never been to the Dome and knew nothing about the diamonds until after he was arrested.

Meredith described himself as having been in 'a nightmare', and in states of shock, panic, fear and devastation around the time of the Dome raid.

35. The Verdict

The Old Bailey, London

On 18 February 2002 at the Old Bailey, after a three-month trial and 35 hours of deliberations, the jury, by a majority 10–2 vote, rejected the defendants' arguments and found Betson, Cockram, Ciarrocchi and Adams guilty of conspiracy to commit robbery.

Betson and Cockram were sentenced to eighteen years each.

Ciarrocchi and Adams were sentenced to fifteen years each.

The jury unanimously found Kevin Meredith guilty of conspiracy to steal. He was given five years. The judge called Meredith's argument that he was acting under duress 'pathetic'.

Addressing the defendants, Judge Michael Coombe said, 'This was a very well-planned and premeditated attempt to rob De Beers of what would have been the most gigantic sum in English legal history – or any other, for that matter.'

Describing the Dome plot as 'a wicked and highly professional crime', the judge told the defendants, 'You played for very high stakes, and you must have known perfectly well what the penalty would be if your enterprise did not succeed.'

Detective Superintendent Jon Shatford announced that he was 'delighted' by the verdicts and sentences. 'They are ruthless, dangerous criminals with no care for anybody,' he told the press. 'Had the police not intervened it's likely there would have been schoolchildren there who could have been seriously injured.'

In contrast to the tone of some press reports that portrayed the gang as 'Dim Raiders' and comically inept 'geezers', Shatford argued that 'They deserve nobody's glorification,' adding that 'if it had not been for the police, they would have driven through children and spectators and this would have been a very different story – society can do with a rest from these people.

'These people have no scruples whatsoever,' he concluded. 'I think they deserve to be in prison for a very long time.'

In a separate case at the Old Bailey that month, accused gang accomplice Lee Wenham was sentenced to nine years after pleading guilty to participating in conspiracy in the attempted Securicor cash-in-transit robbery at Aylesford, in July 2000.

Prosecuting counsel Martin Heslop said that Wenham 'played a knowing part in the preparation for the Aylesford attempted robbery, and in the reconnaissance and preparations for the Dome', but he was not a key organiser. Wenham was also sentenced to a concurrent four years after pleading guilty to conspiracy to steal in connection with the Dome plot.

It is important to note that, while the Nine Elms and Aylesford investigations led police to the Dome plot, Raymond Betson, William Cockram and Aldo Ciarrocchi have not been charged with either the Nine Elms or Aylesford crimes, nor any other crimes beyond those they admitted to in the witness box during the Dome trial.

In May 2001, British and Spanish police on the Costa del Sol arrested the gang's alleged accomplice known as The Boatman. He spent 10 months in a high-security prison near Madrid pending extradition but, four days before the extradition hearing, the Crown Prosecution Service dropped the case due to a lack of evidence.

In February 2002, William Cockram's wife Pauline told journalist Lucy Panton of the *Sunday People* that Cockram had re-mortgaged their house to help fund the Dome raid, leaving her penniless. 'I have no money and no husband,' she said, 'but at least I won't be constantly tearing my hair out wondering what Bill is going to do next.'

'They deserved to go down for what they did,' she declared. 'It was madness, and I don't know how they thought they were ever going to get away with it.'

Aldo Ciarrocchi's girlfriend seemed much more forgiving. Elisabeth Kirsch, the American fashion model with whom Ciarrocchi was living at the time of the Dome raid, devotedly attended the trial and visited him in his new home in South London, Belmarsh prison, where he took up residence as a category A, high-risk prisoner along with Betson and Cockram.

Immediately after the trial, Kirsch gave an interview to journalist Angela Levin of the *Daily Mail*, who described Kirsch as joining 'a long line of daughters from good backgrounds who seem terminally attracted to criminals and chancers'.

Kirsch told Levin that, while in prison, Ciarrocchi asked her to marry him by pulling the ring from a can of Coke, kneeling down and loudly proposing. Struck by his thoughtfulness, she said 'Yes', and some tears flowed from witnesses in the visiting room. It was the third anniversary of their relationship.

'The sweet, well-educated woman,' wrote Levin, was 'not the first and no doubt will not be the last young woman who has chosen to waste her life on a villain – a life that will probably be lonely, seedy and cut off from family and friends.'

'Some people say he doesn't deserve me,' Kirsch admitted, 'but I know how happy he makes me.' Ciarrocchi's crime, she maintained, 'doesn't outweigh all the good in him.' She predicted that the Dome raid would be his last crime.

Robert Adams died in prison of a heart attack later in 2002, after his conviction.

In January 2004, the Court of Appeal in London rejected moves by Betson and Cockram to challenge their convictions on the basis that Judge Coombe nodded off during the original trial, among other grounds.

The two prisoners had tried to challenge their convictions for conspiracy to rob, which they asserted should have been for the lesser offence of conspiracy to steal.

Former judge Michael Coombe, who was by now 73 years old and retired, did admit to nodding off during the final speech of Betson's defence counsel, but denied snoring. One witness, a BBC employee, said the judge appeared to fall asleep six times, as well as snore, and added that 'on one occasion his head fell so far forward as to be almost in contact with the table.'

Another witness, a solicitor's clerk, reported that when she saw a juror doze off, she looked over to Judge Coombe to see if he had noticed. 'Unfortunately he hadn't, as he was asleep himself.' She added, 'He would actually slump in his chair and fall asleep. It seemed to her that 'the sound of his own snoring would eventually wake him up.'

Raymond Betson's defence counsel Edmund Romilly granted that 'anyone can be forgiven for momentary lapses of concentration,' but argued that Coombe's alleged snoring raised the impression that the judge 'had such a dim view of Betson's case that he could not be bothered to stay awake.'

'It is perfectly plain that judges should not fall asleep,' said Lord Justice Rose of the Court of Appeal as he ruled against Betson and Cockram's challenge of their convictions. 'It doesn't matter whether he was snoring or not. If he was dozing off, he wasn't paying the attention he ought to have been.' The court found that this mistake did not prejudice the defendants, or render the convictions unsafe.

The Court of Appeal did, however, respond positively to challenges made by Betson, Cockram and Ciarrocchi against their sentences as being too excessive. In quashing the original sentences, Lord Justice Rose stated that the court should have had particular regard to the fact that 'firearms were not carried, still less used' in the crime.

The gang, the justice found, did not use 'ruthless violence' in the raid. 'Although ammonia, which can be harmful, was carried, firearms, which can be lethal, were not,' he stated.

Betson and Cockram had their sentences reduced from eighteen years to fifteen, and Ciarrocchi's sentence was cut from fifteen years to twelve. And in January 2004, Meredith was released from prison on parole.

'I just want to put it all behind me and lay it to rest,' he said after his release. 'It is all in the past.'

The identity of the gang accomplice who drove the white escort van towards the Dome on 7 November 2000 is unknown. That vehicle was never recovered.

No evidence of the Tony character, as described by the gang, ever surfaced.

The identities of the Money Men who were supposed to rendezvous with the gang after the robbery, if they ever existed, are unknown. Some fragmentary clues pointed towards the possible involvement of Russian mafia figures, but the clues were not conclusive.

The identity of the intended buyer of the De Beers Millennium Star and Millennium Jewels, if such a person ever existed, is unknown to this day.

Epilogue

To Catch a Star

The imminent scheduled closure of the Millennium Dome triggered renewed public interest in the attraction, and visitor numbers picked up in December 2000.

A final total of 6.5 million people visited the Dome during the year it was open. It was a gigantic number for any exhibition, but it was barely half the projected break-even number of 12 million.

A plague of rats overran the management offices of the Dome in the weeks after the diamond raid, prompting Chairman David James to install four large rat traps in his office. An anonymous Dome official quipped to *The Times*, 'I suspect they moved in when they realised that there were not enough humans to scare them away.'

Prime Minister Tony Blair visited the site of his £1 billion pet project only once after its opening, on 19 December, to thank Dome employees. He had already admitted that the Dome had 'not been the success we hoped'.

The Prime Minister boarded the Jubilee Line to get to the Dome, but a fuse blew out that section of the Underground, forcing him to switch to a car and then to another tube train.

At the Dome, Blair graciously hailed those who worked the entrance gates and security guards for their hard work despite constant press ridicule of the attraction, earning their sustained applause and calls like 'Thanks for sticking with us, Tone!'

According to David James, Blair telephoned him in mid-December to ask if the Dome could stay open awhile. 'Look,' James quoted the PM as saying, 'the figures have improved greatly, the numbers of people coming through are at an all-time high for the whole year. Why don't we give it a few more months?'

However, the Dome's executives calculated that it would still burn up an unacceptably large amount of cash if it stayed open, and they went ahead with plans to put the exhibition out of its misery on 31 December.

Epilogue

The Millennium Dome closed permanently as scheduled on 31 December 2000 after a year of poor attendance and savage press ridicule. Dome managers had hoped to hold a big New Year's bash for 20,000 people but, in keeping with the Dome's chronic history of bad luck, a tube strike was threatened and the party was cancelled. And then the strike was cancelled.

On the last day of its life, a capacity crowd of 27,000 people came to the site, including Prime Minister Blair's wife Cherie and their three eldest children, and Lord Falconer, the minister in charge of the Dome. Mrs Blair said she thought the Dome was 'fantastic'. Prime Minister Blair stayed at home, babysitting his youngest son, Leo.

A shower of ticker-tape fell upon the Dome's Chief Executive Pierre-Yves Gerbeau as he took the stage amid exploding fireworks, and a standing ovation, at the climax of the 999th and final show in the Dome's centre stage.

A little after 7 p.m., PY Gerbeau pulled the metal shutters down for the last time.

One of the last visitors, a 39-year-old, John Ryan, declared, 'I am appalled at this enormous waste of money on a very boring attraction. I will go out applauding its closure.'

As if the Dome hadn't suffered enough already, in 2002 it was named the 'Ugliest Building' in the world in a *Forbes* magazine poll of leading architects and critics.

In achieving the top spot on the list of 'greatest architectural atrocities', the Dome beat such powerful contenders as the Rock 'n' Roll Hall of Fame in Cleveland, Ohio, and London's Barbican Centre.

'It would be hard not to hate a building with a $1.25 billion price tag and a pretentious name like the Millennium Dome,' wrote *Forbes*, dismissing the structure as a 'space-odyssey novelty act'.

In the Dome's defence, The Royal Institute of British Architects president-elect George Ferguson said, 'I don't understand how architects can look at the building and say it's ugly. It is an elegant structure and a brilliant piece of engineering.'

Pierre Gerbeau no longer wishes to talk about the Dome, and refuses all requests for interviews on the subject. Today he is Chief Executive of X-Leisure, an entertainment and sports company based in London.

David James went on to become Chairman of the Racecourse Holdings Trust, and was appointed by the Conservative Party to conduct a major survey of Government waste. So far, he reports that he's found £20 billion. And he's just started.

Today, the corpse of the Dome stands empty at its desolate outpost on the Thames. Various schemes for redevelopment of the site have been discussed, including the announcement in the press in mid July 2004 that it is to be transformed into a casino and 600-bed hotel, set to rival anything in Las Vegas, but, as of going to press, no plans have been finalised, and its future is uncertain.

The Flying Squad had a final surprise in store for the Dome Raiders: the glittering object nestled in the centre display case of the De Beers Jewel House at the Dome was not the De Beers Millennium Star. It was a fake.

The real Millennium Star never returned to the Dome after it was smuggled out in a Flying Squad gun ship on 1 September. In its place since that day was the exquisite replica made of plastic and Zircon. The near-perfect copy was created by Nir Livnat of The Steinmetz Group, the same designer who supervised the creation of the actual Millennium Star. The fake was so realistic that it even fooled some of Livnat's colleagues.

'I think it would have been absolutely silly to have allowed the real McCoy diamond to be sitting there knowing full well that we knew an attack was imminent,' said former De Beers security director Tim Thorn.

'Early on,' remembered Dome chairman David James in 2004, 'I had a conversation with De Beers to ask how they stood on it. They were quite relaxed because they had never brought the diamond back to us after taking it away for the exhibition in Japan. All of this was because they were trying to steal a bit of plastic.'

When the gang broke into the vault on 7 November 2000, the real Millennium Star was sitting not in the shattered display case, but in the highly secure De Beers master vault in the City of London. On that day, however, tens of millions of pounds worth of diamonds actually *were* on display inside the De Beers Jewel House, inches from the robbers' noses: the authentic, eleven blue Millennium Jewels, which were never replaced with decoys.

The De Beers exhibit in the Millennium Dome was closed immediately after the robbery attempt and became a crime scene. It never re-opened.

The Millennium Star was sold by De Beers to its affiliated company De Beers LV, a new global jewellery retail joint venture with luxury conglomerate LVMH Group, makers of Louis Vuitton. This extraordinary diamond is now kept in a very secure place in the centre of London. There have not been any further attempts to relieve the company of its most dazzling creation.

It was later displayed at the launch of the new De Beers LV stores in

London and Japan, and is being used to celebrate the opening of the first De Beers LV location in New York, in 2005.

'It will continue to be the flagship diamond of the De Beers brand, and the inspiration behind all of the diamonds which we select,' says De Beers' LV executive Andrew Coxon, 'because, unlike all of the other famous and important diamonds in the world, the De Beers Millennium Star was cut for maximum beauty, not for maximum weight.'

A hair-raising episode did occur though, in 2002, when supermodel Imam wore the Millennium Star for an Amfar Charity Dinner during the Cannes Film Festival.

The diamond triggered a sudden surge of over thirty photographers, causing Imam to teeter backwards off of a 6-inch-high platform. Luckily she fell into the arms of cheering photographers and emerged with her dignity, and the Millennium Star, fully intact.

Unlike other great jewels, like the supposedly cursed Hope Diamond and Koh-i-noor Diamond, the De Beers Millennium Star seems destined to be a lucky stone.

In August 2002, De Beers Diamond Trading Company President, Anthony Oppenheimer, presented the replica diamond to Metropolitan Police Commissioner Sir John Stevens, to be donated to the Met's Crime Museum in New Scotland Yard.

Mr Oppenheimer said, 'We are proud to have been able to co-operate in an undercover operation of such meticulous planning and professionalism.' He added, 'Of course we are also extremely grateful the real diamonds were kept safe.'

In accepting the gift on behalf of Scotland Yard, the Commissioner said, 'The replica Millennium Star will act as a reminder of one of our most successful operations, and I'm delighted to receive it on behalf of the brave and dedicated officers.' Stevens said of the attempted heist, 'Their efforts to pull off one of the largest robberies in the world in broad daylight were utterly audacious, and worthy of a James Bond film plot.'

In February 2003, the Metropolitan Police veterans of the Millennium Dome operation were honoured in a Commendation Ceremony at Scotland Yard, and were given certificates by London Metropolitan Police Commissioner, Sir John Stevens. Over a dozen officers from the Flying Squad, SO11 and SO19 were honoured.

They included Detective Inspector John Swinfield, Detective Sergeant Mark Drew (now Detective Inspector), Detective Constable Sean Allen, Inspector Mark Williams, Detective Constable Gill Blakebell, Sergeant Clive Rew, Sergeant Mark Adams, Press Officer

Angie Evans, Detective Sergeant Jools Lloyd, Detective Constable David Michael Hayward (now Sergeant), Detective Constable Carol Brockelsby, Detective Constable Barry Adams, Detective Inspector Gary Kibbey, Detective Constable John Wood, and Detective Constable Christopher Bishop, as well as Jon Shatford.

Shatford has since been promoted to Detective Chief Superintendent and is now in charge of homicide investigations for north and east London.

De Beers is still the world's leading trader of rough diamonds, but in response to pressure from government regulators in Europe and the US it has recently modernised its business practices to allow for more competition. De Beers is also taking a leadership role in trying to stop the worldwide trade in African 'conflict diamonds' that has helped fuel bloody rebellions in places like the Democratic Republic of Congo, birthplace of the Millennium Star.

In 1997, the nation of Zaire, birthplace of the Millennium Star, changed its name back to the Democratic Republic of Congo. In recent years, the country has collapsed far deeper into a seemingly endless cycle of rebellion, invasions, corruption, starvation and lawlessness.

For security reasons, De Beers has not identified the name of the small African village that discovered the fabulously large gem that became the Millennium Star.

Right after the sale, according to De Beers' executive Andrew Coxon, the villagers 'were harassed by others wishing to share in their good fortune, but all was not lost and the whole village prospered, although not in any way that would attract unwelcome attention.'

'We continue to keep our promise to protect their identity and keep silent about how much we paid them,' says Coxon, 'but we are able to confirm that they kept in touch with De Beers for years afterwards, and they were all still smiling.'

It has been reported that De Beers set up a bank account for the villagers to store their windfall, and that every so often a delegation flies to London to pick up the interest on their millions.

One final enigma lingers around the story of the diamond.

According to experts who examined the Millennium Star in its original rough state, its shape indicated that it could be a fragment that had broken off from a much bigger stone.

Today, somewhere in central Africa, nestled in the soil of an alluvial riverbed, the world's most enormous perfect diamond may be waiting to be discovered.

Acknowledgements

We thank our editor Kerri Sharp and her colleagues at Virgin Books; and our agents at William Morris: Mel Berger, Lucinda Prain and Katy McCaffrey.

We also thank Naomi Moriyama, Marilou Doyle, Nir Livnat of The Steinmetz Group, Tom Moses of the Gemological Institute of America, Mates Witriol, David James, Lesley Coldham of De Beers, Andrew Coxon of De Beers LV, Rachelle Rahme, Ashley Schlaifer, Jesse Selwyn, Wayne Furman, Professor Lawrence Taylor of the University of Tennessee and Eric Lupfer.

Source Notes

The primary sources for this book are Jon Shatford's personal experience of the investigations into the Nine Elms, Aylesford and Millennium Dome crimes, and his memory of the dialogue and events that transpired. Also, the January 2002 trial testimony of Raymond Betson, William Cockram, Aldo Ciarrocchi and Kevin Meredith at the Old Bailey.

The stories of the Millennium Dome and of the attempted robbery were covered extensively in the British press, and the coverage of the BBC, *Independent*, *The Times*, *Daily Express*, *Daily Mail*, *Evening Standard*, *Daily Telegraph*, *Sun*, *Mirror*, *Guardian*, *Scotsman*, *Financial Times* and Reuters was especially useful in our research. Unless noted below, the biographical details of Betson, Cockram, Ciarrocchi and Meredith, and the source for their thoughts, actions and the dialogue between them, is their trial testimony. Additional sources are listed below.

'It seemed unfathomable': Wilkie Collins, *The Moonstone: A Romance*, The Modern Library (New York, 2001), p. 67.

'the docking station': 'Kitch Report', *Time Asia*, 15 November 1999.

'a giant mushroom': 'London's Celebration Flaws', *Scottish Daily Record*, 4 January 2000.

'a very bad hair transplant': *Baddiel and Skinner Unplanned*, ITV, 7 June 2000.

Prince Charles's quotes and opinions on Millennium Dome: Christopher Morgan, 'Charles says Dome is a "Monstrous Blancmange"', *Sunday Times*, 16 January 2000. A spokesman for the Prince soon issued a kind of 'non-denial-denial' of this story, calling it a 'speculative report based on anonymous sources'.

Prince Charles on Millennium Eve: Reuters, 1 January 2000.

'a triumph of confidence': Maureen Johnson, 'Swinging Bridge is Latest London Millennium Bug', Associated Press, 14 June 2000.

Millennium Eve in London: Christopher Leake, Fiona Barton and Dan

Bridgett, 'The Queues that Barely Moved', *Mail on Sunday*, 2 January 2000; Maureen Johnson, 'Swinging Bridge is Latest London Millennium Bug', Associated Press, 14 June 2000; Paran Balakrishnan, 'Real Fireworks Begin on Dome Disaster', *Business Standard*, 8 January 2000; 'The Dome: From Conception to Birth', *BBC News*, 6 February 2000.

'It was like launching': 'Special Report: Our Year at the Dome', *Guardian*, 28 December 2000.

'the largest perfect diamond': Tania Branigan, 'Dome Raid: Star of £200m Collection Replaced by Crystal Copy', *Guardian*, 19 February 2002.

'arguably the most beautiful': 'The History of Diamonds in South Africa', *Birmingham Post*, 8 February 2003.

Livnat's experience: William Doyle interview with Nir Livnat, 3 February 2004.

'When you cut a diamond': William Doyle interview with Mates Witriol, 3 February 2004.

Oppenheimer quotes: undated video interview of Harry Oppenheimer posted on De Beers' corporate website ('History of Diamonds, Millennium Star' section), 2003.

'the most spectacular collection': 'Diamond Gang Betrayed by Informer', *BBC News*, 18 February 2002.

The Nine Elms attack was also detailed in these two articles: John Steele, 'Police Picked Up Scent Next to Battersea Dogs Home', *Daily Telegraph*, 19 February 2002; Justin Davenport and Paul Cheston, 'Only Seconds from Biggest Heist Ever', *Evening Standard*, 18 February 2002.

Datatrak background is from publicly available sources. London crime statistics and police structure: Metropolitan Police Service website. The figure of 1 million crimes a year is from the 1999-2003 crime statistics posted on the website, and represents total 'notifiable offences', crimes that are required to be reported to the Home Office.

Adrian Smales quotes: Louise Powell, 'The Real Sweeney', *Police Review*, 7 November 2003.

Police Federation report: Doug Kempster, 'Man who Will Save the Yard', *Sunday Mirror*, 8 August 1999.

McAvoy spotted by *Mirror*: Tim Luckett, '£27m Man Freed', *Sunday Mirror*, 30 July 2000.

Details and quotes on Winchester attack: 'Bungling British Burglars Burn Fortune', Reuters, 9 May 1995.

'We had to make a decision': Tony Thompson, 'You Don't Mess With the Wenhams', *Observer*, 24 February 2002.

'If you were looking for metaphors'; 'broken, post-Armageddon'; 'looked like the aftermath': Adam Nicolson, *Regeneration: The Story of the Dome* HarperCollins (London, 1999), p.118.

The main source of details and dialogue in 'The Colour of Magic' chapter is an excellent article by Richard Pendlebury in the 23 February 2002 *Daily Mail* on the discovery of the De Beers Millennium Star, the full title of which was 'The Attempted Heist of this Diamond from the Dome was Breathtakingly Audacious, but the Story of Intrigue, Greed and Drama Surrounding its Discovery by two Englishmen is even more Extraordinary'. Additional sources:

Lorna Martin, 'Diamond out of Africa Dazzled even De Beers', *The Herald* 19 February 2002, and 'Lucky . . . the 777 carat Diamond from Dried-up River Bed', *Yorkshire Post*, 19 February 2002.

'There was a room': F Scott Fitzgerald, *The Short Stories of F Scott Fitzgerald*, Scribner (New York, 1989), p. 189.

'diamonds are intrinsically worthless': Alex Duval Smith, 'The Gem Trail', *Observer*, 13 February 1999.

'Every police officer': Keith Lloyd Webb, 'Arming the British Police', *Contemporary Review*, 1 October 1997.

Betson and Cockram on Millennium Eve: Lucy Panton, '£2M Secret of Dome Mr. Big', *Sunday People*, 24 February 2002.

'This famous hotel has put up': Henry Hill with Byron Schreckengost, *A Goodfella's Guide to New York*, Three Rivers Press (New York, 2003), p. 67.

Plaza Hotel historical background: Wade Morehouse III, *Inside the Plaza: An Intimate Portrait of the Ultimate Hotel*, Applause Books (New York, 2001), p. 14-15, 45, 147, 163–164, 167.

Hoover in drag: Anthony Summers, 'Official and Confidential; The Secret Life of J. Edgar Hoover', GP Putman's Sons (New York, 1993), p. 253–255.

Judith Campbell and JFK in Plaza: Judith Exner, as told to Ovid Demaris, 'My Story', Grove Press (New York, 1977), pp. 100–105, 242.

Elisabeth Kirsch background and quotes: Angela Levin, 'She's a Beautiful, Well-educated Middle-class Girl, So What on Earth Made her Fall for a Dome Raider?' *Daily Mail*, 20 February 2002.

'is unique and immediately recognisable'; 'going to the Louvre': Leslie Adler, Reuters dispatch, November 2000.

'Cutting up the Millennium Star': Nick Hopkins and Tania Branigan, 'The Great Dome Robbery', *Guardian*, 8 November 2000.

'Perhaps the most Romantic Notion': Tracey Lawson, 'Daring Theft Of 3M Pound Cezanne May Be Case Of Life Imitating Art', *Scotsman*, 3 January 2000.

'There are some very rich people': Reuters report quoted on cbsnews.com webpage, 'British Diamond Heist Foiled', 7 November 2000.

'I'm sure there are enough people': William Doyle interview with Nir Livnat, 3 February 2004.

'I was working three days a week': Lucy Panton, '£2M Secret of Dome Mr. Big', *Sunday People*, 24 February 2002.

'We will never be caught'; 'We will either come back': 'Champagne Life of Feared Ringleader,' *Daily Express*, 19 February 2002.

'Marbella is an important centre'; 'La Costa del Plomo': Giles Tremlett, 'Marbella Vice', *The Times*, 1 July 2000.

'They're heavy, very heavy': Duncan Campbell, 'Old Lags', *Guardian*, 5 September 1998.

David James biographical details, use of words 'bastard', 'self-opinionated, stuck-up, arrogant prig' to describe himself: Nick Mathiason, 'Final Word: Mammon, Your Driver Speaking', *Observer*, 20 January 2002. Additional biographical details from William Doyle interview with David James, 14 April 2004.

'a national disgrace'; 'This has gone well beyond': Alastair Jamieson, 'We must End this National Joke', *Scotsman*, 6 September 2000.

'an empty, pointless tent': Kate Kelland, 'London Dome's New Saviour Wonders why it was Built', Reuters, 6 September 2000.

'We will never be caught'; 'We will either come back': 'Champagne Life of Feared Ringleader', *Express*, 19 February 2002.

John Walsh quotes: John Walsh, 'Oh, for a Good old Politically Incorrect Thrill', *Independent*, 21 February 2000.

Dome's litany of troubles: 'an upside down rice bowl'; 'There have been an increasing': Adrian Turpin, 'Dome Report – The Grand Delusion', *Independent On Sunday*, 3 December 2000.

'Shit, miss': Michael Hanlon, 'What's New in Old London: Britain's Capital Greets Another Millennium with a Fresh Image';*Toronto Star*, 20 May 2000.

'That was the end of him': Maggie Urry, 'Racing Man bets to win as he Shows it is Never too Late to Gamble in Life', *Financial Times*, 23 January 2004.

'I went out to try': Alison Maitland, 'In his own Words: David James', *Financial Times*, 31 January 2001.

'Not bloody likely': Lucy Baker, 'Demise of the Dome', *Independent*, 4 January 2001.

'Like Everest, it's there': Christopher Adams and Ruth Sullivan, 'Troubleshooter Prepares for Assault on Mount Everest of Corporate Rescues', *Financial Times*, 6 September 2000.

'on the edge of nervous': Benedict Brogan, 'Dome Staff Left on Edge of Nervous Breakdown', *Daily Telegraph*, 2 May 2002.

'was nothing more than the man': Dominic Kennedy, 'Dome Saviour Just Repair Boss at Disneyland Paris', *The Times*, 7 February 2000.

'Bear in mind': 'Dome Raiders', BBC Special, April 2002.

David James Government consultations; 'My first concern': William Doyle interview with David James, 14 April, 2004.

'the most infamous crime family'; 'Britain's most feared gang': Paul Lashmar, 'Adams Family Values', *Independent*, 18 September 1998.

David James in Bronze Control: William Doyle interview with David James, 14 April 2004.

People's opinions on Meredith: 'Dome Downfall of Popular Skipper', *This is Brighton & Hove*, 19 February 2002.

'Van Gogh cornfield yellow': Nicolson, *Regeneration: The Story of the Dome*, p. 154.

'They're coming in'; scene of John Coles in New Scotland Yard control room; Coles quotes: John Edwards, 'A Tale of JCBs and Diamond Geezers', *Daily Mail*, 6 March 2002.

David James in Bronze Control: William Doyle interview with David James, 14 April 2004.

'lower than falling in front of a Tube train': Sonia Purnell, 'The Thames – the River that Bewitches its Sad or Reckless Victims', *Independent on Sunday*, 28 April 2002.

'Eyeball One'; 'stand back': Lucy Panton, 'Minute by Minute Account of the Great Millennium Gems Heist', *Sunday People*, 12 November 2000.

'a terrible crashing noise': Nick Hopkins and Tania Branigan, 'The Great Dome Robbery', *The Guardian*, 8 November 2000.

'It sounded like something': Andrew Cunningham, 'Dome Chef – I Saw Gem Raid', *Mirror*, 17 November 2001.

'I heard this enormous'; stilt walkers scrambled away: Lucy Panton, 'The Biggest Heist Ever, & Only WE Were There', *Sunday People*, 24 February 2002.

'I could remember'; 'a tank in a war film'; 'they looked like terrorists': witness testimony in trial of Dome defendants.

'Eyeball three'; 'Wait for them all in': Lucy Panton, 'Minute by Minute Account of the Great Millennium Gems Heist', *Sunday People*, 12 November 2000.

Scene in De Beers' control room: William Doyle interview with Lesley Coldham, 30 April 2004.

'It really was like'; 'There was a loud crash': Lucy Panton, 'The Biggest Heist Ever, & Only WE Were There', *Sunday People*, 24 February 2002.

'It was a hell of a lot of noise': Mike Taibbi, 'Diamonds are Forever; Scotland Yard Foils Attempt to Steal Millennium Star and Other Diamonds from Millennium Dome', NBC News *Dateline NBC*, 24 June 2003.

David James detail: William Doyle interview with David James, 14 April 2004.

'Eyeball One'; 'You should have seen'; 'six arrests'; Panton's descriptions of post-arrest scene, 'we knew we might get caught': Lucy Panton, 'Minute by Minute Account of the Great Millennium Gems Heist,' *Sunday People*, 12 November 2000.

'It was worth a try': Dan McDougall, 'Five Jailed for Foiled Dome Gem Theft', *Scotsman*, 19 February 2002.

David James descriptions of post-arrest scene: William Doyle interview with David James, 14 April 2004.

'It's another crazy day': Andrew Walker, 'Another Crazy Day at the Dome', *Scotsman*, 8 November 2000.

Pauline Cockram quotes: Lucy Panton, '£2M Secret of Dome Mr. Big', *Sunday People*, 24 February 2002.

Kirsch update and quotes; Levin quotes: *Daily Mail*, 20 February 2002.

'without Operation Magician'; 'I think they were the best robbery team': Mike Taibbi, 'Diamonds are Forever; Scotland Yard Foils Attempt to Steal Millennium Star and Other Diamonds from Millennium Dome', NBC News *Dateline NBC*, 24 June 2003.

'I suspect they moved in': Andrew Pierce, 'Dome Rats Doomed as Traps are Installed', *The Times*, 25 November 2000.

'not been the success we hoped': Lucy Baker, 'Demise Of The Dome', *Independent*, 4 January 2001.

Blair's last visit to Dome: Alan Hamilton, 'Blair and Heseltine bid Dome Farewell', *The Times*, 20 December 2000.

'Look, the figures have improved': Jason Beattie, 'Blair Wanted to Keep Failed Dome Open for a few Months Longer', *Scotsman*, 2 January 2004.

Dome 'fantastic': Steve Boggan, 'Will the Last Person to Leave the Dome turn off the Lights?' *Independent*, 1 January 2001.

'I am appalled': Helen Rumbelow, 'One Final Day ends in Tears for Staff', *The Times*, 1 January 2001.

Forbes poll of architects: Betsy Schiffman, 'The World's Ugliest Buildings', Forbes.com, 3 May 2002.

'I have no money'; 'they deserved to go down': Lucy Panton, '£2M Secret of Dome Mr. Big', *Sunday People*, 24 February 2002.

'I just want to put it': Alexander Hitchen, 'Dome Free!' *People*, 25 January 2004.

'I think it would have been': Mike Taibbi, 'Diamonds are Forever; Scotland Yard Foils Attempt to Steal Millennium Star and Other Diamonds from Millennium Dome', NBC News *Dateline NBC*, 24 June 2003.

'We are proud': 'Reward for Gem of an Operation', *This is Greenwich Borough*, 19 August 2002.

'The replica Millennium Star': Andrew Coxon, email to authors, 8 May 2004.

De Beers set up bank account for villagers: Lorna Martin, 'Diamond out of Africa Dazzled even De Beers', *The Herald*, 19 February 2002.

Postscript on De Beers Millennium Star: from Richard Pendlebury's article in the 23 February 2002 *Daily Mail*. He wrote: 'But there is one more intrigue surrounding the stone. The shape of the rough diamond suggested that it was merely a splinter from a much larger piece. Somewhere in the heart of Africa, the world's biggest, flawless diamond may still be waiting to be found.'

Index

Index